Playwrights for Tomorrow

VOLUME 3

EDITED, WITH AN INTRODUCTION, BY ARTHUR H. BALLET

PLAYWRIGHTS FOR TOMORROW

A Collection of Plays, Volume 3

THE UNIVERSITY OF MINNESOTA PRESS · MINNEAPOLIS

Library of Congress Catalog Card Number: 66-19124

PUBLISHED IN GREAT BRITAIN, INDIA, AND PAKISTAN BY THE OXFORD UNIVERSITY PRESS, LONDON, BOMBAY, AND KARACHI, AND IN CANADA BY THE COPP CLARK PUBLISHING CO. LIMITED, TORONTO

Playwrights for Tomorrow

VOLUME 3

INTRODUCTION

Arthur H. Ballet

In 1963, with financial aid and encouragement from the Rockefeller Foundation and with the blessings of the University of Minnesota, the Office for Advanced Drama Research (O.A.D.R.) was created. Our purpose has been to make the funds and talents of an active theatre community in Minneapolis–St. Paul and suburbs available to playwrights.

The assumptions under which this program has operated are basic: that living theatre must encourage new writers and must not depend solely on either "classics" on the one hand or the established "success" on the other; that between the smash hit and the disastrous failure of the professional theatre there should be room for the developmental and experimental so that the artists of the theatre have an opportunity for growth; and that a major university, in company with a body of active theatre groups, can provide writers with a testing ground for their skills, their ideas, and their talents.

In the four years that O.A.D.R. has operated we have had a reasonably good batting average. In Volumes 1 and 2 of *Playwrights for Tomorrow* were represented such writers as Maria Irene Fornés, Lee H. Kalcheim, Megan Terry, and Terrence McNally, all of whom went from their work with O.A.D.R. in its first year to Broadway and off-Broadway production. In the succeeding years of O.A.D.R., our playwrights have continued to move into the mainstream of the American theatre: Rochelle Owens, Sam Shepard, Jean-Claude van Itallie, Romeo Muller, Herbert Lieberman, and Philip Barber are only a few who built on their work under this program's aegis to achieve professional production.

The financial resources available for the program have not been great:

3

the seed grant from the Rockefeller Foundation, ticket sales for performances of plays presented under O.A.D.R. sponsorship, the university's support through released time for the staff, and, potentially, a share of royalties from the plays first developed here. But, with the dedicated cooperation of the theatres and writers involved, we have been able to use the money to greatest advantage. As Dolly Levi, in Thornton Wilder's *The Matchmaker*, says, "Money — pardon my expression — is like manure; it's not worth a thing unless it's spread about encouraging young things to grow."

Of the hundreds of playwrights considered each year, I try to select those writers who show the greatest promise. I have the aid and counsel of an Executive Committee appointed by University of Minnesota President O. Meredith Wilson. Members are Donald K. Smith, associate vice president of the university, chairman; Peter Zeisler, managing director of the Minnesota Theatre Company at the Tyrone Guthrie Theatre; Willard Thompson, dean of the university's General Extension Division; and Kenneth L. Graham, chairman of the speech, communication, and theatre arts department at the university. The playwrights are selected after careful reading of their work and, insofar as possible, personal interviews. The final decision on which playwrights to try to include in the program is mine, as director of the program; we learned early that committee selection invariably resulted in compromise and mediocrity.

Once a playwright is selected, a previously unproduced play he has submitted is circulated to a number of Twin City theatres, ranging from professional to community to educational. These producing groups are completely free to select those plays and writers in whom they find the greatest promise and with whom they'd like to work. Of perhaps twenty-five plays that I find of interest each year, only eight to twelve are finally produced.

Each playwright selected by a theatre (if he is available to that theatre during the time that it can work with him) is brought to the Twin Cities by O.A.D.R. He is given a modest honorarium (largely to replace salary which might otherwise be earned), a subsistence allowance, and, most important, developmental rehearsals and production before a discriminating and interested audience. We try, also, to bring to the Twin Cities one or more producers, critics, directors, or agents who have expressed interest in the playwright so that they may consult with him and see his work performed, which may lead to the play's being done elsewhere. We publish some of the plays so that an even wider audience may judge them and perhaps bring about additional productions.

The O.A.D.R. underwrites the modest production budgets of the cooperating theatres, which in return share their profits on ticket sales for the new plays with the Office. More significant than any financial returns, the theatre offers the writer a laboratory, and the writer brings to the theatre the excitement and stimulus of working with a new script.

In Volumes 3 and 4 of *Playwrights for Tomorrow* are nine new writers. Five are in this volume and four are in Volume 4.

John Lewin's *Five Easy Payments* is both a sharp observation of and a hilarious satire on middle American mores. As playwright in residence at the Guthrie Theatre, Mr. Lewin wrote this play for a specific stage and company. He has since completed an adaptation of the *Oresteia*, published by the University of Minnesota Press under the title *The House of Atreus*. A production of this work, directed by Sir Tyrone Guthrie, was produced by the Minnesota Theatre Company in the 1967 season.

Jean-Claude van Itallie's *America Hurrah* was a much-discussed and highly praised off-Broadway production of the 1966–67 season. *Where Is de Queen?* is a brittle and wise blending of social comment and abiding compassion.

The Great Git-Away by Romeo Muller is fantasy based on frightening possibility. A collection of theatrical (and real) stereotypes (perhaps the more fashionable word would be "archetypes") face a new world in a highly moral comedy. This play was appropriately produced on the University of Minnesota Showboat and played to capacity most of the summer of 1966. Mr. Muller is a widely respected television writer, and he is in the process of adapting *The Great Git-Away* into a musical comedy.

A modern view of the smart set is wittily presented in John Stranack's *With Malice Aforethought*. The parallel between Restoration form and content and modern sophistication is brought off successfully in one of the jolliest high comedies our audiences have ever enjoyed. Mr. Stranack is South African by birth, American by adoption, and an international traveler by choice.

I, Elizabeth Otis, Being of Sound Mind by Philip Barber has been one of our most successful works, both with critics and with audiences. A mature, knowledgeable, and respected talent in the American theatre, Mr.

Barber takes a view of small-town America that is honest and searing. At the same time his is an "old-fashioned" play in the best sense of that term.

Mary Feldhaus-Weber is a St. Paul poet who has chosen to work in the theatre, and in her *The World Tipped Over, and Laying on Its Side* she brings to the drama a keen and discerning ear and fresh insight. Her words and images shimmer brightly in a brief but penetrating theatre piece.

Visions of Sugar Plums by Barry Pritchard, who was playwright in residence at Theatre St. Paul, bears down unmercifully on the modern market place. Stifling routine and the easy laugh are the targets as Mr. Pritchard focuses sharply on a prevailing theme in modern drama. Mr. Pritchard is now in Hollywood writing for television and the films.

Theatre, drama, momism, identity, and Oedipus in reverse are startlingly — and hilariously — welded together in *The Strangler* by Arnold Powell. The most pathetic of tragedies and the darkest of comedies, punctuated by the wildest of puns, this exciting theatrical piece is miraculously never a pastiche and always a moving experience. Mr. Powell is a teacher and theatre director at Birmingham-Southern College in Atlanta.

Kevin O'Morrison earns his keep as an actor in the Broadway theatre; in 1966 he appeared in *The Rose Tattoo*. His *The Long War*, which was worked with in Minneapolis under the title *Three Days before Yesterday*, is a major work which deals both bitterly and compassionately with questions of war and individual responsibility. The parallels to other eras, including our own, make a Greek heroic theme a modern commentary that is powerful and stirring.

A number of other writers, not included in these volumes for various reasons, also worked with our program. Mark Berman's *A Saxophone for America* was a workshop presentation of the Minnesota Theatre Company, and John Cromwell's *A Breezy Fourth* was given careful rehearsals and production by Theatre in the Round Players of Minneapolis. Sam Shepard's *Fourteen Hundred Thousand* was presented at the Firehouse Theatre, Minneapolis. Rochelle Owen's *Futz*, first presented by the Minnesota Theatre Company, Alfred Levinson's *Socrates Wounded*, produced by the University of Minnesota Theatre, and Herbert Lieberman's *Tigers in Red Weather*, also presented by the Minnesota Theatre Company, are all available in anthologies published by Hill and Wang, Inc.

And the program continues. Each day new scripts arrive, giving promise of an exciting discovery; almost every month a new play opens in the

INTRODUCTION

Twin City area for an audience increasingly eager to make its own judgment of the work of playwrights; each year with pride we watch as "our" playwrights move on in the working world of the theatre. There are also problems and regrets: the struggle to make ends meet is often like something out of a nineteenth-century melodrama; critics are more often than not unsympathetic to new, unproved playwrights; audiences still want "hits" and are disinclined to buy tickets to see pigs in pokes; some of the best plays I read are not accepted by the cooperating theatres.

But over all the venture has been exciting, worthwhile, and, we hope, important. As theatres in the Twin Cities and throughout the country open their facilities to the playwright, there is increasing evidence that significant contributions can be made outside the commercial New York theatre, that amateurs and professionals and educators can join together effectively to work in the theatre, and that good drama can be nurtured. These volumes testify that such drama is not restricted to any one style, form, theme, or place: bouncing and vital and fresh, it is happening in many guises in all parts of the country.

JOHN LEWIN

Five Easy Payments

A SHORT PLAY

for Hazel

Cast of Characters

EDGAR MOMPESSON

PHYLLIS MOMPESSON

MRS. BIERCE (CHORUS LEADER)

DR. FINGERMAN (ONE)

EDGAR'S FATHER (TWO)

MR. KIRSCHBAUM (THREE)

MISS LEMMING (FOUR)

WAITER (FIVE)

MR. FACCIAMATA (SIX)

ANNOUNCER (SEVEN)

BOXER (EIGHT)

REV. DEAN SAMUELSON (NINE)

FIVE EASY PAYMENTS

The stage is dark. The Chorus huddles in a tight group. Dim light on Edgar and Phyllis' bed. Edgar turns restlessly in his sleep.

AMPLIFIED VOICE

The nightmare book of Edgar Mompesson. Entry for Thursday, six forty-five A.M. First there was a station. A shed by a track. There were people on the platform. Then a roaring and a clanging as a black train filled the hollow of the eye. When it had gone there were only black stumps where the people had been standing. (*lights up on Chorus*)

MRS. BIERCE

Hail to the light. I come on Thursday morning
To clean the House of Edgar and Phyllis Mompesson.
This house has stood since 1956,
Built by Wenburg and Sons on a site where another house stood.
In the other house was an old man roaring with cancer
And a white-skinned woman and a child who said awful things.

CHORUS

Nine years since the House of Mompesson
Was clapped on the spot where the other house stood.

SEVEN

In the House of Mompesson you can telephone the kitchen from the bathroom.

NINE

In the other house you could scream and hope someone would hear.

TWO

The old man had a ragged mustache and a stinking pipe.

FOUR

The woman with white skin collected leaves.

EIGHT

The boy wanted to be a boxer.

CHORUS

They baked bread and roasted meat,
And no one knows what they did at night.

FIVE

Under the House of Mompesson are broken bricks,

SIX

Bricks from a house built in 1878
That were not removed by Firkusny and Sons, Wreckers.

ONE

Today these bricks are metastasizing.

CHORUS

Listen.

THREE

The House of Mompesson is entering Thursday morning.
(*A great iron bell is heard tolling.*)

EDGAR

Shut off the alarm. (*Phyllis does so.*) Jesus.

PHYLLIS

Mary.

EDGAR

Pray for us now . .

EDGAR AND PHYLLIS

And in the hour of our death. (*They cross themselves. They kiss briefly.*)

PHYLLIS

Orange juice or tomato?

EDGAR

Tomato. (*pause*) It's cold.

PHYLLIS

It's awfully cold, Edgar.

EDGAR

You know, lately I don't feel like getting out of bed at all.

PHYLLIS

Well, nobody does. Especially in winter.

EDGAR

Yeah, but it's not just because it's nice. It's because it's the only place left that's safe.

PHYLLIS

You shouldn't want to be safe.

EDGAR

I shouldn't want anything I want. That's the trouble.

PHYLLIS

People die in bed.

EDGAR

Thanks a lot.

PHYLLIS

Did you make that appointment?

EDGAR

What appointment?

PHYLLIS

Dr. Fingerman.

EDGAR

Yes. It's for today.

PHYLLIS

Good. If you need me and I'm not in I'll be at the Big Cherry getting groceries or at Mr. Dick's getting my hair fixed.

EDGAR

What do you mean, if I need you?

PHYLLIS

Well, if you call. I'd like to know whether you're coming home for supper.

EDGAR

I don't know whether or not. It depends if they make me work overtime.

PHYLLIS

Why should they do that?

EDGAR

Because I took the hour off work to go to the doctor.

PHYLLIS

They wouldn't make you do that.

EDGAR

You don't know Mr. Bunrath.

PHYLLIS

Stand up to him. Be like you were at the party last night.

EDGAR

I was drunk at the party.

13

PHYLLIS

You were great. And afterwards. Wowie!

EDGAR

What? What do you mean?

PHYLLIS

Well, you practically raped me, if you really want to know. I mean for *you*, you did.

EDGAR

Jesus.

PHYLLIS

Listen, a woman loves that. Then she can really relax. Because she doesn't feel dirty. I mean she feels dirty, but she doesn't feel responsible.

EDGAR

Me? I?

PHYLLIS

It's quarter after. You'd better get going or you'll be late to work.

EDGAR

(*false bravado*) So what?

PHYLLIS

Edgar, you don't want to lose your job. You remember what happened last time you were late. I'll go make the coffee. (*She rises and exits from the bedroom area. Edgar gets up.*)

EDGAR

Hail to the light.

CHORUS

And the bell.

EDGAR

And the bell.

CHORUS

And the dry eye of the day.

(*The Princess phone on the bedside table rings: a bell chime. Edgar answers it.*)

PHYLLIS

Did you say orange juice or tomato?

EDGAR

Tomato. (*He hangs up and goes downstage to the front door.*)

EDGAR

Morning, Mrs. Bierce.

MRS. BIERCE

Hardly worth getting up, is it?

14

EDGAR

Well, have to get the paper, eh?

MRS. BIERCE

Yeah, the paper. I forgot about that part.

EDGAR

Raw, isn't it?

MRS. BIERCE

Yeah. It's raw.

EDGAR

Come in and have a cup of coffee.

MRS. BIERCE

No thanks. I'll just stand here and watch.

EDGAR

Watch what? (*He sees Chorus.*) Who are you people?

SIX

Passersby.

THREE

It doesn't take much to collect a crowd.

EDGAR

Well, I'm going in. It's cold.

FOUR

It's awfully cold, Edgar.

NINE

Cold as hell.

EDGAR

What is this?

MRS. BIERCE

Go have your coffee, Mr. Mompesson.

EDGAR

(*going in*) Jesus Christ, you can't even step outside your own door any more . .

PHYLLIS

Edgar, is something the matter?

EDGAR

No. Nothing. (*She sets out coffee, toast, and juice.*)

PHYLLIS

Read the paper.

EDGAR

"Five Babies Burn in Slum Tragedy."

PHYLLIS

If you don't know what's happening to you, is it still a tragedy?

EDGAR

I don't know. "Mayor Calls Prostitutes 'Undesirable.' "

PHYLLIS

You know Darlene? She says she knows this girl at work who's an Elizabethan. I just can't imagine that . . I mean what's the sense of doing it with another woman?

EDGAR

"Contraceptive Boom Looms, Pope Told."

PHYLLIS

Edgar, are we ever going to have a baby?

EDGAR

I don't know. When we've got something to give it we will.

PHYLLIS

What do you mean? You've got a good job, we've got a nice house — and you know we haven't got forever.

EDGAR

I know, but people have children without thinking what's going to happen to them. And then something goes wrong and the child gets mixed up and he hates you for it and all you've got is a bad feeling and another unhappy person in the world.

PHYLLIS

Edgar, nobody can tell what's going to happen.

EDGAR

I know. And I just don't like to live that way.

PHYLLIS

Would you like it if you knew when you were going to die?

EDGAR

Don't talk like that!

PHYLLIS

Well, I'm sorry. But that's the way everybody lives. You just sort of trust yourself and play it by ear.

EDGAR

Where'd you hear that?

PHYLLIS

My brother used to say it, if you want to know.

EDGAR

Oh, him.

16

PHYLLIS

What do you mean, "Oh, him"?

EDGAR

This is the one who died when you were twelve?

PHYLLIS

He was the only one I had. I mean he and I were the only children.

EDGAR

You never showed me a picture of him.

PHYLLIS

You never asked. I've got one upstairs. You never asked much of anything about me. Since we've been married, I mean. You *used* to act like you wanted to know what I'm like.

EDGAR

Well, I found out. You're wonderful.

PHYLLIS

I'm no trouble, huh?

EDGAR

Maybe you can show me the picture tonight. I haven't got time right now.

PHYLLIS

Maybe. It's a bad picture. I mean *you* wouldn't think it was a good picture. It's overexposed. He was in his Navy whites and it was a sunny day. You can't even see his face very well. Just a big white blaze. I'm in it too. I look awful. A dumpy little girl. Squinting. I said, "Hank, you made me snowblind."

EDGAR

Hm. (*Another pause. He returns to the paper.*) "Photographs Reveal: Other Side of Moon Is Dull."

PHYLLIS

Read "Dear Abby."

EDGAR

There's nothing much *in* "Dear Abby" today.

PHYLLIS

That means you don't want me to see it. (*She grabs paper.*) There. "Chaste Teen-Ager Not So Dumb."

EDGAR

Well?

PHYLLIS

Well.

EDGAR

Look, I'm going. I've got to go. (*They kiss briefly.*)

17

PHYLLIS

Rubbers. (*He puts on rubbers.*)

EDGAR

Take care of yourself today.

PHYLLIS

Edgar . .

EDGAR

What?

PHYLLIS

Am I a woman to you?

EDGAR

You're the most beautiful, sexiest woman in the world.

PHYLLIS

Am I a castrating bitch?

EDGAR

Of course not.

PHYLLIS

Why not?

EDGAR

All right, have it your way. You're a castrating bitch.

PHYLLIS

Are you kidding?

EDGAR

Of course I'm kidding.

PHYLLIS

Sometimes I think I'm just an object. And not even a very useful one.

EDGAR

Honey . .

PHYLLIS

Don't you want me?

EDGAR

Of course I want you . . You mean *right now*?

PHYLLIS

Do I disgust you? Do I not smell good or something?

EDGAR

You smell wonderful (*nibbling*) Nmnmnmnmnmnmnm . .

PHYLLIS

Oh, cut it out.

EDGAR

Well, for Christ's sake . .

PHYLLIS

You know you're just doing that to appease me and then you'll walk right out that door.

EDGAR

Honey, the last thing in the world I want to do is go out today. You were the one who was rushing me to get out of bed.

PHYLLIS

Oh, now it's my fault.

EDGAR

Honey . .

PHYLLIS

Edgar, listen.

EDGAR

What?

PHYLLIS

I had an awful dream last night.

EDGAR

Oh, well — hell, everybody dreams.

PHYLLIS

I was cleaning this chicken and it had nothing inside it, just a plastic bag with a note in it.

EDGAR

A note? What did it say?

PHYLLIS

I don't know; the alarm woke me up then.

EDGAR

Well, I've got to go. (*He starts to leave, then comes back to her.*) You see, what your dream meant was "Edgar will be a chicken, without guts, if he doesn't go out today." Eh? Ha-ha.

MRS. BIERCE

Ha-ha.

EDGAR

What was that?

PHYLLIS

What?

EDGAR

Somebody laughing.

(*Blackout. Lights up as soon as Dr. Fingerman is in Phyllis' place. Edgar does not move.*)

DR. FINGERMAN

What do you mean, laughing?

EDGAR

Ha-ha. Like that.

DR. FINGERMAN

But you did laugh first, didn't you? So it could be feedback.

EDGAR

You mean . . like an echo.

DR. FINGERMAN

Well, a little different. You say your house is about a hundred feet away from a steep hill?

EDGAR

Yes.

DR. FINGERMAN

Well, there you are.

EDGAR

Oh, God. *Thank* you, Doctor. Something else I've been wondering. The trees have these lumps on them.

DR. FINGERMAN

The trees in your yard?

EDGAR

Yes.

DR. FINGERMAN

Mm-hm. Lumps. Well, that's a rather specialized question.

EDGAR

It couldn't be — I mean, it isn't . . you know?

DR. FINGERMAN

You think about that a lot, don't you?

EDGAR

Yes, I do. All the time. It's like . . this smell comes to me. And I close my eyes and I see . . this thing. Black . . and . . and . . puffy.

DR. FINGERMAN

Suppose we lie down. (*He conducts Edgar to the couch. The Doctor sits in a chair.*)

EDGAR

There must be . . something going on I don't know about.

DR. FINGERMAN

Mr. Mompesson, we dance on a bubble of darkness.
It is the sin of Oedipus to stamp on the floor.

20

Better the sin of Onan, the sin of Judas,
Better seasickness and lockjaw than to ask, who am I?

EDGAR

Well, what do we have to do?

DR. FINGERMAN

We must go down into that cyst of night
And bring out fragments of putrefying shadow:
The screaming man in the clean room, the deformed dog and the thin child
who sees death in faces, the hero carved out of soap, the woman in the
dark house, the train that comes into the station sideways and leaves
black stumps where once were people.

EDGAR

(*faintly*) All right.

DR. FINGERMAN

Where were you born?

EDGAR

I was born from a raw place of animal darkness
Into a world that pawed me till I shrieked.
(*a long sigh*) I was born in Toledo.

DR. FINGERMAN

Son of? (*pause; no answer*) Child of? (*pause*)

EDGAR

(*absently*) Babe.

DR. FINGERMAN

I beg your pardon?

EDGAR

(*eyes closed*) Babe.

> "These pretty babes with hand in hand
> Went wandering up and down,
> But nevermore they saw the man
> Approaching from the town."

(*During this Edgar's dead father has come up and is standing at the foot
of the couch. Dr. Fingerman moves quietly out of the light.*)

FATHER

Edgar.

EDGAR

Father.

FATHER

Edgar, I come from the land of shadows.
They do not treat me badly.

21

I have my dry flies, and my sketchbook,
And my thirty-four Sulka cravats,
And the beautiful hosiery buyer from whose bed I saw New York.
But you, the thin child with the great eyes, to whom I tried to teach boxing,
What crooked path has brought you to this man?

EDGAR

Father, I am forty. My cells are scaling from me.
Each morning I pull a pad of hair from my comb.
Each night I wonder: can I coax the blood to its place?
Father, hear me. I am lost on the way to the boneyard.
I am still that six-year-old boy, with a rotten heart.

FATHER

Edgar, Edgar, the dead are unusually truthful.
I have no magic to save you from yourself.
I could not give you the shield of protection, a faery sword, the crown of
   vision;
Only a cloak of darkness, and that you have woven for yourself.
Go back to your great fluorescent office, Edgar,
And curl like a grub in your buttock-hugging chair
While the Univac giggles and plays with itself in the corner
And the pretty receptionist pops a lens from her eye.
For me, I shall return to my own place.
I wish only to remember that beautiful child I knew
And not to dwell on these thirty-four years, the arc
Of joy that fell like an arrow and broke on fear . .
Goodbye, Edgar. Resign from the club, Edgar.
Lie down in the snow, Edgar.
Lie down in the snow and sleep.
(*He exits. Edgar curls in the fetal position. Dr. Fingerman comes over
and touches him on the shoulder.*)

DR. FINGERMAN

Fifty minutes, Mr. Mompesson.
(*Edgar gets up and goes dazedly out. Exit Dr. Fingerman. Enter Mr.
Kirschbaum, the supermarket manager. He wears a red derby and a huge
red-and-white button on each side of his chest, reading, respectively,* BIG-
GER *and* SOFTER. *Enter Phyllis.*)

PHYLLIS

Good morning, Mr. Kirschbaum. (*The stage is drowned in intense white
light. A white sign descends with the red legend* KIRSCHBAUM'S BIG CHER-

RY SUPERETTE *and a big red cherry with an oval, sharp-toothed mouth and no other features. Muzak begins to play.*)

MR. KIRSCHBAUM

Hail to the light.

PHYLLIS

Could I get two rolls of toilet tissue?

MR. KIRSCHBAUM

Come this way. (*Seven enters.*)

SEVEN

(*darkly*) Food for animals.

MR. KIRSCHBAUM

What kind of animal? (*slight pause*)

SEVEN

He could probably eat dog food.

MR. KIRSCHBAUM

Over there. (*Seven moves away.*) Why do you want toilet tissue?

PHYLLIS

I sometimes use it to blot my lipstick. (*They encounter Mrs. Bierce.*)

MRS. BIERCE

Morning, honey.

PHYLLIS

Morning, Mrs. Bierce. Oh, did I give you the key so you can get in if I'm gone?

MRS. BIERCE

Honey, your house is *really* gonna be cleaned today.

PHYLLIS

Good.

MRS. BIERCE

Look at these hands.

PHYLLIS

What?

MRS. BIERCE

Look at these hands. Soft, aren't they? And white? You'd never believe these hands are up to the elbows in other people's crud all week. That's what they mean by a classless society.

PHYLLIS

You're right. And mine are so rough and coarse I hardly dare to touch Henry intimately anymore.

MRS. BIERCE

Edgar, honey. Your husband's name is Edgar.

PHYLLIS

You're right. And mine are so rough and coarse I hardly dare to touch Edgar intimately anymore.

MRS. BIERCE

You know people can't tell me and my daughter apart? Even my daughter's husband can't tell us apart.

PHYLLIS

How wonderful!

MRS. BIERCE

He's a loser in bed. Once was enough. But the principle is good, you know? And you know what it is? It's the soap I use.

PHYLLIS

I can't believe it. I've tried them all . .

MRS. BIERCE

It's this fancy German stuff. It contains baby fat. Kirschbaum doesn't stock it.

MR. KIRSCHBAUM

There's very little of it left. It's not cheap, and you have to send for it special. The guy in New York who ships it in and me are like that, though. For *you* I could get it wholesale, Mrs. Mompesson.

PHYLLIS

It's not a detergent?

MR. KIRSCHBAUM

No, it's soap; the real thing. And I'll tell you something else; this wasn't made by no Communists, so you don't have to worry about that. Put you down for a few cakes?

PHYLLIS

Well, I'll think about it.

MR. KIRSCHBAUM

That's okay, you think about it. This is Free Enterprise System, we don't force nobody to buy. Mrs. Bierce, you want anything you don't know where it is?

MRS. BIERCE

No, I know where everything is.

MR. KIRSCHBAUM

You bet you do. Okay, you just find what you want while I show Mrs. Mompesson some bread.

PHYLLIS

It's toilet paper I want.

MR. KIRSCHBAUM

And it's toilet paper you get. This bread was originally made by a little old crippled-up lady, but she died and her son owns the business now. A genuine enriched old-fashioned loaf, with sodium propionate to retard spoilage. I think that's wonderful, don't you?

PHYLLIS

Yes.

MR. KIRSCHBAUM

Wonderful. What does a pretty lady like you want with toilet paper, anyhow?

PHYLLIS

Could we go on?

MR. KIRSCHBAUM

We sure could. Here's the canned goods. Could I interest you in some crabmeat? We got a special on. What's the matter?

PHYLLIS

Do you . . ah . . smell something funny?

MR. KIRSCHBAUM

What, something funny? No, I don't smell nothing funny. What's the matter?

PHYLLIS

It's . . terrible, it's just awful.

MR. KIRSCHBAUM

Maybe you think it's me?

PHYLLIS

Wait, that's what it is, it's that can of crabmeat. It's all puffy and black.

MR. KIRSCHBAUM

Well. Isn't that funny? Let's go on, all right?

PHYLLIS

All right. (*Four enters.*)

FOUR

Breakfast food.

MR. KIRSCHBAUM

What did you have in mind? Something contemporary, or traditional?

FOUR

I want breakfast in my apartment to be an *exciting* meal.

MR. KIRSCHBAUM

I got just the thing. New from General Mills. You put it in a bowl, pour milk on it, and it moves around. I forget the name but it's in a burnt

25

orange box. That way. (*Four moves off.*) Now here we got toilet paper coming up, but before that we got Kotex. You need Kotex, I'm sure.

PHYLLIS

No, as a matter of fact I don't.

MR. KIRSCHBAUM

You don't.

PHYLLIS

No.

MR. KIRSCHBAUM

Well. I guess that means congratulations, don't it?

PHYLLIS

I don't need any, that's all.

MR. KIRSCHBAUM

Well. How about deodorant?

PHYLLIS

No.

MR. KIRSCHBAUM

Stick, ball-point, squeeze bottle, cream, and aerosol can. (*holding one up*) This one is for special cases.

PHYLLIS

I said I don't need any.

MR. KIRSCHBAUM

Well. That does mean congratulations. Congratulations, Mrs. Mompesson.

PHYLLIS

What do you mean?

MR. KIRSCHBAUM

You don't sweat neither.

PHYLLIS

Mr. Kirschbaum, I don't think that's one bit funny and I think it's in awful taste.

MR. KIRSCHBAUM

Sure. Well, we're not talking about taste right now, we're talking about smell. If you don't smell good nobody loves you, isn't that true? You come in my store and tell me you smell something bad. How do you think that makes *me* feel? So I just want you to know you don't kid me. You don't kid *nobody* . .

PHYLLIS

Stop it. (*music: "Somewhere Over the Rainbow"*)

26

MR. KIRSCHBAUM

Here, here's the toilet paper. Load up. Take lots. To blot your lipstick with.

PHYLLIS

I only want two rolls.

MR. KIRSCHBAUM

Okay, that's fine. This is Free Enterprise System. Here's a good kind. Smells real good, soft, double-ply, won't fall apart no matter what kind of lipstick you have. Squeeze it. Go on, squeeze it.

PHYLLIS

There's a sign that says not to.

MR. KIRSCHBAUM

That's to make you do it.

PHYLLIS

I couldn't. It'd be wrong.

MR. KIRSCHBAUM

Listen, the guy who makes those signs up and me are like that. I know what he's got in mind.

CHORUS

Hey, Mrs. Mompesson. Squeeze it.

MR. KIRSCHBAUM

This is my store. I run it along Free Enterprise lines. Watch. (*He squeezes the toilet paper. Phyllis gasps.*) I do that every day. Five, maybe six times a day.

CHORUS

Squeeze it, lady. (*Phyllis touches the huge roll tentatively.*) Hold it close. (*She does. Music crescendo.*)

PHYLLIS

It's soft.

CHORUS

It's awfully soft, Phyllis.

MRS. BIERCE

Soft as hell.

PHYLLIS

I can't stop.

MR. KIRSCHBAUM

That's right.

PHYLLIS

(*vaguely*) Help.

MR. KIRSCHBAUM

Well. That's what I'm here for, isn't it? To help you. (*He draws her gently away, holding her by both arms.*)

PHYLLIS

What are we going to do?

MR. KIRSCHBAUM

We're going to my place, Mrs. Mompesson. And I'm going to undress you. And afterwards, if you're good, I'll spend the rest of the afternoon pasting green stamps all over you.

MRS. BIERCE

(*calling*) Kirschbaum, you got bad crabmeat.

MR. KIRSCHBAUM

So do you, Mrs. Bierce.

MRS. BIERCE

(*laughing*) Ah, you son of a bitch; you kiss and tell, eh?

PHYLLIS

What about Edgar? I love him.

MR. KIRSCHBAUM

Screw your husband. He's not enough man for you.

PHYLLIS

If I desert him where will he go?

MR. KIRSCHBAUM

To lie with the losers, out in the snow.
This is Free Enterprise System. Come.

PHYLLIS

I wanted to dance to a different drum.

MR. KIRSCHBAUM

This is the land where you follow a star.
Follow me out to my fastback car. (*They exit.*)

CHORUS

Double your pleasure, double your fun:
Thus, though we cannot make our sun
Stand still, yet we will make him run
With double good, double good, Doublemint gum.
Hail to the light, which has lasted through most of Thursday,
And is going into retirement under the earth.
It sits on the top of the tallest building on West Sixty-Second Street,
Waiting for thanks, since it has grown gray in our service.
In houses all over the city yellow lights are going on;

The worker thinks of the welcome sizzle of his Rotissomat and drives a little faster.

On the House of Mompesson a gray bloom has appeared and no one is at home:

The house looks a little old. (*sound of city traffic in background*)

In the city park there is a constant traffic of dead leaves.

The trees stand black and tall.

In the streets there is thunder.

Listen.

The House of Mompesson is entering Thursday evening.

(*Edgar enters, carrying three packages, two small ones and a long cylindrical one, a wrapped-up fishing rod. He sits on a park bench and begins to examine the contents of one of the small packages, a plastic box with a couple of dry flies in it and a fishing reel. He gives the reel a couple of experimental spins. A young woman enters. She carries two wrapped packages — a fifth of liquor and a small white-wrapped drugstore bottle.*)

MISS LEMMING

Careful he doesn't pull you in.

EDGAR

Who? . . What?

MISS LEMMING

That fish. He sounds like a real fighter. How are you, Mr. Mompesson?

EDGAR

Oh. Miss Lemming. Hi. How are you?

MISS LEMMING

I believe I asked you first.

EDGAR

Oh, I'm fine.

MISS LEMMING

That's fine. Now ask me how I am.

EDGAR

How are you?

MISS LEMMING

I'm fine too, thanks. There. Now how are you really?

EDGAR

Oh . . a little depressed, sort of.

MISS LEMMING

What about?

EDGAR

Well . . it's sort of personal, actually.

29

MISS LEMMING

Uh-huh. Well, if it wasn't personal you wouldn't be depressed about it, would you?

EDGAR

I guess not.

MISS LEMMING

No. And yet this morning I read in the paper that they've photographed the other side of the moon and it's dull as can be. And *that* depressed me, a little. I suppose that means there's something wrong with me, doesn't it?

EDGAR

No. I don't think so.

MISS LEMMING

Well, you're a pretty exceptional man, Mr. Mompesson. I mean, I see you around the office looking depressed so much I figure you *must* be exceptional.

EDGAR

Uh, could I . . buy you a drink somewhere?

MISS LEMMING

No, thank you. I've had a great deal too many already. I'd rather just sit here for a little while . . okay?

EDGAR

Okay. Were, uh, were you depressed too?

MISS LEMMING

Yes. I wouldn't say that . . that's . . what I am now, though. (*She slurs this a bit.*) Excuse me. I mean, I made up my mind to something and that helps a lot.

EDGAR

I'll bet.

MISS LEMMING

Really. You should try it sometime. (*Edgar draws himself in a little.*) Look, I didn't mean anything . . personal, you know. I'm not trying to attack your masculinity or anything. Do you know I scare men off, by the way?

EDGAR

(*gently*) You don't scare me.

MISS LEMMING

(*tears suddenly standing in her eyes*) Thank you. (*She snuffles fiercely and looks in her purse.*) Oh, shit, I used my handkerchief for a bar rag. (*He gives her his breast-pocket handkerchief.*) Thanks. (*She blows her nose. There is a sound of auto horns — a wedding procession. At the peak of it Edgar observes:* "Someone's getting married." *It is completely drowned out. The sound starts to diminish. Miss Lemming shouts:* "What?")

EDGAR

I said someone's getting married. (*a long pause*)

MISS LEMMING

What were we talking about?

EDGAR

Decisions.

MISS LEMMING

Well. Anyway. I didn't go back to work after lunch.

EDGAR

Neither did I!

MISS LEMMING

You *didn't*?

EDGAR

No. I wasn't there at all this afternoon. (*solemnly*) Boy, will I get it when I go back in the morning.

MISS LEMMING

(*dully*) You're going back in the morning.

EDGAR

Oh, yes. Sure.

MISS LEMMING

Oh.

EDGAR

Why?

MISS LEMMING

Because I won't be coming back.

EDGAR

You resigned?

MISS LEMMING

I left.

EDGAR

How come you didn't wait till the end of the week?

MISS LEMMING

Oh, that would be too neat. Mr. Bunrath would love that. He would also have loved it if I'd given two weeks' notice. I'd like to see Mr. Bunrath having to sit at the reception desk. I bet nobody'll ask him what *he's* doing after work. They'll say, "What happened to the one who used to be here (*gesturing*), the one with the teacups?" And he'll say, "Oh, she . .

31

ah . . left to get married," or something *nice* like that. "See all those cars going by? That's her wedding party." "Then why aren't they honking their horns?" "Because she was always a lady of exquisite taste." Except when she was drunk. Excuse me. But what I really mean is, you've got to realize that all this neat packaged stuff is the shit it is and either find some way of (*enunciating carefully*) *assimilating* it or . . well, whatever you decide, but stop pretending it's apple butter. Did you know, by the way, that Bunrath Chemicals has developed a synthetic formula that will make *anything* taste like apple butter? Mr. Taggart told me about it this morning. That was one of the things that for me, personally, really tore it. (*pause*) I don't seem to be making very good sense at all, do I?

EDGAR

I think you make very good sense, Miss Lemming.

MISS LEMMING

You know you're the only man in the office who calls . . called . . me Miss Lemming? Even the ones I scared off called me Dorine. *Dorine Lemming.* Isn't that a name, for Christ's sake? Do you know what a lemming is? It's a little furry animal. Do you think I'm like a little furry animal? (*Edgar starts to reply.*) Don't say yes or I'll cry all over you. (*She blows her nose again.*) Let me tell you about the lemming. Then you can tell your wife, "I was on a park bench being told about lemmings." Anyway, the European lemming, *Lemmus lemmus*, every so often shows up in huge numbers and they start moving across the country. Well, eventually they get to the ocean, and, here's the thing, they keep going right into the ocean, and they all drown, every last furry one. And of course the scientists ask, "Why?" But here's the thing. The wise Norwegian fisherfolk, who are right there when it happens, swear they can hear the lemmings crying out, just before they take the plunge, "Why not?"

EDGAR

Dorine.

MISS LEMMING

Oh, Jesus, Edgar. (*She dabs at her eyes, then suddenly starts.*)

EDGAR

What?

MISS LEMMING

I lost my contact.

EDGAR

What?

MISS LEMMING

My contact lens. It's on the ground somewhere. (*Edgar gets down on his hands and knees and begins crawling around.*) Never mind. I don't need them anymore.

EDGAR

No, I'll find it. (*She closes her eyes and sits motionless while he hunts for it.*) Here it is. (*He rises and hands it to her. She rises too. The great bell is heard tolling again.*) Listen, will you have dinner with me?

MISS LEMMING

I'm sorry. At one time I would have but not now. I promised myself something, and that's all there is to it. I have to go now.

EDGAR

(*for the first time savage and passionate, almost in tears, grabbing her arm*) WHY?

MISS LEMMING

(*gently disengaging herself*) Why not? (*She waves.*) Cheers. (*Exit Miss Lemming. Edgar stands looking after her. Phyllis enters.*)

EDGAR

Hi.

PHYLLIS

Hi.

EDGAR

I thought you were going to have your hair fixed.

PHYLLIS

(*too glibly*) Mr. Dick couldn't work me in. (*slight pause*) Why? Does it look awful?

EDGAR

It's all right. (*They start walking.*)

PHYLLIS

I thought you were going to call me from work.

EDGAR

Well, I didn't go back to work.

PHYLLIS

You *what*?

EDGAR

Did you go to the store?

PHYLLIS

Yes. What do you mean you didn't go back to work? Where have you been all day?

EDGAR

I sort of wandered around. I went to the museum, and I looked at fishing tackle and bought myself a couple of neckties.

33

PHYLLIS

Why didn't you go back to work?

EDGAR

I . . had to think things out.

PHYLLIS

Did you?

EDGAR

Uh . . What did you buy at the store? (*Phyllis does a sharp reaction.*)

PHYLLIS

Four rolls of toilet tissue.

EDGAR

What's the matter?

PHYLLIS

I left them somewhere.

EDGAR

Why did you buy so many?

PHYLLIS

WHAT DO YOU CARE? (*a loud blast from the horn of a passing truck*)

EDGAR

YOU DIRTY FUCKER!

PHYLLIS

Edgar!

EDGAR

He was trying to kill us!

PHYLLIS

Edgar! I've never heard you talk like that.

EDGAR

I never had a truck driver try to kill me before.

PHYLLIS

Edgar, he wasn't anywhere near us. He was beeping at the car in front of him.

EDGAR

I don't care. (*pause*) I want to go home.

PHYLLIS

There's nothing to eat at home. I want to go to a restaurant.

EDGAR

All right, all right.

PHYLLIS

Here's a place.

EDGAR
Facciamata's. All right.

PHYLLIS
Does my hair look awful?

EDGAR
It's all right.

PHYLLIS
Because if it looks awful I'm not going in.

EDGAR
It's all right. Come on, it's cold. (*They enter the restaurant area.*)

WAITER
Two?

EDGAR
Yes. (*Waiter leads them to the table.*) Do we get a menu?

WAITER
Hey, Mr. Facciamata! (*Enter Mr. Facciamata, large, dark, and hairy.*) He says he wants a menu. (*Mr. Facciamata surveys Edgar.*)

MR. FACCIAMATA
Give him a menu. (*Exit Mr. Facciamata. Waiter brings a large menu, offers it to Phyllis.*)

PHYLLIS
Oh, I know what I want already. I want the filet steak. (*Waiter passes menu to Edgar.*)

WAITER
And how would you like that?

PHYLLIS
Uh . . medium.

WAITER
Have you decided, Mister?

EDGAR
Um. Sirl . . no. Ummm . . wait a minute. What's this? "The Man's Cut. U.S. Prime. $4.50." That sounds good. I'll have that. Rare. (*Waiter surveys Edgar for a moment.*)

WAITER
Mr. Facciamata! (*Mr. Facciamata reappears.*) He wants the Man's Cut. (*Mr. Facciamata looks at Edgar inscrutably for a moment.*)

MR. FACCIAMATA
Give him the Man's Cut. (*He exits. Edgar looks hard at Phyllis, who has her head turned, looking after Waiter. He reaches across the table.*)

35

EDGAR

What's a green stamp doing behind your ear?

PHYLLIS

Well, I'm sorry, but I don't always have time to take care of myself like when we were dating. I notice *you* don't shave as close as you used to. I remember sometimes you'd have blood oozing out of the pores around your mouth, you'd shaved so close. Whatever happened to those days, Edgar?

EDGAR

(*lighting a cigarette with abrupt movements*) *I* don't know. (*to Waiter*) Say, could I have a double J. and B. and soda?

WAITER

Sure.

PHYLLIS

(*lighting a cigarette*) I'd like a Pink Squirrel.

WAITER

Yes, ma'am.

EDGAR

You'll spoil your appetite.

PHYLLIS

So what.

EDGAR

All right, all right. (*pause*) Who are you being now?

PHYLLIS

I'm not being anybody. What kind of a question is that? I'm being myself.

EDGAR

All right, all right. (*Waiter brings the drinks.*)

WAITER

Which one gets the Pink Squirrel?

PHYLLIS

I do, thank you. (*Waiter distributes drinks and exits.*)

EDGAR

Well. I don't know what we're sniping at each other for.

PHYLLIS

Oh, you know; end of the day . . Mm, that drink helps.

EDGAR

Yuh. (*He drinks.*) Did you go to the store?

PHYLLIS

I told you I was going to the store; why do you keep asking if I went to the store? (*Edgar starts to reply but can't find anything to say.*)

EDGAR

Well . . Jesus. (*He slumps in his chair, chin on chest, staring at the tablecloth. Waiter enters with a tray, calling behind him.*)

WAITER

Mr. Facciamata, the steaks are ready. You'd better be out here. (*Mr. Facciamata enters. Edgar and Phyllis put their cigarettes out together.*)

EDGAR

Ouch.

WAITER

(*to Phyllis*) Did he burn you?

PHYLLIS

No, I burned him.

WAITER

Oh. Okay. (*serving*) Filet steak . . and . . Man's Cut. (*They cut into their orders.*)

EDGAR

It's tough.

WAITER

That's right. We say around here, if you can't eat that steak, Mister, you're not a man. Gable ate it. Cooper ate it. Bogart ate it.

EDGAR

How is yours, Phyllis?

PHYLLIS

It's all right, I suppose. It's too well done. I like it rare.

EDGAR

If you like it rare, why didn't you ask for it rare?

PHYLLIS

If I have to ask for a thing I don't want it.

WAITER

Cagney ate it. Robinson ate it. Jomo Kenyatta ate it.

EDGAR

Jomo Kenyatta?

WAITER

Former head of the Mau Mau.

MR. FACCIAMATA

(*moving in*) They call him Burning Spear.

PHYLLIS

(*transfigured*) Burning Spear.

EDGAR

Are you the manager?

37

MR. FACCIAMATA

That's right.

EDGAR

Well, this is ridiculous. This awful stuff is advertised as U.S. Prime. That means it's supposed to be tender, doesn't it?

MR. FACCIAMATA

You find it not so?

EDGAR

It's tough as shoe leather.

PHYLLIS

Are you going to make a scene?

EDGAR

You want me to stand up for my rights, don't you?

MR. FACCIAMATA

And it is your right that all things must be tender and fluffy?

EDGAR

Listen, what is this?

MR. FACCIAMATA

(*holding up a hand*) Pardon me. To those whose teeth have known the hard bone of reality, this steak is not tough. Look at these teeth. Strong, are they not? And white? They grow from gums that are on the side of life. To such teeth, this steak is merely what we call *al dente*. My uncle Marco, for instance, comes to this country maybe, what, fifteen, twenty years ago. He opens a restaurant, and there he serves pasta in many forms. Farfalle. Mostaccioli. Tirabaci. And his pasta is *real*. In it is the taste of the sun and the air where it is hung to dry; sometimes the droppings of the deep-bosomed pigeons of Tuscany. It is golden and when you bite it, it springs back, like the thighs of a fine woman. But he succumb soon to false values. They send his pasta back to the kitchen. "Softer!" they say: "softer." America destroy my uncle Marco. Soon his soul is mush, like his lasagne. I think: America will never destroy me. I am strong. I am on the side of life. In Puzzaforte, where I come from, is life, savage, pulsing. Little boys peeing against wall. Girls crossing themselves as priest ride by on bicycle. *Real.* And I have this dream. I will come to America, and will have restaurant where only those who are on the side of life will eat. Right, Dino?

WAITER

Right, Mr. Facciamata.

EDGAR

Listen, my money is good; I . .

MR. FACCIAMATA

Hah! You Americans think you can buy anything with money. Here we know better.

EDGAR

This is America we're in right now, buddy. You people think you're so damn smart just because you lost the war. You think you can come over here and tell us how to run our lives. Phyllis. Your steak was tough, wasn't it, Phyllis?

PHYLLIS

It was just a little too well done, that was all.

MR. FACCIAMATA

You like it rare, hey, Signora?

WAITER

Blood raw.

PHYLLIS

Well, yes.

MR. FACCIAMATA

What a woman. The reward of a hero, hey, Dino?

WAITER

Hey, hey, Mr. Facciamata.

EDGAR

You leave my wife alone.

MR. FACCIAMATA

Sit down. SIT DOWN. (*to Phyllis, who is trembling with tension*) I will not fight him. The bull fights only with the bull. But he will hear me out. To my restaurant come many men. Some laughing, some doomed, but all on the side of life. All men. None rotten. All strong. Not like him, eh, Dino?

WAITER

Not like you, Mister. They ate the Man's Cut. Right, Mr. Facciamata?

MR. FACCIAMATA

Right, Dino. They ate the Man's Cut. Of them was one, a writer of books, dead now. Once I said to him, "Words . . I am not good at them. You are a wordsmith; write what is in our hearts. Write what is a man." And he said, "I will write it out for you." (*He reaches in his pocket.*) I am going to read you what he wrote. And then you are going to leave my restaurant forever. You owe me nothing. Only the courtesy to hear this, and then to leave, knowing what is the difference between him who is on the side of life and him who is not. (*He extracts a folded, timeworn piece of paper from his wallet, unfolds it, puts on a pair of steel-rimmed spectacles, and reads.*) "But a man does many things for reasons other men don't need to ask a man why he does them; they know, because they do these things too: maybe not the same ones, or in different ways, but something, something to give a man some reason to do these things for other men to see and not to have to ask him why he does them, or even whether he does them for the same reasons they do, because every man who does them knows it's for different reasons though it may be done, this depends on the man and why he does them, in the same way." Now go. Go; go forever. (*The lights begin to dim. Waiter comes out of the kitchen with shish kebab on a flaming sword. Unhurried, inexorably, like St. Michael, he drives Edgar and Phyllis before him out of the restaurant. Thunder begins to rumble faintly, growing strong with the darkness.*)

WAITER

You can stay if you want to, lady.

PHYLLIS

No, thank you. He's my husband. (*Exit Edgar and Phyllis. Waiter exits, striking the tablecloth as he goes. Mr. Facciamata stands stage center, lit only by flashes of lightning, singing.*)

MR. FACCIAMATA

Vivan le femmine,
Viva il buon vino,
Sostegno e gloria
D'umanità.

(*There is a tremendous roll of thunder.*)

CHORUS

Hail to the light, which is under the edge of the world
And alone in the country of darkness.
This is the land where outcomes are doubtful,
The land of the corpse trying to become an embryo
And the zero struggling to be an egg.
The land is familiar only to the monsters which inhabit it.
There is no advice to be given.
If you say, "It is cold," we can only agree.
If you say, "I hurt," we can only say, "We bet you do."
You are welcome to everything we have in our pockets:
A ball-point pen that writes under water,
A fishing license from last year,
A bottle of pills that are good for a spastic colon,
And four five-cent stamps that show George Washington naked.
Goodbye now. Try to remember your ZIP-code number,
And if you happen to come back, give us a call.

(*Dim area light up. Edgar and Phyllis enter.*)

EDGAR

It's late.

PHYLLIS

It's awfully late, Edgar.

EDGAR

Probably no use turning the set on.

PHYLLIS

Turn it on.

EDGAR

We can't watch it if there's nothing good on. It makes me nervous to just sit there and watch crap.

PHYLLIS

Everything makes you nervous. And anyway, we can't *not* watch it. There's nothing else to do. (*pause*)

EDGAR

What do you mean by that?

PHYLLIS

What do you mean, "What do I mean"? Does everything I say have to mean something?

EDGAR

You used to like being alone with me.

PHYLLIS

Well, why don't you act like *you* like being alone with *me*?

EDGAR

What do you mean?

PHYLLIS

Edgar, if you say "What do you mean" once more I am going to scream.

EDGAR

What I mean is what do you mean by "There's nothing else to do"? You mean I don't make love to you enough, is that it? If I'm so awful why don't you walk out on me? I'm not a . . "Burning Spear," is that it? I'm a loser, is that it?

PHYLLIS

If I didn't love you I wouldn't stay with you.

EDGAR

I didn't say that. I said am I so awful?

PHYLLIS

Edgar, will you either talk sense or just stop talking?

41

EDGAR

Listen, I don't know what's going on. All of a sudden some great big *thing* has started. You're going pick pick pick . . and . . I don't *feel* right.

PHYLLIS

Well, why do you have to take it out on me? Every little thing that happens you act like I messed my pants or . . (*She stops suddenly.*)

EDGAR

Listen, I feel just awful. It's like a great big . . black . . (*a centrifugal gesture*) *snowball* or something . . You know what I feel like? I feel like nothing.

PHYLLIS

What?

EDGAR

Why don't you *listen* to me for a change?

PHYLLIS

Are you hot?

EDGAR

What?

PHYLLIS

Are you hot? I'm burning up. (*Edgar goes over to her and puts his hand on her forehead.*)

EDGAR

Your forehead is cool. (*slight pause*) I'll turn down the thermostat.

PHYLLIS

Turn on the television while you're at it. (*Edgar turns on the television by remote control. Mr. Kirschbaum steps into the resultant pool of blue light.*)

MR. KIRSCHBAUM

(*reading from a teleprompter*) Some of you are probably wondering how to get more food for your money. Well I am here to tell you. I am Nathan Kirschbaum proprietor of Kirschbaum's Big Cherry Superette and I want to tell you about some of the wonderful food values we have for you. Take crabmeat. (*Phyllis leaps up and changes the channel. Chorus appears and begins to sing the Dies Irae.*)

EDGAR

What's the matter with *you*?

PHYLLIS

It was a commercial. You don't want to watch the commercial, do you?

EDGAR

Well, we could have waited, couldn't we? Something good might have been on.

PHYLLIS
He makes me nervous.

EDGAR
Who?

PHYLLIS
Kirschbaum.

EDGAR
For hell's sake, you go in there every day. (*Phyllis does not answer.*) Oh, when something makes *me* nervous we watch it anyway, but when something makes *you* nervous that's different, isn't it? And what the hell have you got on *now*?

PHYLLIS
A little music. I don't suppose we could have a little music, could we? That would be too much to ask.

EDGAR
That kind of music? We can turn on the radio if you want music. But then you'd have to look at me, wouldn't you? And you wouldn't like that.

PHYLLIS
Edgar, what is the matter?

EDGAR
I don't know. All day long I've felt like everybody's after me. Like they won't let me live. I'm not good enough. So I have to be put away. Like a stray dog in a gas chamber. I bet if this was during the war I'm the kind of guy who'd wind up as a bar of soap.

PHYLLIS
Edgar, nobody is after you.

EDGAR
They're cutting the ground away from under me. If I can't be what they want me to be, I want to not feel guilty about being what I am. I mean, is that too much to ask?

PHYLLIS
When I was a child my mother showed me this picture. "The Peaceable Kingdom." She sang something about it. "The lion wild will lie down with the child, and I'll be changed from the thing I am." That's what I wanted.

EDGAR
The Garden of Eden. Handy to shopping center. Yours in five easy payments. (*slight pause*) I guess we didn't make it.

PHYLLIS
Why don't we go to bed?

43

EDGAR

I don't think I could sleep. And I had an awful dream last night. (*pause*)
It's cold in here.

CHORUS

It's awfully cold, Edgar.

EDGAR

What?

PHYLLIS

I'll go make you something hot to drink.

EDGAR

Didn't *you* say that?

PHYLLIS

Say what?

EDGAR

It's awfully cold.

PHYLLIS

You said that.

EDGAR

Phyllis, I'm hearing voices. I think I am going crazy.

PHYLLIS

Edgar . .

EDGAR

Maybe it's the people who used to live here.

PHYLLIS

Edgar, nobody lived in this house before us.

EDGAR

In the house that used to be here. Remember? The old brick house? We
used to pass it all the time when we were going together.

PHYLLIS

Dirty bricks.

EDGAR

They were old bricks. It was a very old house. I always thought it was
empty, but it wasn't. There was a little light on when we went by at night.

PHYLLIS

A little yellow light. I remember. And once when we went by toward dawn
there was a woman walking around under the trees. Remember when we
used to stay up all night? Remember what we did?

EDGAR

I thought we were pretty happy then. What happens? Do you carry a seed
in you like an egg or a cancer and when something touches it . .

44

PHYLLIS

(*shrugs*) That's what you're supposed to be going to the doctor to find out. (*She exits. Edgar pours himself a drink and twists the channel selector. A boxer appears, being interviewed by a sports announcer.*)

BOXER

They call him Burning Spear.

ANNOUNCER

Burning Spear.

BOXER

That's right.

ANNOUNCER

(*archly*) Is that anything like Shakespeare?

BOXER

(*evenly*) Yeah, maybe that's something like Shakespeare.

ANNOUNCER

Well. You got some poetry for us?

BOXER

Yeah.

ANNOUNCER

Let's hear it.

BOXER

> "The sun starts to go down.
> It is time to go home.
> It is time to go home, thou
> who forge the iron.
> We are children of death; we
> cannot get away from it."

ANNOUNCER

That doesn't sound like you.

BOXER

No.

ANNOUNCER

Doesn't even rhyme.

BOXER

That's right.

ANNOUNCER

I like poetry that rhymes.

BOXER

You do.

ANNOUNCER

Yes.

BOXER

Well.

ANNOUNCER

I bet the Garden is sold out.

BOXER

That's right.

ANNOUNCER

And tonight you leave.

BOXER

That's right.

ANNOUNCER

How are you getting there? Flying?

BOXER

I'm going by train.

ANNOUNCER

I bet there'll be quite a reception committee.

BOXER

There will be people
Standing on the platform.
Those who are wise
Will stand far back.
Some won't know
That the big train's coming.
They will be standing
Closer to the track.
(*Edgar stiffens.*)

The lights are sickly
And the floor is dirty,
Black as the floor
In the home of the dead.
They will all look down
To a point in the distance
Where the rails seem touching
The roof of the shed.

And some will know
What's going to happen.
To those who don't

FIVE EASY PAYMENTS

It will seem like a dream;
And they *won't* know
Till the lights are on them,
Till their ears are blasted
By the big train's scream.
(*Under this, the roar of an approaching train, growing to screaming cre-
scendo. Edgar switches set off. Sound continues. Edgar clutches his head
and staggers about. Sound out. Enter Phyllis in robe and slippers.*)

PHYLLIS

Edgar.

EDGAR

Listen, I've got to talk to you. I didn't go back to the office today because
I was afraid to.

PHYLLIS

Afraid of *what*?

EDGAR

I don't *know*. Isn't there some way out of this?

PHYLLIS

Out of what? How can we get out of it if we don't know what it is?

EDGAR

Then you know what I mean. Please, Phyllis. *You know what I mean.*

PHYLLIS

I . . Edgar . . we just can't let ourselves think like this. You know you
can think and think and think until there's nothing left. You can look at
yourself until you see nothing but a piece of . . (*pause*) Listen, Edgar.
We'll just forget it. We'll start all over tomorrow as if nothing ever happened.

EDGAR

Oh, boy. Oh, boy. Ha-ha.

MRS. BIERCE

Ha-ha.

EDGAR

(*rising*) REAL FUNNY, ISN'T IT? A FUNNY THING HAPPENED TODAY . .

PHYLLIS

IT WASN'T MY FAULT WHAT HAPPENED TODAY. I COULDN'T HELP IT!

EDGAR

(*quietly*) I couldn't help it either. I guess nobody could help it. (*pause*)
Jesus.

PHYLLIS

Mary. (*Pause. Edgar turns the set back on, twists the channel selector.*)

47

ANNOUNCER

On the local scene, a fire in a Plymouth Avenue tenement has claimed the lives of five babies. Fire officials were unable to say where the tragedy originated. "It's just one of those things," commented Department Chief Krebs. "The guy who owned the building says it's not his fault. The kids' parents say it wasn't their fault. So I guess it's nobody's fault." And that's the final news roundup, brought to you by Federal Savings and Loan, A Mighty Fortress in Time of Trouble. (*sound of organ: the first two phrases of "Ein Feste Burg Ist Unser Gott"*)

ANNOUNCER

Strength for Tomorrow. Each night before leaving the air this station brings you Reverend Dean Samuelson of Golgotha Episcopal Church with a message for *you*.

REV. DEAN SAMUELSON

In the Twenty-Second Psalm we read, "But I am a worm, and no man; a reproach of men, and despised of the people. All they that see me laugh me to scorn: They shoot out the lip, they shake the head . . Many bulls have compassed me: strong bulls of Bashan have beset me round . . They gaped upon me with their mouths as a ravening and a roaring lion: I am poured out like water . . my heart is like wax; it is melted in the middle of my bowels . . They look and stare upon me . . Deliver my soul from the sword; my darling from the power of the dog." As we enter another Friday morning, may the Lord make his countenance to shine upon you and give you peace. In the name of the Father and of the Son and of the Holy Ghost, Amen. (*Edgar and Phyllis cross themselves.*)

PHYLLIS

Postum or cocoa?

EDGAR

Cocoa. (*She exits. "The Star-Spangled Banner" begins to play. It concludes. The test pattern appears. Sound of a low electric hum. Edgar stands alone as lights dim to blackout.*)

THE END

Five Easy Payments by John Lewin was presented October 10, 1965, at the Tyrone Guthrie Theatre, Minneapolis. It was directed by Alvah Stanley.

Cast of Characters

EDGAR MOMPESSON	James J. Lawless
PHYLLIS MOMPESSON	Evie McElroy
MRS. BIERCE	Ann Whiteside
MR. KIRSCHBAUM	Sandy McCallum
MR. FACCIAMATA	Charles Cioffi
MISS LEMMING	Niki Flacks
EDGAR'S FATHER	Earl Boen
DR. FINGERMAN	William Greene
REV. DEAN SAMUELSON	John Lewin
PHYLLIS' BROTHER	Dean Stricklin
WAITER	Kenneth Frankel
ANNOUNCER	William Greene
BOXER	Tim Christie

(Note. The character of Phyllis' brother does not appear in the final version of the play, as published here.)

49

JEAN-CLAUDE VAN ITALLIE

Where Is de Queen?

Cast of Characters

MAN
WIFE
NANNY
TRAPEZE LADY
FIRST AFRICAN
POET
SECOND AFRICAN
THIRD AFRICAN
PERFECT PLASTIC GIRL

WHERE IS DE QUEEN?

In the dark we hear a loud child's wail. Then in half-light we see a man asleep on a huge child's chair. Dream figures float around him. The setting is a nursery. A couple of regular-sized children's chairs, identical in shape to the one the man is on, are around a small table. The nursery, however, is not a realistic one; it is the environment of the man's dream. There are areas of the stage which are dimly lit or half hidden, as in a forest, where some of the dream characters can hide when the man is only partly aware of them. The entire play takes place in that instant of the man's beginning to awake when his wife calls him on the telephone. The phone rings one time, loudly and violently. Most of the dream figures scuttle away. A light is on in one corner of the stage, which is the wife's. She holds a telephone in her hand, and her setting is, by contrast to the man's, very realistic.

WIFE

Are you there?

NANNY

(*with the voice of a telephone operator*) I'm trying to reach your party. (*Nanny, like all the characters with the exception of the man himself and the wife, is a dream figure and has fantastic masklike makeup. Her hat is particularly awkward and severe. Her costume is white, like a nurse's.*)

MAN

(*starting to say "Are you there?"*) Ahhhhhhh . .

NANNY

One moment please. Keep your hands at your side.

WIFE

I'm calling . .

NANNY

I will connect you in just one . .

MAN

Ahhhh . .

NANNY

Your party seems . .

WIFE

Hello?

NANNY

Your party seems . .

WIFE

Are . .

NANNY

(*slapping the man's wrist*) Keep your fingers out of the jam-pot.

MAN

Ahhhhh . .

NANNY

Just one moment.

(*The light fades on the wife and Nanny leaves. Enter a lady on a trapeze, a few daisies in her hair suggesting a crown. She is a little portly and very self-satisfied. She wears a long white dress and a red ribbon over her bosom.*)

TRAPEZE LADY

Yoo-hoo.

MAN

Where are you?

TRAPEZE LADY

I'm up here. I'm up here, she said.

MAN

Come down.

TRAPEZE LADY

I will not. I will not, she said.

MAN

Come down, he said.

WHERE IS DE QUEEN?

TRAPEZE LADY

Why, you're all excited. Why, you're all excited, she said. (*When she repeats her sentences Trapeze Lady does so directly to the audience, delighting in telling a lovely story about herself that she knows she is telling well. The man is increasingly frustrated by her inaccessibility.*)

MAN

I'm not. I'm not, he said. But I demand to know where the dancing girls are.

TRAPEZE LADY

I made no promises. She made no promises.

MAN

I'm thirsty.

TRAPEZE LADY

Have some cod-liver oil. Have some cod-liver oil, she said.

MAN

Come down.

TRAPEZE LADY

I will never come down.

MAN

Why not?

TRAPEZE LADY

(*singing**)

'Cause I'm on my way to the ball.
As I float, hah, hah
So remote, ho, ho,
I'm on my way to the ball.
In my dress of silk
With the milk chiffon
I'm dressed to kill all the beaux.
See my shoes of glass
See my hair so red . . so long . .
'Cause I'm on my way to the ball.
As I float, hah, hah
So remote, ho, ho
I'm on my way to the ball.
See my shoes of glass
See my hair so red . . so long . .

* A waltz tune for this song and a rock-and-roll tune for the song on page 63 have been written by Gary W. Friedman. Copies are available from Dramatists Play Service, Inc., 440 Park Avenue South, New York City.

Yearn for me,
Pine for me,
Clap for me . .
But, tee-hee,
You can't have me
'Cause I'm on my way to the ball . .

(*She swings happily out of sight, blowing kisses. Phone rings loudly once. The man finds himself in front of a tree which he kicks in pure frustration. The tree dances about a bit when kicked.*)

TREE

(*basso profundo*) Leave me be, said de tree.

MAN

(*surprised, to the audience*) Hah, a tree!

TREE

Dat's right.

MAN

(*looking about, very methodical*) No hammer, no axe. I'd better worship this tree. Oh, sacred tree . .

TREE

Oh, leave me be.

MAN

What?

TREE

A tree. Tall. And den leafy. Wid de sap. And de bark, and de veins and a little bit ob dat purply coloration in de middle ob de trunk. And all ob it, ob course, a-swirlin' around and about.

MAN

I'm busy.

TREE

Wid de sap and de veins . . (*The tree has worked up a little tune for itself which the man interrupts. He sits on one of the small chairs at the child's table which he uses as a desk, carefully ordering out neat piles of imaginary papers.*)

MAN

I have my business to tend, my appointment book, my calendar, my tax agenda, my, my, my telephone, address, checkbook, book, book. My credit cards, and all the diverse perfumes to choose from at the drugstore counter. (*But the tree continues to sway about, humming.*)

TREE

And all ob it a-swirlin' around and about.

WHERE IS DE QUEEN?

MAN

(*delivering the first line to the audience, and then attacking the tree in frustration again*) It's a wonder I don't puke more often from all the perfume I've drunk. If I had an axe I'd chop you up, light you, and do a dance while you burned. (*The man has torn the branches of the tree revealing a sleepy African, who, startled by the lights, does a double take and darts off. The phone rings again. The man makes a great physical effort, tantamount to a sleeping person's lifting an incredibly heavy phone off a mammoth receiver, and tries to say "Are you there?"*) Ahhhhh . . (*Enter an English poet of sixty doing a cartwheel. He wears knickers, and a false beard and mustache. Each time he appears his false beard is different.*)

POET

Have you tea?

MAN

I haven't got time for *you*.

POET

That was very bad. I'll start over again. (*He leaves and returns immediately doing another cartwheel.*) Have you tea?

MAN

I'm frightfully sorry but that particular evening I'm going to be frightfully busy filling in my secretary on new accounts from Africa. How's that?

POET

(*concentrating on working out a soft-shoe number for himself, a little jig*) Not good.

MAN

Can you tell me who I'm waiting for?

POET

For me probably since I'm here.

MAN

I'm busier than that. (*Poet is concentrating on his soft-shoe number.*) I've read your biography, you see.

POET

Yes?

MAN

I congratulate you on its economy and imagery.

POET

Yes?

MAN

Just the right blend of city and country, tweeds and . .

POET

Top hats.

MAN

Tweeds and top hats. Umbrellas in both places but galoshes in the country and rubbers in the city.

POET

(*doing his jig*) Tweeds and top hats.

MAN

I've read your biography, you see, and therefore have no need of you. Bounce off, you twiddle me.

POET

(*suddenly lunging*) See this gnarled cane? Isn't it gnarled enough? Do you want me, an old man, to go through the trouble of putting more gnarls on it? Do you? (*He goes back to his soft-shoeing.*) I'm too old to rectify my image for you to grant it importance in your fledgling lexicon. Much too old to be bothered. And I'm off to see the Queen. (*The man, however, is not prepared to see Poet leave.*)

MAN

Have you any food?

POET

It's I who asked you for tea.

MAN

So you did, you piggy old man. Here. Take this. (*He hits Poet with his cane.*)

POET

I foresee great things from you.

MAN

(*in a sort of trance*) Tiresias and his mammals. A whole Noah's ark. Permit me not to have to count the easier animals, like cows and sheep and goats. I would prefer to stick to aardvarks, norts, poobles, emerald antimodees, and . . and themlike. Orlions with the green spot of the caliph denoting the genus prompt, the genus prompt, and also teeny tiny little orange goldbloats, and their sister-bug, the meow. The purrfect person to count these is me, as I sit on the head of my platinum pin. But as for the cows, let them perish in their own crud.

POET

(*striking the identical pompous pose the man has struck*) You would disgust me to a different degree, more or less, if it weren't that you resemble me so, either now or as I was then.

MAN

Aren't you a bit moldy? Are you thinking yet of heaven? Or is it impolite to burp the word in your presence?

POET

Dear young man, if you were only to know how many i's I've dotted in my time, with and without the aid of a machine and other embellishments to a middle-aged man's cock, you would not speak to me of my death which would only free me from having to endure another moment together with you on this planet.

MAN

Begging your holy pardon, I'm sure.

POET

You'll not get a penny's worth of pardon from me, no, nor holy anything else either. I'm not the sort. I *am* the sort, though, who will dance a gleeful old man's jig. Hee, hee. Hee, hee. (*Poet jigs off.*)

MAN

Jig off then, jog off, you old fruit. (*trying to lift the imaginary mammoth receiver again*) Ahh . . Much pawing about but with one foot still stuck on the ground, in with its original root, so to speak, and that kind of pawing about don't amount to much. Hellllloooo . . (*Enter Africans in a rush, including the one who played the tree. They are very very cool, particularly in their movements, but their stylized makeup indicates violence, and their costumes show them to be revolutionaries.*)

FIRST AFRICAN

Hallo, hallo. Have you bin seein' de Buckingham palace?

MAN

Aw, pushaw. They're going that way, the Queen and the Duke.

SECOND AFRICAN

(*smiling*) And soon she will be receivin' our spears in the fleshy parts ob her body.

MAN

Charge.

FIRST AFRICAN

Already we are de first Negro Disraeli, and now we rush on to Buckingham to be assumin' de eben greater powers ob de Queen.

MAN

Long live the Queen. (*They are on their way out.*)

FIRST AFRICAN

On to de palace.

SECOND AFRICAN

On to de royal twat.

THIRD AFRICAN

Her royal highnee will be a-tinglin', a-warnin' her ob our visit.

FIRST AFRICAN

Hurry, charge.

SECOND AFRICAN

Charge!

THIRD AFRICAN

Charge!!

ALL THREE AFRICANS

Charge!!!

MAN

(*waving goodbye*) So long, my friends. It's very lonely here now. Perhaps I could eat a little grass, pretend it's a cucumber sandwich, very elegant, in a little apartment (*indicates the child's chairs and table*) with a svelte little wife dressed in burnished tinsel, rustling as she pours tea. Surely songs have been written on dat theme. I had better put up an umbrella in the meantime. It won't do to see too much sky, not to feel protected, simply to be alone here under a tree. Surely an umbrella would be better. So much that is comforting has been written about them in English mysteries and children's stories. Perhaps mine is a child's story. We don't exactly choose our own story. We can lean a little to the right or left, add a few embellishments, a little red embroidery here or there, but the story, the story didn't start with me. This umbrella, this dear umbrella might as well be a toadstool and I sitting under it much as one of those comfortable frogs in the children's books, a-philosophically a-waitin' for the next chapter. Dat might be berry nice. I'll just sit here and watch the little raindrops tinkerbell their way into some child's head who's reading about me. Surely somebody is reading about me right now, watching out for me as I sit under this umbrella? Some child is solemnly contemplating me on an expensive colorplate while he or she is being read to aloud? Can anyone deny me that? But then why am I thirsty? (*He begins again to get out his "hello."*) Hehhh . . it ends so well in the books that were read to me. It's only a question of waiting and hehhhl . . help will come. In some form. Hehhhllll . . p will take the very next form that comes along. Anyone that comes along I will love according to my need. But if no one floats by, not a pink girl with a bow in her hair, if she who's reading this story doesn't come by . . Hehhhh . . if there's no one left here . . hehhl

. . if this place is deserted . . Hello!!! (*He has gotten it out finally. The light is up again on the wife.*) Hello.

WIFE

(*on the telephone*) Hello.

MAN

(*still very confused between dream and waking*) Hello.

WIFE

I woke you.

MAN

It's all right.

WIFE

You were sleeping.

MAN

Yes. Something. I'm in the baby's room. (*He is still also in a dream. The Africans tiptoe around him like fireflies.*)

AFRICANS

Glowin' on, glowin' on in de night. (*Trapeze Lady swings by, hovering over him on her trapeze.*

TRAPEZE LADY

Oh, de silly baby. De silly silly baby. Where den is all de laurels? Where is de tree? Here is de tree, de berry tree he is lyin' under. De pore boy, far from his mammy, havin' eaten only a little bit. Dis is de shame. Dis is de shame. How messy, how unexpected, how wounded. And how is de corn growin' on de udder side ob de moon? And dis is only one man to be containin' so much and how many udders, how many millions of others all over de world, cryin' and cryin' ober de milk spilled and dead and gone. In one war how many perish?

AFRICANS

In a revolution?

MAN

And in the blump-dump-moldy-horror of festering in an American suburb?

WIFE'S VOICE

Hello? (*Trapeze Lady goes off.*)

MAN

Fine.

FIRST AFRICAN

(*changing the mood entirely*) Well, dat is enough ob de dat.

SECOND AFRICAN

(*also starting to dance*) Enough ob de dat.

MAN

(*happily finding himself beginning to do a rock-and-roll number*) Baby's fine.

SECOND AFRICAN

Can't get enough ob dat chocolate ice cream with de whipped cream frostin'.

THIRD AFRICAN

Oh, dis is de pleasures ob de palaces. (*They are all, the Africans and the man, having a party together now, dancing.*)

FIRST AFRICAN

We is very happy about becomin' de Queen. Natcherly it can't be done wit'out a little rollin' ob de heads in de gutter . .

SECOND AFRICAN

A few ob de little white heads . .

THIRD AFRICAN

And especially dat ob de Queen.

FIRST AFRICAN

Well, boys, who shall slice de cake first? (*The Africans approach the man, threatening in mock fashion to slice him up.*)

FIRST AFRICAN

Eh, tell be dat.

SECOND AFRICAN

Who is going to slice off a bit o' dis delicious white cake?

THIRD AFRICAN

De Queen's buttock.

SECOND AFRICAN

Dat would surely make a fine meal for any ob us cannibals.

FIRST AFRICAN

Wid de bread . .

SECOND AFRICAN

. . and de butter . .

THIRD AFRICAN

Or even wid de notting.

WIFE'S VOICE

Hello?

MAN

She's going to look like you.

FIRST AFRICAN

Eatin' de curds and de wheys.

THIRD AFRICAN

Dis is de life.

MAN

(*as the rock and roll comes up louder*) This is *de* life. Teen-age life at its very best. (*singing and dancing*)

> Something slick,
> Something slimy,
> Is a-comin'
> Is a-comin' and a-huggin',
> Is a-comin' and a-huggin' and
> a-searchin' for me.

(*speaking*) And boy, will she ever be a doll.

PLASTIC GIRL

Yoo-hoo, Daddy, here I am, all muddled and pooh. (*She is a perfect plastic sort of girl wearing a perfectly tailored transparent raincoat, and a perfect plastic daisy in her hair.*) Wanna kiss? Wanna little kiss, Daddy? Why when you're an old sweety of a grandpa, Daddy-o, I'll still be smoking Newports. So long, Daddy. (*She leaves.*)

MAN

I'm having some difficulty keeping cool. I need something.

FIRST AFRICAN

Well then, have something, honey.

MAN

Thank you. (*Man lights up a joint of marijuana and inhales it. Poet enters, sniffing suspiciously. The Africans leave. Poet looks at the man.*) And so here I am, inside a painted egg, begging your pardon for my existence, living as I do down here, doing nothing much at all that you can count on our fingers.

POET

(*pointing at the marijuana*) What's that?

MAN

It's a pillow.

POET

It's a giraffe.

MAN

It's a pillow.

POET

It's a toy giraffe.

MAN

I'm nursing on it. It's a pillow.

63

POET

Pillows are soft and washable and white.

MAN

Not mine.

POET

And why, pray tell, do you want a toy giraffe when you could be earning five hundred dollars a week?

MAN

(*very much interested*) As much as that?

POET

Mmmmmm. I should say so.

MAN

Well, you should have said so before. Here goes.

(*Poet leaves. Man puts up a sign that reads "The Other Life." In the following television sketch he plays Mister, the Trapeze Lady plays Missus, and the Plastic Girl plays Little Dear. The First African plays Robinson Trousseau, doing calisthenics in one corner, and the two other Africans hold imaginary television cameras. In the television sketch the characters play to the television cameras rather than to each other.*)

MISSUS

(*She wears a few huge plastic curlers and an apron over her dress. She is discovered dusting with a pretty feather duster as her husband comes home from the office.*) Good evening, my dear. My dear, good evening. Did you have a good day, my dear. Oh, my.

MISTER

Ugh.

MISSUS

I want to speak to you about something, dear. I don't know quite well how to put it but, oh my. Take off your jacket, my dear, and I'll hand you your reading glasses, oh my dear. Oh, my, my dear.

MISTER

Where boy?

MISSUS

It's a girl, dear. Don't you remember? Oh, my. (*She calls upstairs.*) Your father's home, Little Dear. (*She comes back to her husband.*) She'll be right down. She has something to tell you. Oh, my. Did you have a bad day at the office, dear?

MISTER

Ugh.

MISSUS

Oh, my. Here she is, dear. Little Dear. Oh, my.

LITTLE DEAR

(*is constantly posing sexily*) Hi, Daddy.

MISTER

Who this?

MISSUS

Your daughter, dear. Little Dear. Don't you remember? Little Dear and I went out today and what do you think we bought? Tell your daddy, Little Dear.

LITTLE DEAR

You tell him, Moms. I can't.

MISTER

Me hungry. What to gnash?

MISSUS

Your favorite, dear. Steak. With steak.

MISTER

(*pointing to African in the corner*) Who that?

LITTLE DEAR

A friend of mine.

MISSUS

Don't be angry, dear. Oh, my.

MISTER

Who that!

MISSUS

Daughter bought a trousseau today, dear. Oh, my.

MISTER

Me no want no Trousseau in my hut!!

LITTLE DEAR

Daddy, I'm married. I'm married to that great big Robinson Trousseau over there. So you can simply lump it. And also I'm pregnant.

MISTER

(*completely outraged, like a wild caveman*) Moo Goo Gai Pan!! (*In fury he chases Trousseau and his daughter around and around as the light fades on them and focuses on Missus, as in a television closeup.*)

MISSUS

(*seated at the dinner table, staring soulfully at the spot she knows the camera to be*) Yet another trial. How, dear God, can I, a beautiful woman in her forties, go on, quarter hour by quarter hour, day after day, facing life in front of millions? Help me, O Lord, to realize The Other Life.

(*There is now a television commercial sung by the Africans. They sing, in high angelic voices, to the tune of "Holy, Holy, Holy."*)

AFRICANS

Hawley, Hawley, Hawley, All the Paints Preservhed.

All the Paints Preservhed. Hawley Paint Preserver.

(*When they are done, one of them holds a frame in front of Trapeze Lady's head and shoulders, making her appear as she would to the home viewer in closeup. Here Trapeze Lady is still the actress from the television soap opera but she doesn't wear the apron and curlers. She is a perfect exaggerated television personality, or several of them.*)

TRAPEZE LADY

Good night, ladies and gentlemen. This is Lilly Heaven. I hope you've enjoyed us tonight. I've certainly enjoyed being with you. "The Other Life" has been brought to you by our sponsors who wish to add their good wishes to my own in wishing you all a very warm good night. Good night. (*Each of the lines in this speech must appear to be definitely the last.*) This is Lilly Heaven saying good night, and to all a very good night. Good night everybody. Here's wishing you pleasant dreams. Sleep tight. From all of us to all of you, a warm good night. And now we must, I'm afraid, say good night, good night, ladies and gentlemen, and good night. Thanks a lot and God bless you. This is Lilly signing off and wishing all of you out there from all of us in here the very best possible good night. I can only hope that you enjoyed watching us as much as we enjoyed being here. Good night. Pleasant dreams. Sleep tight. It's been wonderful being with you, and I hope you'll invite us into your living room again tomorrow night. From the actors and myself, from the staff here, I want to wish you all the best possible night and day before we meet again. It's been wonderful being with you. It's been truly grand. I only wish we could go on but I'm afraid our time is up, and so this is your Lilly saying good night to you. Pleasant dreams. Good night all. Good night to you all. Good night to all of you. Good night. Good night. Good night. Good night. Good night . . Good night. Good night. Good night. To all of you out there from all of us in here, good night. And pleasant dreams till we meet again. Good night to you all. Good night. Good night. Good night. Good night. (*She sweeps off, singing the last line of "I'm on My Way to the Ball!"*)

THIRD AFRICAN

(*sitting in the middle of the stage, like an announcer*) The war in Viet Nam. (*The First and Second Africans approach each other threateningly from either side of the stage, meeting in defiance in the middle, smashing down the Third African with their fists while still only looking at each*

*other. When he's thoroughly beaten down they snort at each other, as if at
a fight well fought, and walk away.*)

THIRD AFRICAN

(*sitting up again as an announcer*) The Second World War: a retrospec-
tive exhibition. (*The three Africans and the man line up in trenches, two
facing two, making battle noises — shooting, explosions, etc.*)

FIRST AFRICAN

Get him.

MAN

Get him.

SECOND AFRICAN

Get him.

THIRD AFRICAN

Get him. (*They throw grenades at each other.*)

FIRST AFRICAN

Bonsai!

MAN

Heil!

SECOND AFRICAN

Heil!

THIRD AFRICAN

Long live de Queen! (*They make war noises and motions.*)

FIRST AFRICAN

Get him!

SECOND AFRICAN

Get him!

THIRD AFRICAN

Get him!

MAN

Get him! (*One crawls from a trench, pulls an enemy out of the opposite
trench and grapples with him. Another takes an imaginary bayonet and
stabs his opposite number. He stabs and stabs. As this action proceeds
Nanny enters, wearing, this time, a large red cross over her breast. She is
very clean and crisp but behaves as if she were being buffeted about by an
increasingly greater wind.*)

NANNY

Excuse me. Excuse me. Pardon me. Oh, dear. (*They are frozen, or almost
frozen, for her entrance. Now they start stabbing and fighting again.*) Oh,
dear. (*The four of them grunt and groan in warlike fashion. She isn't flus-*

67

tered by the war but she would like to get someone's attention to ask a question. She is worried about something. She talks very clearly. She steps over bodies, etc., as if there were many more than four on the battlefield. The men freeze when she speaks.) Have any of you seen a child? Four years old. Curly hair. Black. Red shorts with a white top. Jumper. I've mislaid him. I only went off for a second to the johnny. I can't find him. It's dreadful. Isn't it? Yes. Have you, sir, seen a small girl with long yellow hair, a daisy in it, wearing a white skirt and patent leathers? I'm afraid she's run off. Or perhaps it's I . . in any case I can't seem to . . she's apparently, she's not . . in any case I can't seem to . . the child and I, to reach our party now. Can you help me? Oh, dear. (*The men who have been frozen in rapt attention now start to moan softly, wounded.*) I'd be glad to offer you ice cream as a small reward. I have a nickel in my purse. Or a cigarette? Would you like that? That would make you feel good, wouldn't it? It's . . I would like to find the child. Yes. If any of you could . . It's my job, you see, my liveli . . that's at stake. Perhaps some ice cream to make you feel better? Oh, dear. (*They are all wounded, as if waiting on the battlefield for an ambulance and she were the nurse.*) If you can just hold on for a little bit now. There's nothing going to happen. I'm just looking for a child. Oh, dear. Trust me. They're coming very soon with the ambulance to take you to safety and dry socks. The doctor will be here just as soon as he can. You're being very brave. I'm Nanny. That's right. You're being very brave. Could you help me? I'm looking for a child.

MAN

Are you there?

NANNY

Four years old.

WIFE

Hello?

NANNY

You're being very brave.

WIFE

Are you there?

MAN

Hello.

NANNY

(*wandering off*) One moment please. I've got your party now. One moment . .

WHERE IS DE QUEEN?

WIFE

Could I have your attention for one moment? I would like your undivided attention for *just one moment.*

(*All the lights suddenly go off and one comes up on Poet who is discovered in a new beard, sitting lotus-fashion, like a Buddha. He speaks in a completely colorless tone of voice.*)

POET

But they say the most important events aren't in the histories. They say the most important events happen to four or three, and mostly two. They say these most important events remain unrecorded. And misremembered.

(*The lights go out on him. They come up on the man and the wife.*)

MAN

(*into the telephone*) Are you there? (*silence; into the telephone*) Are you there? (*silence*) Are you there? (*There are long silences between these questions.*)

WIFE

Are you there? (*silence*) Are you there? (*silence*) Are you there? (*silence*)

MAN

Yes.

WIFE

Ah. Tell me again. Where are you? Where are you?

MAN

I'm here.

WIFE

Ah. (*He quietly moves his chair back a little.*) Where are you? (*silence*) I just wanted to know where you were.

MAN

(*very rapidly*) Here.

WIFE

Oh, you frightened me. You moved, didn't you?

MAN

Yes, I moved.

WIFE

I know where you were before. I remember exactly. And I know where you've moved.

MAN

You're right. I have.

WIFE

Two can play that game. Call me now.

MAN

Where are you?

WIFE

(*very clever, standing on her chair*) I'm here.

MAN

You're high.

WIFE

That's exactly right. And I'm enjoying it very much.

MAN

No reason why you shouldn't. I enjoyed moving around.

WIFE

(*swinging her arms*) I'm waving my arms about.

MAN

Shall I look at you?

WIFE

Do, do. I'm looking very well. Aren't I? Tell me how I look.

MAN

Be quiet. (*She slows her arms down to slow motion.*) I've seen you. (*He looks slowly away.*)

WIFE

Well? How was it?

MAN

It was a summer afternoon, not too hot, with brilliant sun and cotton clouds. You wore the dress with the goldfish on it. "Come," you said, and you got up and walked through the field of daisies, looked back, smiled at me, and stretched out your hands.

WIFE

Oh, yes. And how was that?

MAN

It was good.

WIFE

It was. It might well have been the best moment of my life. I recall it now like a photograph.

MAN

And the *next* moment . .

WIFE

And the next moment I tried to see myself as you were seeing me. I became embarrassed. I tried to smile more but it was a strain. The sun was too bright. (*She sits again on her chair.*)

MAN

And I felt I had to live up to something. I wanted to stretch my legs, get up, run, but I was afraid of hurting you. You looked so odd, abandoned.

WIFE

I stopped thinking of you at all, looking uncomfortable, like a stranger there, on the ground, and I retired into a private landscape of my own, a gray garden in my mind.

MAN

I got away too. I thought of Swiss cheese.

WIFE

Was *that* what it was?

MAN

Yes.

WIFE

I'm so glad to know. I've always wondered.

MAN

I was terribly hungry. I suppose that was it. But I remember saying to you as gently as I could, "Where are you?" And you said wistfully, "I don't know."

WIFE

In point of fact I was in North Reading. I was raised there.

MAN

Hah! Why didn't you mention it?

WIFE

I don't know. Why didn't you mention Swiss cheese?

MAN

I didn't think you'd be interested, I guess.

WIFE

It might have been a lot of fun.

MAN

Maybe.

WIFE

Well, tell me now.

MAN

About what?

WIFE

Swiss cheese.

MAN

You really want to know?

WIFE

Yes, I want to know what's on your mind!!! finally!!!!

MAN

Well . .

WIFE

(*excited, encouraging*) Yes, yes, go on.

MAN

It's yellow, soft yellow.

WIFE

How about buff? (*The man begins by speaking to her but gets carried away and speaks instead directly to members of the audience.*)

MAN

Very good. Swiss cheese is buff. Well, perhaps not exactly buff, a shade or so lighter and brighter, but soft . . the color has a soft quality. You know, if you hold a candle behind a piece of Swiss cheese you can see the soft light through it . . Swiss cheese is translucent. Gentle. And the holes are smooth, perfect for running the tongue around . . absolutely smooth ridges. And then it's "all right." It's "acceptable." There's not a thing vicious about Swiss cheese. There isn't anybody on earth who would refuse to have it in their house, who would feel disgraced or put out by it. It isn't exactly a luxury, although it's true a lot of people would be glad for anything at all to eat, but it is nonetheless somewhat special. It's a little like Switzerland itself, or milk. It's not as frivolous as, say, butter, which is also made from milk. When you think of Swiss cheese you think "comfort," overstuffed armchairs, cool larders, wood and glass cheese dishes, quiet breakfasts, a picnic, a snack from the icebox. Swiss cheese, you know, is never fancy. It isn't something you'd find at a banquet, except perhaps melted and unrecognizable. But, on the other hand, it's not so undifferentiated as water, not *that* undifferentiated. It's blander than most cheeses, but not so faceless as cottage cheese or farmer's cheese or sour cream, not so flighty and versatile as eggs . . you know you can often define a thing by what it's not . .

WIFE

That's true.

MAN

And, well, I like the patterns the holes make, like wells on a smooth buff-colored field; neatly drilled wells on a desert. The holes really define the cheese. You can't taste the holes but it's on account of them, the empty spaces, I don't know, that the cheese is, I guess.

WIFE

I always knew you had a mind. Want to hear about North Reading?

MAN

Not especially.

WIFE

Why not?

MAN

I'm not really interested.

WIFE

(*the light fading out on her as the man gets up*) But North Reading can be as fascinating as Swiss cheese.

MAN

(*very full and proud of himself*) I must have a wider forum for my ideas. (*again, shouting*) I must have a wider forum for my ideas! (*He makes large, rallying gestures. One dubious African peers from behind a tree. He speaks importantly.*) Humph. Humph. (*He pronounces the word fully — "humph" rather than making the sound.*)

PLASTIC GIRL

Ohhh. (*During this part Plastic Girl plays the role of an ambitious wife. She wears a wide-brimmed, transparent plastic hat to match her raincoat. It has a plastic daisy in it.*)

MAN

Swiss cheese. My subject this morning, my friends, is Swiss cheese: the properties, natural and unnatural; the philosophy and psychology thereof. And may I present my dear wife without whose absence I would be nothing at all.

PLASTIC GIRL

(*throwing him a kiss*) I'm so happy.

MAN

(*professorial*) Our first subheading will be rotundity. Rotund. Rotundity. (*He plays with the word, rolling it in his mouth, giving it different rhythms, like a rooster.*) Ro-tun-di-ty. Rotundity. Ditty. Ditty. Rotund. Rotund ditty. (*The African yawns and starts off into the wings. Desperately the man tries to hold his interest by perking up the lecture.*) Not rotund ditty. Dirty ditty. Let us study the dirty ditty. (*There is a faint interest at "dirty." Plastic Girl holds her breath. The man sings.*) She stood out there in the cold night air while the wind blew up her nighty. (*The African starts to saunter again.*) Let us leave Swiss cheese for a while and

73

turn to . . to . . to ice cream. (*This is not completely without interest for the African.*) Now ice cream . . ice cream gives you kicks. (*a definite perking of interest*) And it is said to be the favorite food of the Queen. (*The Second African comes out from the wings.*) Yes, yes, gentlemen, of the Queen herself.

PLASTIC GIRL

(*to the audience*) And I am his wife and later will be his widow.

MAN

Ice cream. Ice cream. Ice cream. I warm to my subject. Come and get royal ice cream here currently at an enormous discount. Come and get your ice cream. (*The Third African appears. The man speeds up like a salesman.*) Put iron in your blood and iron in your blood, and stand your feet in the air, eat everything, buy everything, buy ice cream and be the Queen!!

PLASTIC GIRL

(*to the audience*) Oh they're listening. I'm so excited. Soon we shall be crowned. He'll play at the palace and I in a low-cut will lower my boobs to her maj. Eek-squeak. I can't wait.

MAN

Eat your royal ice cream here. It'll turn you white.

AFRICANS

Ahhhhhhhhhhh. (*He is mobbed by the Africans who snap his picture, and finally lift him up on their shoulders. He waves to Plastic Girl and audience.*) Hail, hail to the Queen.

FIRST AFRICAN

It is she de first Negro Queen of England to turn all the Negroes white.

SECOND AFRICAN

Hoorah for Queen Ice Cream.

POET

(*appearing from sidelines, speaking to Plastic Girl*) My, my, is that him? Truly? How he's grown. Although when I first met him I knew there was something there. I said so at the time. Ice cream, eh? Well, I must try some of that. Excuse me. Some ob de dat. (*The Africans parade around with the man on their shoulders. He waves and poses as if for news cameras.*)

FIRST AFRICAN

Hoorah for Queen Ice Cream.

SECOND AFRICAN

Long may she reign.

WHERE IS DE QUEEN?

THIRD AFRICAN

Long may she reign ober us.

FIRST AFRICAN

Happy as a lark and victorious.

THIRD AFRICAN

Victorious.

AFRICANS

Victorious. (*They carry him behind a screen where he can't be seen by the audience. Poet steps forward.*)

POET

Somewhere in our memory, calamitous in our past, poisoning our present, stone-like, colossal, venerable, ancient and terrible, completely certain, like a rock: Victoria.

AFRICANS

(*in awe and recognition*) Ahhhhhhhhh.

POET

(*to the audience, each title going up a little in pitch, like a prime minister on a state occasion*) Empress of India. Queen-Empress. Empress-Queen. High and mighty Prince of her Dominions and Peoples and Umbrellas across the Street. Her Imperial Royal Majesty the Queen Victoria of England and Somaliland, Ireland and Liverpool, Duchess of Dakaar, Countess of Kent, Dikibaa of Pradripoor, Thorwatch of Igglespent, Prush of Prosh, Howbigah in the Desert, Serene Patipah of the Salvation Army, Greedy Great-Grandma of Everyone, Savior of the Gray Noses, Grand Duchess of Rock and Roll, Jewel of the Southeast Desert, Imperial Imperium of Imperiosity, Granule of Farth and Penelope of the Sages, Oregano in the Pot, Chicken in the Plate, Homily of Homilies, de Queen ob England, Victoria Vagina!

EVERYBODY

(*cheering and cheering*) Long live de Queen. (*The screen is removed from in front of the man who is discovered seated on the huge child's chair as Queen Victoria. He wears an enormous gray crown in the form of a daisy, tied on to his head with a black velvet ribbon. A few panels of gray material hang from it, like Queen Victoria's veil. He speaks in a grave voice.*)

MAN

Thank you. We are much moved. The dear soldiers are fighting in the Crimea. The dear officers too. How *distressed* and *warm* it makes us feel. I have sent them some chocolates. The middle part of our body became exposed today as John Brown pulled us up out of the mud after the pony cart overturned. I was *most* amused and *very* brave. I believe that people are *better* today: men more brave, women more virtuous, and domestic animals more restrained. Lord M. thinks I am mad. He calls me his Faery Queen. I think he is an old caramel myself, so *dear* to me, and so Important to the Nation. The Irish presented me today with a castle near Dundee. Very drafty and cold but *quite* charming. I think I shall have it painted pink and black, dear Albert's favorite colors, aside from orangish brown, which, of course, we shall keep for our own privates. Another Opening of Parliament. Princess Beatrice and dear Alfie helped me hand out prizes to the Lords. The Lords were *most* grateful and *loved* the embroidered handkerchiefs. Unfortunately there was a *great* mixup and only one could be found. But Lord Burleigh got on his *knees* to me and said that he would tear that single *one up* with his *teeth* into as many *pieces* as there are *Lords*. I was very touched, but of course the idea was ridiculous. We merely bowed. He professed himself more honored than if we had given him a Dukedom. I *hope* that was not a *hint*!

AFRICANS
Long live de Queen!!

MAN
(*still as Victoria*) Thank you. We are much moved.

POET
(*leading a cheer*) Hip, hip for the Queen.

AFRICANS
Hip, hip, hooray for de Queen.

MAN
Thank you. We are much moved.

FIRST AFRICAN
De great Queen!

MAN
(*trying to move but unable to do so because of them*) Thank you.

SECOND AFRICAN
De gracious Queen.

MAN
We are much moved.

THIRD AFRICAN
De pretty Queen.

ALL THE AFRICANS
De Ice Cream Queen! (*The Africans have become seriously threatening. They continue to smile but they pinion the man to his chair.*)

WHERE IS DE QUEEN?

MAN

God save the Queen!

FIRST AFRICAN

De white Queen.

MAN

Scatter her enemies!!

SECOND AFRICAN

De Negro Queen.

THIRD AFRICAN

De red Queen.

MAN

Frustrate their knavish tricks!!! (*The Africans begin to eat the crown.*)

FIRST AFRICAN

De tasty Queen.

SECOND AFRICAN

De all-purpose Queen. De Queen.

AFRICANS

Hip, hip . .

OTHER DREAM CHARACTERS

'Cause I'm on my way to the ball.

WIFE

Are you there?

AFRICANS

(*The rhythm is interrupted, as if in mid-air.*) Hip . .

OTHER DREAM CHARACTERS

'Cause I'm on . . (*The lights go out completely, suddenly, along with the interrupted refrain.*)

WIFE

Are you there?

MAN

Are you there? (*There is a loud child's wail, identical to the one at the beginning.*)

THE END

Where Is de Queen? by Jean-Claude van Itallie was presented March 11–13, 18–20, 25–27, April 1–3, 1966, at the Firehouse Theatre, Minneapolis. It was directed by Sydney S. Walter. Music for the Trapeze Lady's song by Paul Boesing.

Cast of Characters

THE MAN	Marlow Hotchkiss
HIS WIFE	Martha Roth
NANNY	Carol Swardson
THE TRAPEZE LADY	Martha Pierce
THE POET	Mike Monson
THE AFRICANS	Paul Boesing
	Scott Nielsen
	Don Young
THE GIRL	Muniera Jakobi

ROMEO MULLER

The Great Git-Away

ALL PLAY AND A YARD WIDE

to Captain Frank Whiting, who launched and
skippered and navigated so beautifully

Setting

The entire action of the play takes place around and about the rather re-markable house of Carrousel Jones. The play is in two acts, more or less.

THE GREAT GIT-AWAY

ACT ONE

As the play is about to begin, Carrousel Jones, a rotund fellow, dressed in corduroy, comes down the main aisle of the theatre. He chats with members of the audience until the houselights start to dim. Then he gets up onto the stage and begins to tune an old beat-up guitar, which has been placed by the left proscenium. Finally, he strikes a chord. The houselights go out and a spotlight hits him. He bows to the audience.

CARROUSEL

Thank you, folks. My name's Carrousel Jones. (*strums guitar*) Name of the show's *The Great Git-Away.* (*another strum*) Now, was I you, I'd jest set back, relax, untie your shoes . . loosen yer girdles, make yourselves comfortable, while I tell ya about this dream a few of us had. Yeah . . a dream. (*sings with guitar*)

> Once upon a winter's night
> I dreamed a dream so true.
> And, if the dream's familiar, folks,
> Then you were dreaming too.
> Yes, the glory of this dream I dreamed
> Was you were dreaming too.

(*in brighter tempo*)

> Had this old dream 'bout
> The Great Git-Away.
> Happened one March

81

In the middle of May.
On a bright sunny morning
Out under the moon.
Never could happen,
But it's gonna happen soon.

(*The curtain rises slowly. Lights come up on a rather sketchy representation of an old, weathered farmhouse with a big front porch. The set is very colorfully done in a simple, American-primitive style à la Grandma Moses or Joseph Pickett.*)

CARROUSEL

On the banks of a river
That led to the sea,
Had me a house
'Bout big nuff for me.
River was rising
As rivers will do.
Swishin' and swirlin'
All twirlin' and blue.

(*He continues to play under dialogue. Henry, a good-looking but excitable country boy, rushes on.*)

HENRY

Hey, Carrousel! Run for the hills!

CARROUSEL

What for?

HENRY

Stop plucking that guitar! The river's rising!

CARROUSEL

Yeah, so I heard.

HENRY

(*climbs onto porch, and then onto roof; produces a spyglass, which he looks through*) Wow-eee! Washed out the drawbridge. And that statue of Thomas Edison is up to its kneecaps in raging water!

CARROUSEL

Nothing to worry about I can see.

HENRY

Nothing to worry about? (*He jumps down from roof.*) I swear, the world could be coming to an end and you wouldn't move. You wouldn't wiggle a toe if all the stars in the heavens collided and blew up into little quarter-inch bits.

CARROUSEL

I happen to believe in the eventual triumph of the secure.

HENRY

Where's Infinity?

CARROUSEL

Damned if I know.

HENRY

You know you never let him get out of your sight.

CARROUSEL

Infinity lives his life and I live mine.

HENRY

You gonna let that poor, half-witted old man get et up by those rampaging flood waters?

CARROUSEL

(*strumming guitar*) Aw, Infinity's far and away the most intelligent individual in the world. And the bravest. You won't get him to run from mere H_2O.

HENRY

You don't seem to realize that the river's rising. (*He calls.*) Infinity! Infinity! (*Infinity, a huge and powerful bald-headed old man totters from the house. He carries a comic book.*)

HENRY

Infinity, the river's rising! Run for the far-off high ground! (*Infinity looks to Carrousel. Carrousel shakes his head no. Infinity does likewise. He sits on the porch.*) Don't you guys realize . . ? (*Infinity makes some rather elaborate gestures.*) What'd he say?

CARROUSEL

Says please don't disturb him. The Mad Scientist has got Superman in one hell of a fix. (*Infinity starts to read the comic book avidly.*)

HENRY

How can ya sit there and let nature overtake you? (*furious*) Ain't ya got no pride? How come you ain't awed and terrified by this manifestation of the Lord?

CARROUSEL

Simple. I float.

HENRY

Oh.

CARROUSEL

Everything I own floats.

HENRY

Infinity. He don't float!

CARROUSEL

I float enough for two!

HENRY

Well. Well, doggone! I'm running from it. (*starts out; stops*) Seems like the only decent thing to do. (*looks off*) Hey, down the road! There's one of them shiny convertible cars coming. Maybe I can hitch me a ride to safety. S'long. Don't say I didn't warn ya. (*He runs off.*)

CARROUSEL

(*strums his guitar and sings some more*)

> Now this was the start
> Of the Great Git-Away.
> I'd been thinkin' and thinkin'
> For many a day . .
> That the world was too frenzied
> And worried for me
> My house and my guitar
> And Infinity.

(*He continues to strum.*) Infinity? You ready for it? (*Infinity nods yes.*) It's gonna be a long, long trip, old feller. (*Carrousel removes his hat and looks upward.*) May the Lord bless our caulking. (*Henry enters again.*)

HENRY

Hey!

CARROUSEL

I though you were well on your way to the safety of altitude.

HENRY

Folks in the car want to talk to you. They gimme this twenty-dollar bill just to get to talk to you. (*shouting off*) Right this way. (*Max Ellis, a dark, glowering man in an expensive, hand-tailored Italian suit, enters, followed by Sarah, a mink-draped, impossible sexy blonde.*)

MAX

My name's Max Ellis and I need water.

CARROUSEL

My name's Carrousel Jones, and you'll get plenty in a few minutes.

MAX

My radiator's boiling. I been speeding. You got a spigot?

CARROUSEL

Got a pump back there by the privy. But relax. Take it easy.

MAX

Gotta get outta here. Flood! Been down the river a few miles. That new plant I'm building . . ya know? (*no reaction from Carrousel*) I'm Max Ellis. The industrialist!

CARROUSEL

Can't say I ever heard of you.

MAX

(*furious*) Don't anybody read *Fortune*?

CARROUSEL

I'm sure you're everything you say.

MAX

I'm a self-made man. Nobody ever gave me a dime. Made a fortune in the past twenty years. Even with taxes. Capital gains! That's my middle name. Max Capital Gains Ellis! (*laughs, delighted with himself*)

SARAH

Ahem . .

MAX

That's my stepdaughter, Sarah. I made her what she is today. Ain't nothing too good for her. Say hello to the man, Sarah.

SARAH

Ever so pleased.

MAX

See? Manners, poise . . the works.

SARAH

Ya got a john?

MAX

What! You'll never get class.

SARAH

It's chilly. (*to Carrousel, pointing*) This way?

CARROUSEL

(*nodding yes*) Second to the right and straight on till morning.

MAX

(*hollering after her as she exits*) One more slip like that . . and so help me God . . back to finishing school.

SARAH

Hah! (*She exits.*)

HENRY

(*on roof with spyglass again*) Hey, that water is up to Edison's hip pockets!

MAX

It's the end of that plant for sure. But what the hell . . I'll write it off.

HENRY

It's up to his belt buckle!

MAX

Yessir, soon as this flood goes down . . I'll reorganize everything.

CARROUSEL

Everything?

MAX

Nothin' halfway about *this* baby. I'll rebuild this whole crummy landscape. Then subdivide it and make a fortune. That's my motto. No matter what happens . . *use* it.

CARROUSEL

Mr. Ellis, you are an inspiration.

MAX

(*delighted*) Yeah? Nobody thinks positive like me!

HENRY

Up to old Mr. Edison's vest pocket. You better hurry. The road outta here's gonna be washed away pretty soon.

MAX

Yeah. We gotta scram. Wait out the flood. Then come back, and . . operate! (*Infinity makes a gesture.*) What's he doing?

CARROUSEL

He says you might have some long wait.

MAX

Huh? Can't he talk?

CARROUSEL

He can. But he just don't want to at the moment.

MAX

What?

CARROUSEL

Infinity's a phenomenon of our age. A genius to end all geniuses.

HENRY

Aw, don't let him give you none of that, Mr. Ellis. Infinity's just an old man that don't say or know nothing.

CARROUSEL

Infinity don't say nothing 'cause he's just about said everything there is to say.

MAX

No kiddin'?

CARROUSEL

He knows everything there is to know. He's found out everything there is to find out. And, accomplishing all of this, he set down for about a year and a half to figure out what to do with his vast knowledge. After careful deliberation he figured the safest thing to do would be to shut up. Hence he is a model citizen and I find him invaluable.

HENRY

(*sarcastic*) The swelling crest has just covered up Mr. Thomas Edison's bow tie, if anyone's interested.

MAX

Maybe I could use him. Put him on my board. Nah, I never hire anyone over forty. Balls up my pension plans. I might have to pay before I liquidate.

CARROUSEL

Infinity don't need work. He's got his hands full just being Infinity!

HENRY

All ya can see is Mr. Edison's wavy hair.

MAX

We better scram. Vamoose. (*Sarah enters carrying a bucket of water.*)

SARAH

The pump's back there. While I was at it, I brought water.

MAX

(*takes it and runs off*) Good!

SARAH

I must compliment you on your accommodations. Back to nature motif, huh? Very touching. Authentic . . eh . . Americana.

CARROUSEL

A privy's a privy.

SARAH

(*disturbed*) I ain't putting you on . . really. I was only . . I mean it's just one of those books Max made me read. *A Treasury of Colonial Homes*. Real class. It wasn't bad . . lots of pictures. That's where I learned that word. "Americana." (*desperately*) I entertain for Max. Boy! You should see me pour tea. Real class.

MAX

(*returning*) Cut the gab. I got the water in. Come on, let's go.

HENRY

(*hand over heart*) Farewell, Mr. Edison. Gone, but not forgotten!

CARROUSEL

Crest'll be here any minute. (*checks pocket watch*) Yup.

SARAH

(*annoyed*) Always on the rush.

MAX

(*to Carrousel*) Ain't you coming? There's room. I happen to own the biggest goddamn car in the U.S.A.!

CARROUSEL

Naw. I'm gonna stay.

MAX

What are you? Some kind of hero?

CARROUSEL

Well, I tell ya. The only reason I'd go with you for would be to escape from the flood. The question arises, "What would I be escaping *to*?" Just the outside world. Hell, I'll take the flood!

MAX

Well, I'd worry about you, but I don't know you that good.

CARROUSEL

Don't waste those precious worries, friend. When that old river starts seeping up around the legs of this chair, I intend to move several feet up onto the porch. Infinity will set alongside of me.

MAX

Then what?

CARROUSEL

If all goes right, she'll displace water.

MAX

What?

CARROUSEL

My house here. Soon as I heard about the flood crest coming this way, I had Infinity make my homestead seaworthy. When the flood waters and me meets, this'll become a vessel.

HENRY

You're plumb crazy, Carrousel.

CARROUSEL

Hell no. I'm sick of this neck of the woods, anyway. Ever since my apple tree died and stopped producing bountiful harvests, I been meaning to push on. I hate automobiles, and I ain't much for walking. So this is as easy a way as any to see a bit of the world.

MAX

You mean you're gonna float down river on your house.

CARROUSEL

Down river. Up river. Whichever way the current chooses.

MAX

That's impossible.

CARROUSEL

Impossibility don't awe me in the least.

HENRY

Hey, come on. There's water seeping over the roads.

CARROUSEL

I'd be mighty pleased if you folks cared to join Infinity and me.

SARAH

I took a cruise once. To the Virgin Islands. Hah!

MAX

(*edging out*) Come on, will ya?

HENRY

Goodbye, Carrousel. (*Henry and Max exit.*)

SARAH

(*hating to go*) Bon voyage. Now ain't that class? It means . . Bon voyage. (*She shrugs her shoulders and exits.*)

CARROUSEL

(*starts singing and strumming guitar*)

> Now if you don't think
> Ya can travel this way,
> Wait till ya hear of
> The Great Git-Away.
> Sit back and enjoy
> This old tale that I tell
> Them that don't want to
> Can go plum to . .

(*Suddenly he cuts off his song and jumps a bit.*) Hey! I just felt the unpleasant sensation of cold liquid touching my feet. Better move up on the porch. (*He does so.*) Yessir, Infinity . . the time's je-e-e-est about come! (*Infinity nods yes, enthusiastically.*) We ready for it? Got everything battened down? (*Infinity nods yes.*) Toothbrushes, mail-order catalogues, playing cards, and canned goods!!? (*Infinity nods yes.*) Beer, checkerboard, and toothpaste? (*Infinity nods yes.*) Then, by gawd . . we *are* ready for it!! (*Infinity jumps up and down, excited.*) Waaaaaaahoooooo!! (*We can hear the sound of rushing water. Then we make out a girl's cry for help.*)

GIRL'S VOICE

(*off*) Carrousel. Oh, Carrousel!!

CARROUSEL

Who's that? (*looks off*) It's Emmy Pleasant. She's out in that soggy field
. . all alone . . with her . . child. (*Infinity shakes his head sadly.*)
This way, Emmy! Hurry!!

EMMY

(*off*) Hurryin' fast as I can!!

CARROUSEL

Faster! C'mon, you can make it, gal. Don't just run, Emmy. Hop from
stone to stone! There! That's it. (*Emmy, a fragile girl of about nineteen,
enters, carrying a small baby wrapped in blue blankets.*)

EMMY

Carrousel, oh Carrousel! Thank the heavens I found somebody left. I
thought that flood would just swaller me whole.

CARROUSEL

Hop aboard!

EMMY

Glad to. (*She gets on porch.*) My folks all pulled out in their Chevrolet
panel truck. Wouldn't take me unless I left Roger behind. (*indicates baby*) I just couldn't do that.

CARROUSEL

'Course not, Emmy.

EMMY

They don't understand. They thought by driving off for a bit they could
scare me into leaving him. But I wouldn't leave Roger for all the eggs in
China.

CARROUSEL

Now you just calm down.

EMMY

Not for all the broken bulbs on Broadway.

CARROUSEL

Sure . . sure.

EMMY

I ran and hid behind a cow. They came back for me, all right. But they
couldn't find me. Soon the flood water was lappin' at their heels. They just
had to leave.

CARROUSEL

Yes, Emmy?

EMMY

How do you intend to ward off the awesome aquatic calamity headin' our
way?

CARROUSEL

I intend to give before it.

EMMY

I suppose that's as good as any way. When my Roger grows up, he'll be able to reinforce a levee singlehanded. They'll be sorry they treated him this way then.

CARROUSEL

They'll probably hire the entire National Broadcasting Company and make a public apology.

EMMY

No, sir. I wouldn't leave my baby. Not for all the hay in the sunshine. Hold Roger while I fetch my bundle. It fell out in the field there. It contains my blue dress and various other things I cherish. (*She hands Carrousel the baby and exits. Carrousel unwraps the baby from the blankets and looks at it sadly. It is a shabby teddy bear. He looks to Infinity, who looks away and frowns. Carrousel wraps it up again. He sighs. The sound of oncoming water is quite loud. Suddenly, Henry, Max, and Sarah enter. Max carries several strongboxes.*)

MAX

That road was washed out.

HENRY

We just made it back in time.

CARROUSEL

Hop on board.

MAX

All right. But let me just say that it'll never get off the ground. I want to be on record! (*Emmy enters with her bag.*)

CARROUSEL

Folks, this is Emmy Pleasant. And this here's her son, Roger. Anybody makes any comments can swim! (*Suddenly there is the great sound of rushing water. The stage becomes darkened.*)

HENRY

Here it is!! Jump on, everybody. All aboard!

(*The water sound is very loud for a few seconds . . then recedes. The lights come up. Across the apron of the stage is a neat row of rolling waves. They are stylized and look as if they might have been cut out from an old Popeye comic strip. From these waves we might gather that Carrousel's house is on its way.*)

HENRY

Hey! HEY! We're afloat. By damn! We're really travelin'. How many knots would you say we're traveling?

CARROUSEL

How many knots, Infinity? (*Infinity makes a gesture. Carrousel turns to Henry.*) Classified information.

SARAH

Mmmmmmmmmmm . . smell that sea air. (*She strikes a pose right out of some cruise-ship advertisement.*)

MAX

I don't know about anybody else, but *I* feel silly.

HENRY

We're drifting downstream. How far, Carrousel?

CARROUSEL

I ain't rightly figured that one out.

MAX

(*giving an order*) There's a town over there. I own the mayor! Steer over!

CARROUSEL

Can't. Ain't got no rudder.

MAX

Ye gods!

CARROUSEL

(*to Infinity*) Ya better pull in the lines and make sure everything's fast. (*Infinity goes to the back of the house and starts pulling a long rope.*) We got about everything anybody could need. We'll pick up pork, salt, and provisions along the way.

MAX

(*appalled*) Pork, salt, and provisions?

EMMY

It's lucky my Roger isn't fed by formula. (*Infinity finishes pulling the rope. It is attached to a small, brightly painted privy, floating merrily along. He ties the line fast to the house. He tests it to see that one can hop across to it easily.*)

MAX

All the comforts! Oh boy!

CARROUSEL

Why don't you just sit back and enjoy life?

MAX

Waste of time! (*alarmed*) Did my boxes wash overboard? (*He sees*

92

them.) Thank God for that. They're full to the brim with negotiable securities and tax records!

SARAH

I shoulda brought something to read. (*The top of a telephone pole suddenly juts out from behind one of the side-wing flats. It bounces around as if it were floating along. Clinging to it is a rather timid young man, dressed in leather motorcycle clothes. This is Jesse.*)

EMMY

(*pointing to him*) Look yonder!

MAX

Yonder?! Who talks "yonder" nowadays?

EMMY

On yonder telephone pole. A soul in distress. (*All look to the pole. Jesse looks away from them.*)

CARROUSEL

Howdy, stranger!

JESSE

(*pretends not to see them; sings casually*) "Me and my shadow, strolling down the avenue . ."

CARROUSEL

I say . . howdy!

JESSE

Ya mean me?

CARROUSEL

Certainly.

JESSE

(*suddenly violent*) Watch out how you talk to me, stranger. I'm a wild, woolly, hard-shooting fugitive from all the law-enforcement agencies!

CARROUSEL

You sound right interesting, son. Hop aboard.

JESSE

Hah! When I spit, I spit bullets. And I feel like spitting now!

EMMY

(*turning away*) Thank you and goodbye. What has become of the chivalrous male?

JESSE

You making fun of me?

EMMY

For a moment you reminded me of the father of my child and I felt tenderness.

SARAH

That's life, honey.

CARROUSEL

We offer you hospitality. Take it or leave it.

JESSE

Any stoolies aboard? Can you all keep mum? I hate squealers!

CARROUSEL

We are all members of Stoneface Anonymous.

JESSE

All right! Ya got me! (*He jumps on board. The pole bobs off behind the wing flat and disappears.*) My name is Jesse Dalton Dillinger James! (*He pulls out a pile of damp posters.*) Take a look at this! (*He shoves one of them into Carrousel's hands.*)

CARROUSEL

(*reading, as Jesse hands out a few more posters*) "JESSE DALTON DILLIN-GER JAMES . . Public Enemy Number One."

JESSE

(*delighted*) See!

HENRY

(*reading over Carrousel's shoulder*) "Wanted in forty-nine of the fifty states." (*impressed*) He's Number One, all right!

JESSE

And it's tough keeping up there . . let me tell you that!

EMMY

I never heard of him. I never saw that poster! And I've spent many after-noons in post offices!

JESSE

(*snarling at her*) Anything I can't stand . . is a yappy broad! (*Emmy steps away from him with distaste.*)

HENRY

(*reading poster*) "Sought in every state of the Union except Indiana."

JESSE

Crazy, big-hearted Hoosiers. (*bellowing — pulls out revolver*) I'm a fierce, wild, mixed-up youth! I live for dough and dames. And if my gun wasn't soaked clear through, I'd show you all what a tough guy really is like! (*He starts to stick one of his posters up on the wall, using handle of revolver as hammer. Max clutches his boxes and cowers.*)

EMMY

(*whispering to Carrousel*) I think he's a show-off. (*Infinity comes up to Jesse and offers his hand kindly.*)

CARROUSEL

This here's Infinity . .

JESSE

I don't shake with strangers. (*He pushes Infinity's hand away. Infinity quickly flips him halfway across the deck with a judo maneuver. Infinity slowly retires. Jesse lands on the ground — hard. He sits there for a minute. There is a silence. Carrousel strums his guitar a bit. Jesse suddenly breaks down and starts to cry like a baby.*) Awww . . why must I always blow my cool?

EMMY

Oh, dear!

JESSE

Awww . . it always turns out this way!! Always!!

EMMY

(*going to him*) I can never bear to see a man cry.

JESSE

All this wouldn't have happened if my name wasn't really Casanova Potts. (*He gets up, bitterly hurt. He starts to take down his poster.*)

EMMY

No, don't. I'm sure it wouldn't have.

JESSE

(*turning to her, unbelieving*) You understand?

EMMY

(*putting poster up again*) I have great compassion. It's terribly hidden sometimes, though.

JESSE

Casanova Potts. My mother died when I was born and my father named me that to get even. By the age of ten I had fought every kid on the block. I always lost. (*He cries again.*)

EMMY

I wish there was something I could do. I haven't even a Kleenex to offer you.

MAX

See! Not even a Kleenex. Cut off from civilization!

JESSE

I showed my old man. I soloed. Cut off. Disengaged. I turned my back on the world. I showed them all! Hah! But . . but . . (*starts to cry again*) the world didn't even notice. I felt so damn silly. (*snarls*) So I became its enemy. An outlaw. A rebel with about twelve and a half causes! I broke

95

speed laws. I walked on the grass. I stole more money than . . oh I guess, anybody . . *ever*! (*desperate to be believed*) Really I did.

EMMY

But did you rob from the rich and give to the poor?

JESSE

Of course!

EMMY

I just knew it! (*We hear a cry from offstage.*)

WOMAN'S VOICE

(*off*) Yoo-hoo. Yoo-hoo.

HENRY

We're being hailed!

CARROUSEL

(*shouting off*) Ahoy! What can we do for you?

WOMAN'S VOICE

Can you help a poor, loving mother in distress?

HENRY

It's an old dame floating on a chicken coop.

CARROUSEL

Care to come aboard?

WOMAN'S VOICE

You'll take also my friends, the chickens?

CARROUSEL

We'd be delighted to welcome your chickens.

WOMAN'S VOICE

Swear you won't eat them?

CARROUSEL

(*to others*) Everybody hereby swear they won't eat this old lady's feathered friends? (*They are all about to.*)

WOMAN'S VOICE

Make it legal. Use a Bible.

CARROUSEL

Ain't got a Bible.

WOMAN'S VOICE

Pity. (*Infinity points to his head.*)

CARROUSEL

Oh hell, we got a Bible. Infinity's got it in his head. (*gestures them over*) Come on now, folks. (*They place their hands on Infinity's bald pate.*)

ALL

We hereby swear.

MAX

(*turning away*) Wait till they hear about *this* at Dow Jones!

CARROUSEL

Infinity, give that fine, God-fearing mother an assist. (*Infinity takes a rope. He twirls it around his head and throws it off, behind one of the side-wing flats.*)

MAX

You gonna let another nut on board? Ahhh. I'm puttin' these boxes inside where they'll be safe! (*Infinity pulls the rope back. Holding onto the other end of it is a tiny old lady. She is seated on the edge of a battered chicken coop, which pokes out from behind a wing.*)

CARROUSEL

Easy now, easy.

WOMAN

What's with the easy? You think, maybe, I'm made from glass? (*Henry and Infinity go to help her on board, but she waves them off and makes a remarkable leap over from the coop.*) When a woman gets to be my age, she's *got* to be self-sufficient.

CARROUSEL

Glad to have you on board, ma'am.

WOMAN

The name's Martha Golden. You wouldn't believe how I got in this situation. (*She catches her breath.*) The chickens . . I don't know personally. They were nice enough to happen by just as I was going down for the third time. They saved a mother's life . . so how could I desert them?

CARROUSEL

Gratitude needs no explanation.

HENRY

(*bellowing excitedly*) NOW HEAR THIS! NOW HEAR THIS!!

MARTHA

(*jumping; looks up at Henry*) That young man's got troubles?

HENRY

Make way! Make way for the AMERICAN RED CROSS. The Angels of Mercy are right off our port bow.

CARROUSEL

I'd say this is an honor. (*Max re-enters. We hear the sound of a motorboat offstage.*)

MAN'S VOICE

(*off*) Stand by. Don't be frightened. We'll save you. (*The bow of a small motorboat appears from behind one of the wing flats. A tall man, with an umbrella, stands in the bow. He gets out and nimbly steps onto the floating house. We can hear the motor idling.*)

MAN

(*speaking with a Rotarian assurance*) I'm Higgens of the Red Cross, and there's nothing to fear.

CARROUSEL

How do, Mr. Higgens.

HIGGENS

(*closing his umbrella and cleaning his rimless glasses*) Now then, we can fit you all into that boat. We'll have you ashore in no time.

MAX

Thank God.

HIGGENS

Nooo. Just thank the American Red Cross. (*He chuckles smugly.*) You can always count on us in times of disaster. Fires, Earthquakes, Floods, Holocausts! Come, come now. Women and children first.

MAX

(*exiting*) I'll go get my boxes!

MARTHA

Not me. I just got here.

HIGGENS

Eh?

JESSE

(*suddenly tough*) Get lost, you fink!

EMMY

Shhh.

HIGGENS

I beg pardon?

CARROUSEL

I think what they're trying to say is that they don't want to go.

HIGGENS

I beg your pardon? Don't want to go? To dry, safe land? That's absurd.

EMMY

(*smiling brightly*) Yes . . isn't it.

HIGGENS

Wha . . ? Now, now. Enough of this nonsense. You're disaster victims and I'm the Red Cross. You know the rules. Don't you ever watch the newsreels?

98

CARROUSEL

Hell, we ain't victims of anything but our own happy desires. We're having a fine time, and we'd love you to join us.

HIGGENS

Me join you? No. No. It's the Red Cross's mission to help troubled people. See?

CARROUSEL

Then maybe you can find some on the shore . . and bring them out to us.

HIGGENS

(*suddenly composing himself*) This is your last chance. (*dead silence*) You're going to stay? (*All turn away. Carrousel strums his guitar.*) Do you realize what you're doing to me? How can I face them at headquarters?

EMMY

Don't be distressed. Please.

HIGGENS

I'm not distressed. Disenchanted maybe, but not distressed. (*reaching for a straw*) Can we give you some of our coffee? Hot coffee and doughnuts?

CARROUSEL

We got plenty of victuals. Can we give you some of ours?

HIGGENS

You won't even take our coffee? (*He is shaken and almost in tears.*) Gee whiz.

CARROUSEL

I'd be pleased to make a slight contribution though, if you got a can.

HIGGENS

Of course. (*He produces a small red and white collection can.*)

CARROUSEL

Mighty fine organization, the Red Cross.

HIGGENS

You're double-doggone right about that.

CARROUSEL

I'm sorry we couldn't oblige you.

HIGGENS

Not even coffee!

SARAH

Kind of awe-inspiring, aren't we?

HIGGENS

Holy cow.

CARROUSEL

(*gives Higgens the full can*) Here you are.

HIGGENS

Thank you. Thank you so much. Oh, I almost forgot. (*He reaches into his pocket.*) Your buttons. (*He passes out Red Cross buttons and starts to go.*)

HENRY

(*from above — sad but proud*) Hail to thee, "AMERICAN RED CROSS."

HIGGENS

Yeah. (*He steps into his boat, the motor starts, and he shouts off to someone on shore.*) They wouldn't even take our coffee. (*As he disappears behind the wing flat, he opens his umbrella. He is gone.*)

MAX

(*rushing on with boxes*) All right, Red Cross. Let's go.

MARTHA

(*settling herself down*) Relax. Enjoy.

MAX

What? (*looks off, after the Red Cross man*) Hey! Come back!! (*surprised*) He just stuck his tongue out at me!! (*realizing*) Oh no. And the payoff is I'm still with you!!

SARAH

Poor Max. My heart bleeds.

MAX

AW SHUT UP YOUR SARCASMS!! Don't you saps realize what you're doing? A flood is a catastrophe. Not a joyride. Read the papers.

EMMY

I read a newspaper once, and I can promise you it will never happen again.

MAX

Very cute. Very cute. So we're all a lot of fairies on the way to Never Land.

JESSE

Who you callin' a fairy?

MAX

SHUT UP!! Now look . . somebody's got to take charge here!

SARAH

You?

MAX

Of course *me*!! I'm a natural-born boss! Now first thing we do . .

JESSE

Nuts to you, mister.

MAX

NUTS TO ME!!? NUTS TO . . MAX-CAPITAL-GAINS-ELLIS!!!!!?

MARTHA

Please . . Please . . Stop with the shouting. Have a little consideration for a mother's peace of mind.

MAX

Aw, for cryin' out loud! (*general hubbub*)

CARROUSEL

Now, now . . there seems to be a difference of opinion. I think we need an election. A little democracy might clear the air.

EMMY

An election? Oh good. With bands and bonfires and parades. Roger . . pay attention.

MAX

(*completely confused*) Bonfires? What?

CARROUSEL

I hereby nominate Infinity.

MARTHA

I second.

CARROUSEL

All in favor say aye. (*All, except Max, say, "Aye." Much enthusiasm.*) All against . .

MAX

Nay! Damn it to hell! Nay!

CARROUSEL

(*to Max*) Your man lost.

MAX

My man? I DON'T EVEN KNOW WHO I VOTED FOR!!!

EMMY

That sir, is *not* our problem.

MAX

Next chance I get, I leave.

MARTHA

If there is anything I can't stand it's a sore loser. (*Max exits into house with boxes.*)

CARROUSEL

Infinity. I hereby commission you captain of the ship, mayor of the community, spiritual leader . . (*Infinity makes a gesture.*) All right. And general manager.

SARAH

Hurray! Speech. Speech! (*All cheer. Infinity shakes his head.*)

MARTHA

So couldn't you just sum up our situation? (*Infinity gives an awed whistle and retires to his comic book.*)

CARROUSEL

Oh, we've got a born leader of men there.

HENRY

(*who has been looking ahead*) Here comes another one! (*A bobbing tree pops out from behind one of the side-wing flats. Seated in the branches is a dedicated looking man in buckskin, with a long, red beard.*)

CARROUSEL

Howdy.

MAN WITH BEARD

Howdy.

CARROUSEL

Care to come aboard?

MAN WITH BEARD

Which way you heading?

CARROUSEL

East at present.

MAN WITH BEARD

I'm aheadin' West!

CARROUSEL

Sorry.

MAN WITH BEARD

Don't mention it. (*He bobs off again behind wings and is gone.*)

CARROUSEL

Too bad. I bet he could have told us all kinds of wonderful things. (*Carrousel starts to strum his guitar. Things settle down aboard the house. Everyone has found himself a spot and has made himself comfortable. Henry is on the roof, looking ahead through his spyglass. Martha brings out some knitting. Sarah lets her legs dangle over and puts her feet into the water. Emmy starts to nurse her baby. Jesse cleans his gun.*)

SARAH

(*after a pause, dreamy*) Carrousel?

CARROUSEL

Yes, Sarah?

SARAH

(*smiling beautifully*) It's getting late in the day.

CARROUSEL

Sure is.

SARAH

(*leaning back*) Wow! Just look at that sunset. First one I saw in years.

CARROUSEL

Really.

SARAH

Once, when I was just a kid . . I bet I wasn't no more than sixteen, I saw this other sunset. And it was so beautiful . . I had to sit down . . and just feel good all over. Like clean and peaceful . . and good. But I couldn't get nobody else to look at it with me. They said they was too busy watching where they was going, and watching out for the other guy. So I went to a movie show. And when I came out it was dark. And I never had the time to see a sunset like that again.

CARROUSEL

Look at it now, little lady, look at it now.

(*He strums his guitar and the lights slowly dim. The guitar continues in the darkness for a few seconds, and then the lights come up. The stage takes on the glow of early morning, just before dawn. Morning stars begin to twinkle in the sky. Carrousel is strumming his guitar. He looks out over the river, which can barely be seen through the dim, misty light. Henry is on the roof. He has a rope with a rock tied to the end of it. He continually measures the depth of the river. Occasionally we can hear Max snoring and mumbling in his sleep. Emmy and Jesse are together in one corner. They are asleep in each other's arms.*)

HENRY

(*shouting like an old river-man*) By the mark twain, three fathoms! Safe water.

CARROUSEL

Henry, keep it down.

HENRY

(*taking measurements, whispering*) By the mark twain, four and a half fathoms. Safe water. Flood ain't receding none.

CARROUSEL

I don't look for this one to recede. (*strums a blues sort of melody*)

> Lonesome morning
> Why am I here?
> Lonesome morning
> Why am I here?
> Thinking in the morning

> Long before the light of day
> Thinking in the morning
> Lord drive these devils away.

HENRY

Sun's gonna be rising any minute now.

CARROUSEL

> Come on sunshine
>   Git out of your bed.
> Come on sunshine
>   'Fore I kill me dead.

(*He continues to play and look out over the river. We hear Max mumbling in his sleep.*)

MAX

So I sez to him, sell steel and buy aluminum. Buy aluminum! Buy aluminum!

HENRY

What kind of dreams does *that* man have, anyway?

CARROUSEL

(*continues to sing*)

> Need me a hope, Lord,
>   For to see the light of day.
> Need me a hope, Lord,
>   'Fore I die and pass away.

HENRY

By the mark twain, three fathoms. Safe water. (*Carrousel continues to strum his guitar and hum his blues melody. The light on him dims slightly and comes up on Jesse and Emmy, who have been sleeping in one corner of the porch. Jesse opens his eyes and looks down on Emmy, whose head rests on his shoulder. Emmy starts.*)

EMMY

Oh . . (*sees where she is*) Goodness. (*sits up*)

JESSE

No, don't.

EMMY

I didn't mean . . (*looks around*) Where's Roger? (*picks up teddy bear*) You must think me a brazen hussy.

JESSE

No, I didn't think that. And I didn't mind one little bit. (*He tries to lean on his arm. It collapses under him.*) Must be asleep.

EMMY

How long was I in that . . that compromising position?

JESSE

Not long. About three hours.

EMMY

You make me blush. You should have awakened me.

JESSE

I was afraid.

EMMY

Afraid?

JESSE

Afraid if I startled you or touched you, I mean . . you're just about the tiniest, most fragile woman I ever seen.

EMMY

Have you seen lots of women, Jesse?

JESSE

(*almost an apology*) Emmy, I'm Public Enemy Number One.

EMMY

Oh.

JESSE

But I never seen any like you. Restful and happy-like, ya know?

EMMY

Am I? Yes, you *do* remind me of the father of my child. (*Jesse looks sadly down at Roger.*) You should take that as a compliment.

JESSE

Sure. (*awkwardly*) Were . . were you married to him?

EMMY

No. No, we were never wed. He was called away to . . to . . (*not too sure of herself*) war.

JESSE

He was killed in battle?

EMMY

Defending his country. He died saving his company of men . . and many refugees, including tiny children.

JESSE

Did he look like me, Emmy?

EMMY

No, he was tall. Not really tall. He had red hair . . or blond. Oh, I don't know. It depends on how I think of him, I guess. (*She hides her face.*)

105

JESSE

Emmy?

EMMY

There *was* a man.

JESSE

Sure, Emmy.

CARROUSEL

(*singing softly in background*)

> Lonesome morning
>> Why am I here?
> Lonesome morning
>> Why oh why am I here?

JESSE

Emmy? (*She turns to him. They look at one another for a long moment, then kiss.*)

CARROUSEL

> Need me a promise
>> For to see the light of day.
> Need me a promise
>> 'Fore I die and pass away.

(*They break.*)

JESSE

So tiny. So tiny you'd think a breeze would whisk you away. (*Emmy puts Roger down, sees that he is safe. Jesse gently speaks.*) Emmy, I know now that from now on, I'm gonna worry like anything about you. I'm gonna worry that something will happen to you. And I'm gonna see that nothing does. (*She looks up at him.*) And you can believe me, Emmy.

EMMY

I believe you, Jesse. (*Jesse leans back. Emmy lies alongside him and rests her head on his shoulder again. She closes her eyes. The lights on them fade.*)

CARROUSEL

> Come on sunshine
>> Get out of your bed.
> Come on sunshine
>> 'Fore I kill me dead.

HENRY

By the mark twain . . three fathoms. Safe water.

MAX

(*mumbling in his sleep*) We unite with United and sell our Amalgamated.

(Martha comes out of the house. She is wearing a neat apron and carries a steaming cup of coffee.)

MARTHA

Mr. Jones? Here. I thought maybe a hot cup would warm up the morning.

CARROUSEL

Why thank you, Mrs. Golden.

MARTHA

For what? I been a wife and mother so long I do it automatic. Drink it down . . before you get a chill.

CARROUSEL

Yeah. Dawn on a river can be a mite damp.

MARTHA

I'd make chicken soup . . but suddenly I'm involved. (*points to coop*)

CARROUSEL

Well, old sun will be up soon and take care of everything.

MARTHA

(*sitting next to him*) Personally, I haven't felt so rested since the bank holiday way back in 1933.

CARROUSEL

You come from around these parts?

MARTHA

Just passing through on my vacation. My first one. I figured after all these years, Martha Golden, why not?

CARROUSEL

Have a good time?

MARTHA

Some good time. What's Miami? Brighton Beach with fancy plumbing. Grand Canyon . . a hole in the ground with cowboys. So . . I was on my way home when the river intervened.

CARROUSEL

Where's home?

MARTHA

A two-by-four in Flushing, New York. It's not so bad. Every once in a while they build a world's fair and I can see it from my window. When I feel like it.

CARROUSEL

You live alone?

MARTHA

Just me and the television, and the *Daily News* gets delivered every morning. I'm widowed.

107

CARROUSEL

Sorry to hear that.

MARTHA

You're sorry? (*She sighs.*) His name was Irving. Irving Golden. What can I say? He was a fine man. An elevator operator all his adult life. And dedicated? I tell you, there wasn't a man around who knew or cared more about his elevator than my Irving.

CARROUSEL

I'm sure I would have enjoyed knowing him.

MARTHA

It was a good life. He died a happy man. On his job. Going up. (*sadly*) Now they got a self-service there. Kinda breaks your heart . . but what are you going to do? (*sighs*) Then the kids moved away. The second declaration of independence. Oh boy. Married, careers, psychiatrists, suburbs. You name it, them kids got it. So . . I went on a vacation. And . . (*There is a long pause, broken by Henry.*)

HENRY

By the mark twain . . three and one half fathoms!

MARTHA

(*snapping out of it*) Well, I can't just sit and schmoose when there's work to be done. (*She rises.*) I'll cook up a substantial breakfast. Believe me, when everybody wakes up, are they gonna have stomachs!

CARROUSEL

You go right ahead. Don't know if there's any fire in the stove.

MARTHA

I saw to that already. Could I function without a hot stove? (*She smiles, in her glory, and then exits into the house.*)

CARROUSEL

(*singing softly*)

> Sittin' in my chair
>> Watchin' life go by.
> Sittin' in my chair
>> Teardrop leave my eye.

HENRY

Hey, Carrousel, we must have drifted miles and miles. Don't recognize this landscape nohow. We're probably in a different state of the union. Looks like delta land. By the mark twain . . four fathoms. Safe water.

MAX

So we'll amalgamate with Amalgamated, sell out United, and work on a cost plus . . (*Sarah enters from the house.*)

SARAH

Max's been talkin' in his sleep all night. It's a wonder anybody got any shut-eye.

HENRY

By the mark twain, two and a quarter fathoms. Safe water.

SARAH

(*pointing to Henry*) Why don't he calm down?

CARROUSEL

Henry's a concerned young man with his eye on the future.

SARAH

I know his eyes are somewhere, 'cause they're certainly not on me.

CARROUSEL

I'm afraid the pickings are pretty poor on this voyage for a gal like you.

SARAH

I really ain't too hard to please. Ya know, that little gangster's cute, only I stand a head taller than him without heels, even.

CARROUSEL

He looks pretty spoke-for at the moment.

SARAH

I been watchin' them on and off through the night. They've been sleeping together. And that's all they do . . sleep.

CARROUSEL

Eh . . well a woman could do worse than a good, hard-working country boy like Henry.

SARAH

Meat and potatoes, huh? (*looks up at him*)

CARROUSEL

Backbone of this here nation.

SARAH

Why not? Will you excuse me, please?

CARROUSEL

Go right ahead (*She climbs up on the porch rail and then onto the roof. Henry looks surprised. He glances down at Carrousel, who strums a chord and sings.*)

> If a purty li'l gal
> Sez how-de-doo . .
> Then take it from there, boy,
> It's up to you.

(*Lights on Carrousel dim slightly.*)

SARAH

(*coming up to Henry with an absurdly sexy gesture*) Hi there, big boy.

HENRY

What's the matter? You got the jumps?

SARAH

What are you doing up here by yourself all night?

HENRY

(*eyes glued to his rope*) I'm keeping tabs as to the depth of this river so as we don't run aground.

SARAH

Must be cold and lonely?

HENRY

Can't help that. Something or somebody's got to give a damn in this old world or we'll all go back to the dark ages.

SARAH

(*running her hand along his arm*) I never noticed how strong you were until just now.

HENRY

I'm as strong as the next man. (*bellowing*) By the mark twain, three and a half fathoms. Safe water.

SARAH

I was listening to you all night long and I felt so safe.

HENRY

Pleased to hear that, ma'am.

SARAH

(*very close to him*) I was down there . . in my bed. All alone in my bed. And I heard you all night long. While I was alone . . in my bed.

HENRY

(*swallows hard*) By the mark twain.

SARAH

You got a girl friend?

HENRY

(*shocked*) Shucks no! I got lots to do. Plowing and milking and taking produce to town!

SARAH

Ain't ya got spare time?

HENRY

That's all took up with my basketball, baseball, and coin collection.

SARAH

You *never* had a girl friend?

HENRY

Miss, I'd be much obliged if you'd let me attend to the important chore I have at hand here.

SARAH

You ought to learn to relax. (*She touches him.*)

HENRY

(*loud and quick*) Yes, sir. It looks like it's gonna be a long, long day.

SARAH

Sun's coming up any minute. (*She kisses him. He is startled, to say the least.*) That's just thanks for looking out for us all night.

HENRY

(*confused*) Well . . that sounds reasonable!

SARAH

I think . . that you and me . . are gonna get along just fine.

HENRY

(*swallowing hard*) Well . . I never had no trouble before makin' friends with strangers.

SARAH

(*whispering to him*) You know, I sleep in that little room under the stairs.

HENRY

So what?

SARAH

I'll be there tonight.

HENRY

Sure, if ya sleep there. (*Suddenly it dawns on him.*) Oh. Gee whiz.

SARAH

(*sultry*) This house is too small for basketball.

HENRY

(*He comes closer to her. His arm goes around her. They are about to kiss, when he breaks away.*) No, sir! Not me!

SARAH

Huh?

HENRY

Ma'am, you sure are lucky I'm a gentleman. You'd be shocked if ya knew the thoughts I was entertainin' for a few seconds there. (*He smacks his head.*) Where'd the hell those thoughts come from, anyway?

SARAH

But listen . .

HENRY

(*smacks his forehead*) You better get down from here, ma'am.

111

SARAH

But . .

HENRY

Right down.

SARAH

(*hurt*) Okay . . okay (*She starts to get down.*)

HENRY

Wait! You know somethin'?

SARAH

What?

HENRY

You know somethin'!? I think you're somethin'!! That's all! Really somethin'!

SARAH

(*burning*) Thanks!

HENRY

Don't mention it. (*Sarah starts to climb down, when suddenly Infinity comes out of the house. He makes some gestures and points off.*)

CARROUSEL

What now? (*From offstage we hear the rather boozy tones of a man singing.*) Another one?

HENRY

He's within grapplin' distance.

CARROUSEL

Lord, what's keeping him up? Ahoy! Ahoy off starboard!

HENRY

That ain't starboard. It's port.

MAN'S VOICE

(*off*) If you attempt to detain me, I shall call the Coast Guard!

CARROUSEL

Peace, brother. Care for a lift?

MAN'S VOICE

No. Care for a drink?

CARROUSEL

Certainly.

MAN'S VOICE

Then toss me a line.

HENRY

Man, has he got a bun on! (*Infinity tosses him a line, then starts to pull it in. From behind one of the wing flats appears a tall, angular fellow of*

112

about forty-five. He wears horn-rimmed glasses and Ivy League clothes. He is riding two crates tied together.)

CARROUSEL

Settle him in gentle, Infinity. He don't look too stable to me. (*Infinity and Henry bring him in. They help him onto the deck of the house.*)

MAN

Don't lose those crates. One contains the *Encyclopaedia Britannica*, and the other . . gin.

CARROUSEL

Fine.

MAN

I come prepared to inform and to obliterate.

CARROUSEL

Fish them on board, fellows. (*The men start to do so.*)

MAN

I suppose you think it strange that a person of my academic background should be found floating all night on a set of the *Encyclopaedia Britannica* and a case of gin.

CARROUSEL

Well, I hadn't . .

MAN

If you do, I simply do not give a damn.

CARROUSEL

Hell, we don't . .

MAN

My name is Edgar, but you can call me Herman.

CARROUSEL

How do. I'm . .

HERMAN

I am a teacher. I attempt to . . teach. (*He passes out.*)

CARROUSEL

Lift him gently to some soft place. (*The men carry him into the house. Suddenly, a rooster crows.*) There it comes. Another twenty-four hours punches the clock.

SARAH

Hmmmm, the sun smells good. Smells good and fresh and clean. Hey! Hey look!

CARROUSEL

(*not rousing himself*) What?

113

SARAH

There ain't no more land ahead.

CARROUSEL

Yeah, I was expecting this old river to run out sooner or later.

SARAH

(*with a little wonder in her voice*) The ocean!

HENRY

(*comes running out*) Hey! You see what I see!

CARROUSEL

Don't get excited. Every river's got a mouth.

HENRY

Gawd-a-mighty! We're headin' right out for open sea. A mile a minute! (*We hear the sound of wind.*)

CARROUSEL

(*delighted*) Looks like we're gonna get more than we bargained for.

HENRY

You mean we're going out there?

SARAH

(*happy*) Abroad? (*Infinity comes out of the cabin, smiling. He gestures to Carrousel.*)

CARROUSEL

The Captain has asked me to announce (*shouts out*): All ashore that's going ashore.

SARAH

(*laughing*) Lotsa luck.

HENRY

This house can't take the raging sea!

CARROUSEL

How about that, Captain? (*Infinity kicks the house to show its solidity and nods yes.*) There's your answer. They don't build houses like this anymore. (*Infinity has roused Jesse and Emmy.*)

JESSE

(*catching sight of the ocean*) My God. Freedom. Real freedom at last.

MARTHA

(*coming out of the house*) Yoo-hoo. Breakfast will be ready in a trice.

HENRY

We're heading out to sea.

MARTHA

That's nice. (*She goes back in again.*)

EMMY

I've never seen the ocean. Would you believe that? I've never seen the ocean. Roger, see the ocean?

CARROUSEL

It certainly is awe-inspiring.

EMMY

I wish we could have stopped for a bit, and gathered shells on the beach.

HENRY

We couldn't stop for time or tide. Look at us! We're heading right into the middle of the ocean.

SARAH

Henry, if you'd only calm down! (*Suddenly Max stumbles out of the house. He is half-asleep. Snarling at the others, he makes his way to the privy, which still bobs up and down beside the house. He mutters angrily.*)

MAX

No privacy. How can you live with no privacy? (*He slams the privy door shut and locks himself inside.*)

SARAH

Aw, don't pay any attention to him.

HENRY

(*suddenly lyric, arms outstretched*) The ocean! The great, all-knowing sea! "Oh what mysteries doth thy depths reveal? What fortunes, hopes, and dreams conceal?"

JESSE

Oh good grief!

SARAH

You ought to write that down, honey.

CARROUSEL

I got to warn ya. We may run into enemy submarines, great denizens of the deep, all kinds of unpleasant weather.

HENRY

What about them Vikings? They wouldn't take no for an answer.

SARAH

Atta boy!

JESSE

Hey! Look out . . we're gonna hit that . .

HENRY

What?

JESSE

Right over there!

SARAH

It's a boat of some kind.

EMMY

A raft. A tiny, beautiful raft. We're headin' right for it. Oh Roger!!

HENRY

LOOK OUT! (*Suddenly, from behind one of the side-wing flats, there appears the bow of a strange log raft with a great, colorful sail. It slams into the side of the house with a great bang. Everyone is knocked off his feet. There is the clucking of chickens.*)

HENRY

Collision! Collision at sea!! (*Everyone has fallen to the floor. Now all start to pick themselves up.*)

MAX'S VOICE

(*from privy*) What's goin' on out there for cryin' out loud!!? (*The wind noise dies down.*)

JESSE

Where's the life preservers?

EMMY

Roger.

HENRY

We'll all sing hymns as we go down.

EMMY

Where's Roger? (*She finds him.*)

CARROUSEL

Now wait a minute . . wait a minute. We don't look like we're sinking. (*Suddenly from the raft appear Lo and Le, a delightful Tahitian husband and wife. They wear tiny, colorful sarongs.*)

LO

Many apologies for this intrusion.

LE

We might sorry.

LO

We not look where we go.

LE

We necking below.

CARROUSEL

No need for apologies. We were the ones following an erratic course.

LO

Must compare drivers' licenses. Make reports. Most official. You insured?

CARROUSEL

No.

LO

Me neither. So what the hell. Nice to have met you. (*He starts off with Le.*)

CARROUSEL

Look, as long as you're here . . why don't you stay for breakfast?

LO

Okay . . wife too? (*Carrousel nods yes.*)

LE

If all the same to you we may stay for weeks and weeks. (*They climb onto the house. Infinity ties up the raft.*)

LO

My name is Lolama Hulikalama. You call me Lo. My wife's name ridiculous also. You call her Le. (*Everyone exchanges greetings.*)

LE

We Tahitian.

CARROUSEL

(*mouth watering*) I bet you have all kinds of tropical fruit aboard.

LO

Only watermelon.

LE

We not from tropics.

LO

We come from Norfolk, Virginia.

LE

On our way to tropics.

LO

Come from tropics four years ago on Northwest Orient Airlines.

LE

Come to seek fortune in U.S.A.

LO

"Fortune" much outdated commodity.

LE

Go back to tropics.

LO

No money for Northwest Orient.

LE
(*explaining*) No money — period.

LO
So built the raft from old family plan.

LE
Handed down from generation to generation . .

LO
Most ethnic.

LE
Much better than Northwest Orient.

LO
No stewardess to stop necking.

LE
Lots of time for necking.

LO
We like necking.

LE
That's our story.

LO
What's yours?

CARROUSEL
Well —

LE
Enough formalities. Let's have feast. (*At this moment Max chooses to come out of the privy.*)

MAX
What's all the excitement? (*He glances around.*) Hey! We're right in the middle of the ocean. You damn bunch of idiots!

LO
Me too?

MAX
Who the hell are you?

LO
It long, long story. But since you ask . .

MAX
Aww . . listen, I got interests to protect back there. Turn back, you jerks, turn back.

CARROUSEL
You know we can't.

MAX

(*furious*) Max Ellis does not take no! (*He lunges for Jesse's coat which is lying on the floor. He finds the revolver.*)

JESSE

Hey! He's got my gat!

MAX

(*waving revolver at the others*) Now turn back. Turn back! I'm giving the orders.

JESSE

No, don't. Don't pull that trigger.

LO

How'd we get mixed up in this?

MAX

I'M GIVING THE ORDERS!!!

JESSE

(*pleading*) I can't explain. Please don't pull that trigger!

MAX

Nuts! Take this!!

JESSE

No, don't!! (*Jesse lunges for Max.*)

EMMY

(*screaming*) Jesse! (*Max jumps back and Jesse misses him, landing on the floor in a heap. Max points the gun at him and pulls the trigger. A little red flag pops out and spells "Bang." There is a shocked silence. Max is flabbergasted. Jesse starts to sob.*)

JESSE

Now you all know. How can I face any of you?

LO

I don't follow this plot.

LE

Is why I always hate to come in the middle.

EMMY

(*rushing over to Jesse*) We understand. You're among friends. (*He sobs on her shoulder.*)

MAX

You bunch of creeps. Think you're smart, don't ya? Well, just you watch out for me! I know how to operate. That's all I gotta say. Just watch out! (*Herman appears from the house, hung over.*)

HERMAN

I have an apology to make.

119

MAX

(*reeling around*) ANOTHER ONE!! Aw . . nuts (*He storms into the house.*)

HERMAN

I don't usually imbibe.

MARTHA

(*calling from door*) Breakfast's ready. Eat now . . talk later!

CARROUSEL

Good!

LO

Come quick, Le. Looks like hungry mob. (*Lo and Le go into the house.*)

EMMY

(*to Jesse*) Food will make you feel better.

JESSE

If only he hadn't pulled the trigger. (*He goes inside with Emmy.*)

HENRY

Man, I could eat a seahorse. (*He leaves Sarah flat and bolts into the house.*)

SARAH

Henry, wait for me.

HERMAN

No one will ever listen. That's the story of my life.

CARROUSEL

Later, my friend. Go on in and meet the folks.

HERMAN

I have so much to tell. (*He goes into the house.*)

CARROUSEL

Well, Infinity, we made it. (*Infinity nods.*) You looked pleased as punch. (*Infinity smiles.*) You sure we're doing the right thing? Leaving the mainland . . and its inevitability . . like this? (*Infinity shrugs his shoulders.*) Well, if you don't know . . who does? (*Infinity makes an all-encompassing gesture.*) Oh. (*He looks up.*) Lord, I ain't doubting you. But I sure do hope you know what we're doing. (*He goes into the house with Infinity. The stage is empty for a second. Then the door to the house opens. Max comes out and looks around suspiciously. He holds a few bottles in his hand. He takes out several notes and pushes them into the bottles.*)

MAX

Think these bird-brains can out-fox Max Capital Gains Ellis? Hah. This baby knows how to survive. (*holds up notes in bottles*) One of these messages is bound to get back to the mainland. And when it does . . this excursion'll be over before it starts. (*The sky darkens. We hear the ominous sound of thunder in the distance. Max laughs like an old-time tent-show villain, and starts to drop the bottles into the water. The curtain quickly falls.*)

END OF ACT ONE

ACT TWO

Houselights dim to half. Carrousel steps in front of the curtain and starts tuning his guitar. He ad-libs a few comments to the audience. Waits for them to be seated. Then he calls for a spotlight. It catches him.

CARROUSEL

Well now, where were we? (*He strums a loud chord and frowns.*) One minute. (*He tunes guitar some more, strums a chord, and smiles.*) That's better. (*as if trying to remember*) How'd it go from where I left off? (*begins to play "Git-Away Song"*) Oh yeah . . (*sings*)

> The water's still rising
>> All over the earth.
> Of humidity, folks,
>> There sure ain't no dearth.
> There's a powerful difference
>> 'Twixt right and 'twixt wrong.
> If the world doesn't realize
>> It will before long.

(*The curtain slowly rises.*)

> So, ya see what I mean
>> By the Great Git-Away.
> We're half the way through
>> This ridiculous play.
> It won't likely happen
>> Again anymore.
> I promise you that, folks,
>> For positive sure.

(*Lights on stage come up. It is a brilliant afternoon. There is a great activity aboard the house. Infinity has hauled in a net containing all kinds of useful things. He has a clipboard and some papers in his hand on which he is taking inventory. Sarah and Henry, in swimsuits, are sunbathing on*

121

the roof. Jesse and Emmy are in their corner playing a game of Monopoly. Lo and Le are in the opposite corner, necking. Martha is happily sweeping, humming along with Carrousel as he sings. Max is by one of the railings — surrounded by papers. Carrousel, finishing song, lets himself down into his chair. Herman is standing stage center talking to everyone and no one, with his back toward the audience.)

HERMAN

(*turning front, as if finishing a lecture*) . . And that finishes my little talk on the ancient Inca civilization. (*Max snorts and tosses a bottle overboard. He grins wickedly.*)

CARROUSEL

It was right interesting.

HERMAN

It was always one of my best lectures. I have many of them moldering in the archives. (*He taps his head.*)

MAX

(*grunting at him*) Damn misguided egghead. They're all alike. Sick! (*goes back to papers*)

SARAH

Turn over, Henry. Don't get burned all on one side.

HENRY

You sure are takin' a mighty big interest in me, ma'am.

SARAH

Just being helpful.

HENRY

I sure do appreciate it. Yessir, you and me are gonna be great chums.

SARAH

(*turning away, disappointed*) Oh boy.

JESSE

(*having just thrown the dice*) Seven. That lands me on Atlantic Avenue. You got a Monopoly and three houses there. What's the rent?

EMMY

(*evasive*) Oh, 'bout five hundred or so. But you don't have to pay.

JESSE

I insist.

EMMY

If you do, I'll just give it to charity.

JESSE

(*annoyed*) But Emmy, all you do is give your money to the Community Chest!

EMMY

Owning all this land and houses and hotels makes me feel self-conscious, kind of.

JESSE

That's the silliest thing I ever heard of!

EMMY

Well it may be silly, but I *am* winning the game.

JESSE

That's right!! Throw it up to me!!

EMMY

I don't know what you're referring to. Ladies do not throw up!

JESSE

Now you watch out how you talk to me . . hear? Remember, I'm Public Enemy Number One!!

EMMY

Well, that's what you *tell* everyone!

JESSE

(*hurt*) What do you mean by that?

EMMY

I do not wish to discuss the matter. (*musses the board*) Game's over! (*She turns away from him, very upset. Picks up Roger.*)

JESSE

Over! I was just about to heist the bank! (*grabs some of the colored money*) Awww doggone! (*turns away from her; pouts*)

MARTHA

(*finishes sweeping*) Well, that about does it. (*to Max*) You'll clean up that mess when you're done, please.

MAX

Mess!!? My income tax . . a mess?!

MARTHA

You're impressing me? (*sees a speck under Herman, sweeps*) Feet up, please. (*Herman raises them. She sweeps.*) I been listenin'. Smart boy. Where'd you teach school?

HERMAN

(*evasive*) in the minds and hearts of youth everywhere.

MARTHA

Specifically where?

HERMAN

(*trying to change subject*) Would anyone care to hear me sing the first

123

five chapters of *Finnegans Wake*? I've set them to a Celtic folk tune transposed into a twelve-tone scale.

MARTHA

Not . . necessarily.

MAX

Brother! This boat ride ain't bad enough. He's gotta turn it into a floating teach-in!

HERMAN

Oh, what's the use? I might as well inform you all . . it will be found out sooner or later. I was relieved of my duties.

CARROUSEL

Heck, I been canned many times myself.

HERMAN

I placed a far too liberal interpretation on the first amendment to our Constitution, and I taught something I shouldn't.

CARROUSEL

The Communist myth?

MAX

Are you pink?

MARTHA

Mr. Darwin's theory?

HERMAN

No. Echelmeyer's Comet.

CARROUSEL

Sounds interesting.

HERMAN

A flaming chariot in the heavens. Most amazing body that every visited us from space. It reduces Halley's Comet to a pedantic fizzle.

CARROUSEL

Never seemed to have heard of it.

HERMAN

No one has. And that is the tragedy. The only man ever to sight it was my paternal grandfather, August Echelmeyer. It was the year he was afflicted with bursitis of the neck . . an annoying malady which caused him to go around constantly with his face toward the heavens (*He demonstrates.*) That is how he happened to see it one autumn, when everyone else was watching the World Series. That was forty years ago.

MARTHA

He couldn't get nobody to believe him?

124

HERMAN

He was promptly damned for his solitary truth. A curse he has passed down through the generations. The irony of the whole thing is that the comet is due to appear once more, shortly.

CARROUSEL

Infinity, you keep a lookout. (*Infinity nods yes. Max looks around and tosses another bottle overboard. He snickers to himself . . obviously having a ball.*)

EMMY

A genuine heavenly body! Good gracious . . how awe-inspiring. (*Unconsciously, she draws closer to Jesse.*) Oh! I forgot. We're not speaking. (*She draws away from him.*)

JESSE

(*miserably, holds up handfuls of the Monopoly money*) Aww . . Emmy. It's no fun this way. (*puts money down*) I'm sorry I barked at you before, Emmy.

EMMY

(*pause . . then*) I'm certainly glad you said that, Mr. James (*quickly pulls closer to him again*) Jesse? I'm . . I'm sorry I won. I promise you it will never happen again. (*Carrousel strums a chord on his guitar. Max throws another bottle over. He can hardly contain his glee.*)

HERMAN

(*still lost in thought*) Echelmeyer's Comet. The world has yet to see the likes of Echelmeyer's Comet. (*All is quiet for a moment, when suddenly Sarah jumps and looks up.*)

SARAH

Hey!

CARROUSEL

Now what?

SARAH

I just felt a splash of water. (*Then all jump and look up.*)

CARROUSEL

Me too.

HENRY

Can't be rain. Ain't a cloud in the sky. (*All jump.*)

JESSE

There it goes again. What gives?

HERMAN

Meteorologically, what we are experiencing is an impossibility. Unless of course, some related phenomena . .

HENRY

HEY! (*dashes down front and looks over audience*) There's some kind of great stirring out there.

JESSE

(*running down to Henry*) Yeah! See? Whatever it is it's spouting water!

LE

(*looking up from Lo*) What's all the excitement?

LO

Only the whale.

CARROUSEL

A whale!

LE

Oh yes. We watch him all day this afternoon, between necking.

HENRY

He'll capsize us. Whales are mean critters!

LO

I never think of that. Why I never think of that?

LE

You not American.

LO

(*saddened*) Oh.

HENRY

(*in the spirit of the thing*) Thar she blows!

SARAH

(*flatly*) I bet you got *all* the merit badges, honey.

MARTHA

Could *anything* be that big!

HERMAN

No. No. Whales are not found in these waters. Whaling is an industry of the Arctic and Antarctic seas.

CARROUSEL

This one must be an individualist. (*Infinity can contain himself no longer. He jumps up and down, delirious with joy.*)

EMMY

Mr. Infinity is at long last cracking under the strain of his tremendous responsibility.

CARROUSEL

Naw, he's just feeling good. Ain't ya, Captain? (*Infinity nods yes.*) This is his first chance to talk to a whale. Infinity, you go right ahead. Ask that whale what business he has with us. (*Infinity whistles loudly. There is silence.*)

HENRY

(*awed*) Why . . he's caught that monster's attention. (*Infinity takes a stance. He raises his arms like a great symphony conductor. All are impressed. Then he swiftly brings his arms down and starts to jump up and down and wiggle his fanny. He accompanies all of this with a virtuoso's selection of groans, grunts, and whistles.*)

EMMY

Look! The whale is answering with a spout. (*Infinity turns and gestures to Carrousel.*)

CARROUSEL

The whale says, "How"!

HENRY

How? (*Some more dialogue is exchanged between Infinity and the whale. Infinity relates it to Carrousel.*)

CARROUSEL

(*as Infinity translates*) His name . . is Big Rainbow. He is a . . a scout from the . . the *tribe* of Antarctic whales. And he wishes . . he wishes to . . smoke the pipe of peace with us. Well, I'll be darned. Tell him okay. (*Infinity jumps and wiggles. Infinity watches for a second, then smiles. He turns back to Carrousel and makes some more gestures.*) He's heap-glad to talk to . . Little Spouts. I guess that's us. He's got . . powerful much to tell. Listen long. It will take many moons. (*Infinity turns back to the whale.*)

HENRY

What'll we do?

CARROUSEL

(*amazed; scratching his head*) I don't know about you. But I intend to "listen long"!

(*They all lean forward. The lights on them dim. Carrousel strums his guitar in the darkness. When the lights come back on, the bright daylight has turned to the red and golden hues of sunset. All are gathered around Carrousel, who holds a great piece of paper in his hands.*)

MAX

I tell ya it's impossible. It's a hoax of some kind.

JESSE

But I saw it with my own eyes.

MAX

I'm a businessman. I know double-talking when I hear it.

HENRY

It's at great odds with all the research I've done.

CARROUSEL

Here it is. Drawn up as neat and pretty as you could want it. A plan. A blueprint for paradise. (*He holds up the paper.*) The Promise. The Promise I been waiting for. I knew it would come . . somehow.

MAX

Bunk! If I'd a been here I'd a harpooned that fish and mounted him on my wall.

HERMAN

(*correcting him*) A whale is a mammal. It suckles its young.

MAX

Sue me.

MARTHA

Personally, I'm in favor of the whole idea.

MAX

Nobody calls Max Ellis a "Little Spout."

SARAH

Whales don't read *Fortune* either.

HENRY

Maybe if we'd go through the whole thing again, Carrousel.

JESSE

Yeah. Read it again, Carrousel. I still ain't got the setup.

CARROUSEL

Well briefly, from what we've been able to gather, this here whale, Big Rainbow, has been trying to talk with humans for his entire adult life. All whales try to. But they end up with a harpoon in them . . 'cause us Little Spouts are usually either greedy or afraid. So far, we've been the first brave enough not to get violent.

MAX

Nuts enough, ya mean.

EMMY

What's that part about the Happy Happy Hunting Grounds?

SARAH

Yeah. Read what he said about that again, Carrousel.

CARROUSEL

Well, it was kind of a promise. (*opens paper*) He told me to put it down on paper so that it would be legal. (*reading from the paper*) "In the great land far below . ." Must mean Antarctica. "Deep behind the wall of bitter ice, in the land of many snows, there will exist for you the Happy Happy Hunting Grounds. A sweet, forgotten valley, guarded by a thousand miles of unknown coldness, yet warmed by a runaway sunbeam. A paradise . . untouched. Sobbing lonely . . just waiting to be claimed by Little Spouts. A crystal of hope and laughing air, drowsing at the tip of a silvery frozen river, which love will thaw . . when Little Spouts arrive. Only warrior whales know the way. And Little Spouts too jackal-hearted and faithless to follow."

SARAH
And he wants to take us there.

MARTHA
Sounds beautiful. Like I used to think Florida was . . before I seen it.

CARROUSEL
He says he'll take one of us back to the mainland for provisions. And then we can hitch up to him and he'll pull us down there.

LO
Fine.

LE
When we leave?

MAX
There's a gimmick somewhere.

CARROUSEL
What'll we do, people? He said he'd return when "the great ball of fire sinks beneath the sea."

MARTHA
Me . . you can count in.

LO
Okay by me.

LE
Likewise.

JESSE
If I got down there I could change my name and live a regular life.

EMMY
You could become Casanova again. We wouldn't laugh.

HENRY
I say let's go ahead.

MAX
I can see it's no use *my* saying anything.

CARROUSEL
Sorry we can't turn back, Mr. Ellis. You can ride to the mainland with Big Rainbow, if you like.

MAX

Catch me doing that? I ain't no Jonah. I got my own plans to get out of here! No, I'll stay. I'll stay and watch you come crawling to me with apologies. "You were right, Mr. Ellis. Please take us back with you." That's what you'll say.

SARAH

Max, for cryin' out loud!

MAX

Awwww!

CARROUSEL

Well then, I guess we know who's best suited to go back with Big Rainbow. (*Infinity salutes.*) Then it's settled! (*All agree.*)

HENRY

(*spotting something behind house*) Thar she blows! Big Rainbow's back here.

CARROUSEL

Tell him the answer is yes, Infinity. (*Infinity whistles and nods his head.*) Good luck, old feller. We'll be waiting for you. (*Infinity hops over the back of the porch. He disappears behind the house.*)

HENRY

Wow. There he goes. Mile a minute.

MAX

This is all nuts.

JESSE

He's under the water now. Gone.

HENRY

(*awed*) Wow. (*There is a moment of silence. Carrousel strums a chord*)

CARROUSEL

The Happy Happy Hunting Grounds.

SARAH

I don't know why, but suddenly I feel like crying.

HENRY

(*putting his arm around her*) Aw, don't you do that. (*She looks at him, amazed.*)

EMMY

This is like a dream. A dream I've had so many times. A sad dream. Things, life, love . . get an inch away from perfection . . just an inch . . and I'm almost happy, but I always wake up too soon. Will I wake up this time, Carrousel?

CARROUSEL

(*slowly*) Nobody has to wake up from this dream . . unless they want to, little girl, unless they want to. (*He strums a gentle chord on his guitar. Then there is silence and the lonely sound of wind. The lights dim on all save Carrousel.*)

CARROUSEL

(*sings softly*)

Sometimes it's an earthquake
    To show us his might.
Sometimes it's most nothing . .
    A sigh in the night.
Sometimes it's like fire . .
    A great burning tree.
Lord, I know where I'm going
    But why'd you pick me?

(*then more brightly*)

So the fable goes on, folks,
    I'll sing ya the rest.
There's some of us sinners,
    And others are blessed.
That don't make no difference
    To them or to me.
As we wait for a whale
    In our house on the sea.

(*The stage lights come up brightly. It is mid-morning. Carrousel moves up to his spot on the porch. Herman is up on Henry's perch, looking toward the sea. Martha is upstage, hanging out some laundry. Jesse and Emmy are in their corner holding a deep conversation.*)

HERMAN

Not a glimpse of Big Rainbow.

CARROUSEL

Give him time. That's a big distance he has to traverse. (*Henry steps out of the house and stretches. Seeing him, Carrousel smiles.*) There you are, boy. I been wonderin' what happened to you.

HENRY

(*a bit nervous*) Yeah . .

CARROUSEL

You're usually up and swinging at the crack of dawn.

HENRY

(*shaken . . awed . . mystified*) Yeah? Well . . (*Suddenly we hear Sarah's voice from inside the house.*)

131

SARAH

Henry darling, will you bring me back a cup of coffee? (*Henry winces and smiles sheepishly.*)

HENRY

Well, Carrousel.

CARROUSEL

Well . . ?

HENRY

Yup. (*He turns and swiftly exits into the house.*)

MARTHA

(*singing heartily as she hangs out wash*) "When you wore a tulip . . a big yellow tulip . . And I wore a big red rose . ."

CARROUSEL

You sure sound joyful.

MARTHA

I wouldn't be surprised if I was.

EMMY AND JESSE

(*come over to Carrousel*) Carrousel, we've got an announcement to make.

JESSE

We want to post nuptials. Emmy and me wants to marry.

EMMY

(*amplifying*) Each other.

CARROUSEL

That's the most encouraging thing I heard in ages.

EMMY

But everything must be proper.

JESSE

It's got to be a formal wedding.

EMMY

After a suitable engagement.

CARROUSEL

When's the happy event?

EMMY

Tonight.

JESSE

We figure Infinity will be back by then to do the honors.

MARTHA

A wedding! I'll make a cake.

EMMY

We plan to hold the reception at home.

JESSE

On the front porch.

EMMY

(*sadly*) 'Course, we'll have to use a cigar band for a ring. But that'll be proper.

CARROUSEL

I just so happen to have a dollar cigar inside. I'll strip that down.

JESSE

Everything's beautiful. I'm gonna bawl.

CARROUSEL

(*with mock gravity*) Well now, you know a weddin' is a mighty serious proposition. There's a lot of formalities and regulations.

JESSE

Formalities? Regulations?

CARROUSEL

Yeah! You had your blood test?

EMMY

Oh dear, I knew we forgot something. Do we have to, Carrousel?

CARROUSEL

We want this to be legal-like. I can use this. (*takes a pin out of his lapel*) Stick out your thumbs. (*They do. He pricks them both while they hide their eyes.*) Now take a look. What's it like?

JESSE

Mine's red and sticky.

EMMY

So's mine.

CARROUSEL

Yeah, that's blood all right. I guess you both pass. (*strikes a chord on his guitar*) There's gonna be a wedding tonight. Big celebration!

LO

Lots to eat and drink!

LE

Much color and presents!

LO

Best of everything. (*Their enthusiasm is interrupted by the sound of an airplane.*)

CARROUSEL

I believe I hear something that sounds like civilization.

MARTHA

Up there! A sea plane.

JESSE

Gee, it's circling around.

EMMY

I do believe that the aircraft is going to land.

CARROUSEL

Seems to be signaling us.

MARTHA

I'm no expert, but I'd say that's a good landing.

CARROUSEL

Taxiing right up to us as nice as anything. Infinity, throw him a line. (*looking around . . remembering*) How I miss that man!

JESSE

I'll take care of it.

EMMY

Watch out for the propeller.

JESSE

(*angry*) Emmy, I'm no baby. When will you remember who I am!

EMMY

I do my best to forget. (*Jesse groans and tosses a line off. The motor sound cuts out. The tip of a silver wing juts out from behind one of the wing flats. Standing on the wing is Miss Unit. She is a tall, attractive — but severe-looking — girl in her late twenties. She wears a fashionable business suit and has an old-fashioned aviator's helmet on her head. She carries a large briefcase and an attaché case.*)

CARROUSEL

Welcome.

JESSE

(*trying to give her a hand*) Careful now.

MISS UNIT

(*pushing his hand away with contempt*) Entirely unnecessary. (*stepping aboard, very businesslike*) I am Miss Unit. I am *the* Miss Unit. I am Mr. Max Ellis' personal executive secretary and well-known Girl Friday. I have come to save my boss. Where is Mr. Ellis?

MAX

(*calling from privy*) Somebody mention my name?

CARROUSEL

Mr. Ellis is in conference.

MISS UNIT

(*sitting, businesslike*) I'll wait. (*She takes off her helmet and gloves. She folds them neatly.*)

CARROUSEL

Uhh . . nice weather we've been having.

MISS UNIT

I find it wet! (*another long pause*)

EMMY

Do you fly that machine by yourself?

MISS UNIT

(*quite smug*) But of course. (*Another pause. Carrousel tries to make polite conversation.*)

CARROUSEL

How'd ya know Max was here?

MISS UNIT

One of *Mr. Ellis'* bottled messages finally got to me. It was found on a beach by a shabby native boy who is now a multimillionaire.

CARROUSEL

(*impressed*) Well, I'll be . .

MISS UNIT

But of course you will. (*She sits quietly, not talking.*)

CARROUSEL

(*friendly*) My name's Jones. Carrousel Jones.

MISS UNIT

I know that, Mr. Jones.

CARROUSEL

Hell, call me Carrousel. (*starts to introduce others*) And this is . .

MISS UNIT

I'd *really* rather not make contact today if you don't mind. (*She looks away. Carrousel shrugs and the others more or less give up and return to their activities.*)

HERMAN

(*looking out to sea again*) Still no sign of our whale friend.

CARROUSEL

You'll see him when he gets here. Whales are hard critters to miss.

MISS UNIT

(*looking up*) Whales?

CARROUSEL

Beg pardon?

MISS UNIT

Did someone mention whales?

CARROUSEL

Yeah. Why?

MISS UNIT

(*thinks about this for a moment, then gives a short, high-pitched, silly giggle; catches herself*) Ridiculous!

MAX

(*rushing on from the privy*) Miss Unit!!

MISS UNIT

(*rises, faces Max, and produces a seaweed-covered bottle*) You called?

MAX

(*pleased*) I knew I could count on you, Unit. You never let me down!!

MISS UNIT

(*modestly*) Please, Mr. Ellis.

MAX

(*to others, like a ringmaster*) Miss Unit! The World's Most Efficient! (*There is a fanfare. Miss Unit bows stiffly. All applaud.*) Now you nitwits will see some organization! (*to Miss Unit*) Get rid of them.

MISS UNIT

(*briskly to others*) If you will excuse me, please. I have work to do with Mr. Ellis.

MAX

See how slick she does it! (*He turns away from others.*) Now let's get to it, Miss Unit! Appointments?

MISS UNIT

Chase Manhattan. Four thirty this afternoon.

MAX

(*delirious*) A bank. I been so homesick. (*smiling*) How's the good old Chase Manhattan?

MISS UNIT

As most everything nowadays . . under water.

MAX

Are we adjusting to it?

MISS UNIT

But of course.

MAX

Did you bring the reports like I asked?

MISS UNIT

(*opening briefcase, taking out papers*) The computers worked overtime to get these ready.

MAX

Good old computers.

MISS UNIT

They *care*.

MAX

Let's go. How's our mines?

MISS UNIT

Submerged. (*hands over papers*)

MAX

Issue scuba outfits to the miners.

MISS UNIT

I already have.

MAX

Right! Our factories?

MISS UNIT

(*handing over more papers*) We're converting exclusively to rubbers, raincoats, rafts, and snorkles.

MAX

Dandy! Railroads?

MISS UNIT

Rusting . . but still running.

MAX

Newspapers?

MISS UNIT

Soggy . . but still selling.

MAX

Profits?

MISS UNIT

(*hands him a huge sheaf of papers*) Enormous.

MAX

(*choking up*) Beautiful. Kinda gets ya, don't it? (*holds papers to his heart, blissfully*) Losses?

MISS UNIT

(*handing him a tiny postage-stamp-sized paper*) Unavoidable.

MAX

(*outraged*) HOW COME!!?

137

MISS UNIT
Our garden sprinkler division. Bottom fell out of the market.

MAX
FIRE EVERYBODY!!

MISS UNIT
I already have.

MAX
My vitamins?

MISS UNIT
(*handing him a bottle*) Your vitamins!

MAX
Lunch?

MISS UNIT
(*handing him a tiny sandwich*) Your lunch.

MAX
(*a disappointed little boy*) Aww . . this all?

MISS UNIT
(*his conscience*) Two hundred and twenty-two calories.

MAX
Ahhhhhh. (*businesslike again*) How's the consolidation?

MISS UNIT
We amalgamate.

MAX
The amalgamation?

MISS UNIT
We consolidate! (*pause*)

MAX
And . .

MISS UNIT
And?

MAX
Uhhh . . Libido?

MISS UNIT
Arranged. (*produces a photograph*)

MAX
Who?

MISS UNIT
Linda. A starlet. She'll meet you at nine.

MAX
Ya sure.

MISS UNIT

Her contract and her bauble. (*bringing forth more papers and a sparkling diamond pin*)

MAX

(*pleased*) You think of everything, Unit baby. (*pats her on shoulder*)

MISS UNIT

(*steps away politely*) Please.

MAX

Now let's get off this ferry boat. (*He hands everything back to her.*) Here, take this junk and file it! Warm up the plane while I get Sarah and the rest of my stuff. (*Miss Unit walks back to the plane. Max goes to his papers.*)

MISS UNIT

(*putting aviator goggles back on; to others*) Good day. (*She exits.*)

CARROUSEL

Yeah . . so long.

MAX

See? I told ya I'd get off this scow. And not on no whales neither! And when I get back, I'm gonna sue you for every cent you got! All of ya!

CARROUSEL

Happy hunting. (*We hear the engine trying to rev.*)

MAX

(*exiting into the house*) Sarah! Sarah! Sarah! (*The motor coughs a little more. Max comes out again.*) Where is she? Sarah?

CARROUSEL

Aw, let Sarah stay. She seems to like it here.

MAX

Catch me! Environment is very important to a growing girl. Sarah!

CARROUSEL

But . . (*The motor tries once more — unsuccessfully.*)

MAX

I'll have to drag her out! Where the blazes . . ? (*He starts into the house, but Miss Unit suddenly reappears. Her face is ashen.*)

MISS UNIT

Mr. Ellis . .

MAX

(*stopping*) Yeah?

MISS UNIT

The motor won't start.

MAX

Huh?

MISS UNIT
The auxiliary gas tank.

MAX
Yeah?

MISS UNIT
Empty.

MAX
How could it be empty. (*She squeezes up her face as if to block out this awful thing.*) Answer me, Miss Unit!

MISS UNIT
(*a tragic declamation — Joan at the stake*) For the first time . . in an otherwise faultless life . . I . . I . . I . .

MAX
Yeah?

MISS UNIT
(*in ringing tones*) DEAR GOD IN HEAVEN . . I GOOFED!! (*She moans and faints.*)

CARROUSEL
Grab her! (*Herman rushes over and catches her. Jesse and Lo follow.*)

MARTHA
The poor darling. (*They lead Miss Unit to a chair.*)

MAX
(*exploding*) This is impossible. She always works right. She never louses up!

HERMAN
(*angry*) Things are breaking down all over! (*Emmy rushes over to Miss Unit. Le follows.*)

EMMY
(*kindly*) There. There . .

MARTHA
Give the poor thing some air.

JESSE
She's coming around.

MAX
(*shaken*) I don't believe it. I just don't believe it.

MISS UNIT
(*coming out of it, miserably trying to avoid the others' eyes*) No . . no . . no . .

MARTHA
Calm down, child. I'll make you something hot.

MISS UNIT

No . . no . . nothing.

MAX

Miss Unit, what the hell happened?!!

MISS UNIT

I . . I . . don't know. The flood . . the rains . .

MAX

Things like that don't shake you, Miss Unit. You've been on big deals be-fore. Like that time we almost bought Africa.

MISS UNIT

I know . . I know . .

HERMAN

(*kindly*) We're all entitled to one good goof.

MISS UNIT

(*turning away*) Inexcusable. Don't touch me! Go away. Go away, all of you!

MAX

Miss Unit, I'll expect you to turn in your pencil when we get back.

MISS UNIT

(*burying her head in her hands*) Just go way. Just go way. Just go way.

LO

(*whose attention has wandered off to the side, looks out to sea — jumps*) Hey look! Big Rainbow!!

MAX

That damn fish again. I'll never forgive you, Miss Unit. (*Emmy runs up behind Max and kicks him in the shin. Max reels around.*)

EMMY

Don't you dare strike a woman! (*turns around to Jesse*) I do believe that's the first positive thing I've ever attempted.

LO

They be here any second.

LE

Then we be on our way?

CARROUSEL

Then we'll be on our way.

MAX

(*exploding*) The South Pole! For cryin' out loud!!

JESSE

(*shouts out*) Over here. He's pullin' in right behind the house!! (*Henry and Sarah come out of the house. All the men rush to the rear and help In-*

141

finity up onto the porch. Miss Unit looks back, sees the whale. She gives a little giggle. Stops.)

MISS UNIT

It *is* a whale! (*giggles again, stops*)

JESSE

Hi, Infinity. Great to see you. (*Infinity smiles.*) Great to see you too, Big Rainbow. How!! (*He holds up his hand in an Indian gesture.*)

CARROUSEL

Bring back all kinds of wonderful things? (*Infinity gestures.*) He says to give him a hand, fellows. I'll make the work easy. (*He strikes a chord on his guitar.*)

SARAH

(*seeing Miss Unit*) Unit, what are *you* doing here?

MISS UNIT

(*giggles*) It's a whale. (*Carrousel plays a rousing melody on his guitar. With great, lusty, gleeful whoops, the men all rush to Infinity and help him unload. They lift up a rocking chair, packages of food, a water fountain, magazines, a ship's compass, more food, candy bars, lampshades, and a packet of mail.*)

MARTHA

(*taking mail*) Letters from my children. Now everything is complete! (*Then come books, a record player, a fire extinguisher, seeds, a kite, more food, liquor, hammers, saws, a catcher's mitt.*)

HENRY

Man, Big Rainbow. You got heap lots capacity. (*Miss Unit becomes more and more wide-eyed as Infinity keeps unloading and the men stow the stuff away into the house. There's a bass fiddle, typewriter, bugle, more food, clocks, bicycle, and an espresso coffee urn. Infinity then reaches back and brings on a large tank of gasoline. He walks over and bows gently to Miss Unit. He hands it to her. She looks up at him. Her eyes fill with grateful tears.*)

MARTHA

It's the little things that make a woman happy.

MAX

Well thank God! Let's get going! (*He grabs the tank from Miss Unit and pulls her to her feet*) Get this juice in . . and we'll be out of here! SARAH! Pack up. We're leaving.

SARAH

But . . (*Miss Unit takes the gasoline and goes toward the plane. She looks back, then turns suddenly, and steps onto the wing and exits.*)

CARROUSEL

Any more provisions? (*The men bring up a kitchen sink, more food, a filing cabinet, a bag of money, a fully decorated Christmas tree, and a large theatre poster announcing "The Great Git-Away."*) We certainly are well provided for. Ready for anything! Including the wedding tonight!

HENRY

Wedding? Who?

LO

Them?

CARROUSEL

Right! (*Infinity remembers something. He reaches into his pocket and produces a ring box.*)

JESSE

A wedding ring? But how? (*Infinity gestures.*)

CARROUSEL

He says he just figured. (*Miss Unit reappears on the wing. She watches.*)

JESSE

(*rushing to Emmy*) Look, honey!

MAX

(*who has collected all his junk in his hands*) Ya got the gas in? (*Miss Unit shakes her head no.*) Well why not? Come on, will ya. Get back on the ball!

MISS UNIT

(*to others, weakly*) He *is* a whale, isn't he?

CARROUSEL

That's what he is.

MISS UNIT

A whale! A whale! (*She giggles again. This time she allows it to linger.*)

MAX

So what! A whale! We gotta get going!

MISS UNIT

(*turning to him, after a long pause*) But I wish to see the wedding. (*to Emmy, sincerely*) That is, if I am invited.

MAX

What? You? A wedding? Come on, stop this nonsense, Unit baby. You're the only one who can fly this crate.

EMMY

(*to Miss Unit*) We didn't have time for formal invitations. But had we, you would have been one of the first to have received one.

143

MAX

Hey! I gotta get back for them appointments!!

MISS UNIT

I haven't a thing to wear.

MAX

Industry's just gonna stop dead without me!!

EMMY

I can loan you something. It's blue.

MISS UNIT

(*as if it were one of the most beautiful of words*) Blue. Bluuuuuueeeee . .

SARAH

And if it doesn't fit, Miss Unit . .

MISS UNIT

Not Miss Unit . . (*magically*) Gwen.

SARAH

Beg pardon?

MISS UNIT

(*She can tell the world.*) My name is Gwen. Gwen Joyce Unit.

MAX

What's with the Gwen Joyce all of a sudden. Come on!

MISS UNIT

(*giddy, standing with her new friends*) No. He's a whale.

CARROUSEL

(*hitting a chord*) Glad to have you aboard. Meet the folks, Gwen. (*The others gather around her upstage, babbling welcomes.*)

HERMAN

(*We hear him above the others.*) May I escort you to the wedding tonight?

MAX

(*not believing his eyes*) This bunch of creeps could contaminate I.B.M. Where the hell is that bottle? (*No one pays him any attention. He grabs his bottle and takes it into the house. Infinity gestures and brings Carrousel down front. The lights on the others dim.*)

CARROUSEL

What's on your mind? (*Infinity gestures and produces a small radio.*) You want me to listen? (*Infinity turns on the radio.*)

RADIO VOICES

(*a series of newscasters*) The flood waters show no sign of receding. So far the entire Atlantic and Pacific coasts have been inundated. (*Infinity switches station.*) The United Nations General Assembly this morning had a session which will go down in history. Knee-deep in water, the hip-

144

booted delegates threw aside yesterday's plea for unity and flew at each other's collective throat. (*Infinity switches station.*) The East puts the blame on the West's current series of satellite launchings. However, the West blames the East's launchings last week. (*Infinity switches station.*) Furious, their delegate tore into our representative. He accused him of imperialism, power politics, and splashing. In response, our delegate dunked him. (*Infinity switches station.*) Disarmament talks have been called off, and the arms race has started anew. (*Infinity switches station.*) . . says we'll be able to resume testing next week . . (*Infinity switches station.*) And it's every man for himself!

> CARROUSEL

(*grabbing the radio angrily and turning it off*) I knew it was gonna be this way back there! Nothin' could stop it. (*Infinity shakes his head no.*) What's it look like to you? (*Infinity makes a gesture like a big explosion.*) Then let's get the holy hell outta these parts. (*rushes to the porch rail and shouts*) GIDDYAP, BIG RAINBOW. BLAST IT!! GIDDYAP!!

(*Blackout. Martial music is heard for a few seconds. Then this slowly blends into a cheerful, buoyant tune. Lights come back up. It's night, and the stars are out. A slightly off-kilter moon hangs in the heavens above. Its light bathes the scene. The stage is empty, but lights burn brightly inside the house. Then Lo and Le enter. Both wear incongruous hats — their one concession to the formality of the occasion. They carry stepladders and paper lanterns. Doing a little dance to the music, they proceed to hang the lanterns and decorate the stage for the wedding. At the very end, Lo climbs to the top of the ladder while Le steadies it. Lo straightens out the moon. The music stops.*)

> LE

Most wedding-like.

> LO

I still think should be more yellow lanterns.

> LE

Should be more pink also.

> LO

All we have left is blue.

> LE

What the hell. Blue beautiful too.

> LO

I'm glad we have blue. (*They finish.*)

> LE

Ahhh. You great artist, Lo.

LO

You too, Le.

LE

Let's neck. (*Carrousel enters. He wears a dinner jacket over his old clothes.*)

CARROUSEL

(*meaning jacket*) I was saving this to be buried in. Didn't think I'd need the pants.

LO

You make very handsome stiff.

CARROUSEL

Well, this place sure looks wedding-like.

LE

Just what I said.

CARROUSEL

(*shouting front*) How 'bout it, Big Rainbow. (*worried*) No . . no. Don't slow down. You keep right on goin'. (*Miss Unit — we'll oblige her now by calling her Gwen — enters. She wears a lovely blue dress and golden slippers. She carries a glass of champagne, and is slightly radiant.*)

GWEN

(*twirling her skirt around*) It's blue.

CARROUSEL

Sure is.

GWEN

(*grinning broadly, holding out foot*) They're golden.

CARROUSEL

Damned if they ain't.

GWEN

(*holding up champagne*) It fizzes.

CARROUSEL

Now that's a fact.

GWEN

There's a wedding! And . . and . . (*She bursts into a wonderful laughter and points front.*) He's . . he's . . a *whale* . . (*She doubles up with laughter. It is infectious. Carrousel, Lo, and Le join in.*) Most wonderful thing in my life! (*She just about gets this out and bursts into laughter again. Lo and Le are rolling on the floor with laughter. Slowly, they all control themselves. Finally the laughter subsides. But Gwen catches Carrousel's eye again, and . . *) A whale! (*They all laugh again. Sarah enters in a low-cut strapless gown. The results are fantastic.*)

146

SARAH

Look. No hands.

GWEN

(*laughing*) It's beautiful.

SARAH

Hey. You don't look so bad yourself, cookie.

GWEN

It's blue.

SARAH

(*delighted*) Yeah, you bet your little old bottom it is. (*Gwen twirls around in a little waltz step. Carrousel accompanies her on guitar. She gets a bit too intricate, and loses her balance. Fortunately she is caught by Herman, who enters from the house at that moment.*)

HERMAN

I'm sure I could be of some assistance.

GWEN

(*leaning on him*) It's a wedding!

HERMAN

Yes.

GWEN

(*holding up glass*) It's empty.

HERMAN

There's more inside.

GWEN

Such a long way to go.

HERMAN

I'll help you.

GWEN

(*looks at him for a moment — does not quite know what to make of him; then grins broadly*) Check. (*pause*) Check. Check. (*She laughs. Then she turns to the others and is most dignified.*) We'll be back shortly.

SARAH

Take your time, tootsie. We all gotta live sometime and you might as well start now.

GWEN

(*thinks for a moment, then takes off Herman's glasses*) You're beautiful! (*Herman offers her his arm. They start in. Gwen turns and looks at the others.*) He's a whale. (*She goes into another spasm of laughter as she exits. Herman shrugs his shoulders, grins broadly, and follows her. Sarah laughs, and Carrousel strums a loud, happy chord.*)

147

CARROUSEL

(*to Sarah*) And how's our maid of honor?

SARAH

This is a new spot for me.

CARROUSEL

I was thinkin' we might be having another collaboration by and by.

SARAH

(*a warm smile radiating through her*) Ya mean me and Tom Swift? Oh, I don't know. He's real sweet. Ya know what he says to me last night? He says, "God Almighty, Miss Ellie, but you got beautiful hands." Hands? I mean . . after everything . . Hands? I could have beaned him one there for a minute. And then I think. And I feel like bawling. I ain't never been so touched in my life. And why? Hands? (*Carrousel strums a gentle chord.*)

HENRY

(*shouting from a window*) Hey, Sarah, the function is about to start!

SARAH

Ya got the ring?

HENRY

'Course I got the ring. Come on. Ya holding up the works. (*He disappears.*)

SARAH

Ain't he just wonderful. (*kisses Carrousel on top of head*) Well, honey, see ya after we do the bit.

(*She exits into the house. Lo enters. He and Le take positions on either side of the door. Both wear solemn expressions befitting the occasion. Carrousel strums "Oh Promise Me." The wedding guests arrive. Herman and Gwen are shown to their seats by Lo. Martha and a disgruntled Max are shown to their seats by Le. Then Le shows Lo to a seat. Then Lo rises and shows Le to a seat. Infinity, resplendent in a white captain's uniform, takes his place at a litle improvised altar. Carrousel strikes up the wedding march. Jesse and Henry enter and go down and stand to one side of the altar. All eyes turn back as Emmy, in a magnificent wedding gown, comes through the front door. Le is evidently doubling in brass, for she walks ahead and strews flowers. Emmy still holds the teddy bear, Roger. Sarah, behind her, takes Roger before Emmy walks down the aisle. Emmy protests for a second, but Sarah is firm. Sarah places Roger on the rail of the porch. Emmy looks back longingly — holds for a second. Then Jesse clears his throat. She turns, sees Jesse, then continues down to the altar. Emmy and Jesse take the correct position before Infinity. Lights dim. Spotlight*) *illuminates Jesse, Emmy, and Infinity at stage center. Infinity delivers the wedding ceremony by gestures which Carrousel translates from the darkness.)*

CARROUSEL
Now look here. You two both love each other?

BOTH
We do.

CARROUSEL
No kidding?

BOTH
No kidding.

CARROUSEL
You gonna miss each other when you're parted?

BOTH
You bet.

CARROUSEL
You gonna make up after you fight?

BOTH
We will.

CARROUSEL
You gonna try not to hurt each other's feelings?

BOTH
We'll try.

CARROUSEL
You gonna believe each other?

BOTH
We will.

CARROUSEL
You gonna make it as nice as possible for each other?

BOTH
Yes, sir.

CARROUSEL
For as long as you possibly can?

BOTH
Yes.

CARROUSEL
And above all, you both gonna do your best?

BOTH
We will.

CARROUSEL
(*singing, following Infinity's gestures, as he turns to Emmy*)
Will ya eat the same food?
    Will ya share the same key?
Will ya darn all his socks?
    Keep him happy and free?
Will ya cherish his love?
    If ya will . .
Then he's your husband.

Will ya always be near?
    Will ya make his life gold?
Will ya tell him he's strong?
    And when ya grow old . .
Will ya still feel the same
    If ya will . .
Then you're his wife.
Do ya say "I do," little Emmy?
    EMMY
(*seriously*) I do, oh yes, I do.
    CARROUSEL
Do ya know what that means, little Emmy?
    EMMY
Not exactly . . but I'm willing to find out. (*Infinity turns to Jesse.*)
    CARROUSEL
(*translating*)
Will ya cry the same tears?
    Will ya laugh the same fun?
Will ya light up her night
    When the long day is done?
Will ya treat her kind?
    If ya will . .
Then you're her husband.

Will ya hope the same hopes?
    Will ya dream the same way?
Will ya tell her she's pretty
    'Least ten times a day?
Will ya mean what ya say?
    If ya will
Then she's your wife.

150

Do ya say "I do," Mr. Jesse?

JESSE

Sure! Yeah sure, I do.

CARROUSEL

Do ya know what that means, Mr. Jesse?

JESSE

(*bravely*) Ain't nothing ever licked me yet! Much. (*Infinity gestures.*)

CARROUSEL

The ring. (*Henry steps into light and gives Jesse the ring. Then he steps back out of light.*)

JESSE

(*placing ring on Emmy's hand*) With this ring I thee wed ya good and proper! (*They kiss, Infinity gestures and Carrousel sings.*)

CARROUSEL

> So kiss each other
> And sing the same song.
> Hold tight to each other
> All your life long.
> This is only the start . .
> Little husband and wife.

(*The stage lights come up strong and the ceremony is over. Lo and Le are ready with boxes of rice as the newlyweds rush up the aisle. Then there is a great commotion. Much kissing of the bride and shaking hands with the groom. Herman takes the wedding photograph with a large, old-fashioned flash camera which goes off with a great puff of smoke. Lo and Le rearrange the chairs to form a little reception. Martha remembers something, gives a hoot, and dashes into the house. Emmy, by this time, has taken off her veil. She is ushered with Jesse to the place of honor. Martha comes back out of the house triumphantly with a huge wedding cake.*)

MARTHA

Could I pass up an opportunity like this! (*All cheer.*)

LO

Cut cake, Emmy.

LE

After all the fuss, time for feast. (*Emmy is about to cut the cake when Carrousel strikes a few loud chords on his guitar.*)

HENRY

(*a bellow*) HOT DAMN! A HOEDOWN!!

CARROUSEL

(*starts to play a rip-roaring square dance*) Everybody choose up her part-

151

ner. And clear the deck! (*Jesse and Emmy are partners, as are Sarah and Henry, Lo and Le, Herman and Gwen. Martha even manages to get Max into it. All go into a wild square dance. Carrousel shouts out the calls. When Carrousel stops playing and shouting, all the dancers flop to the deck in various stages of exhaustion.*)

EMMY

Carrousel . . can you play a waltz?

CARROUSEL

Why sure, Emmy. (*He starts to play "Down in the Valley."*) How's that?

EMMY

Thank you so much. (*goes to Jesse*) Jesse . . please . . (*Jesse looks at her — and she is the most beautiful thing he has ever seen. Slowly he gets up, puts his arm about her, and the two of them begin to waltz.*)

EMMY

Goodness . .

JESSE

What?

EMMY

We're wed.

JESSE

Sure looks that way.

EMMY

Were you scared . . before the ceremony?

JESSE

Heck no, Emmy.

EMMY

I was. Scared to death.

JESSE

(*after a long pause*) Me too. (*As they continue to waltz, it becomes obvious that they are oblivious to everyone else. Carrousel indicates to the others that the newlyweds should be left alone. The others all softly steal off. Martha is the last to leave — she has to be torn away from weddings. As they all go, the lights are slowly dimmed, and Emmy and Jesse dance alone in the soft glow of the moonlight. The music slowly fades. They are alone.*)

EMMY

What'd you think about . . during the ceremony?

JESSE

I don't know. The ocean, I guess. All around us like it was the universe. And the house here . . like a new, scared little star. And you and me.

152

And it was like . . a . . I mean . . like you and me was setting out alone on that little star, and . .

EMMY

Oh Jesse . .

JESSE

(*catching himself*) Aw heck, I didn't think nothing of the kind. I thought about us getting married . . and . . uh . . the responsibilities of being a married man, and . .

EMMY

I thought about my calendars.

JESSE

Huh?

EMMY

On the wall in my room. My folks didn't allow no pictures except if they were of God or angels or Jesus. And I never liked those poor dimestore likenesses. So I used to take them down and put up calendars instead. Old calendars, you know? And they were beautiful . . because each number was a day that most everyone forgot. But I wouldn't. I'd look at each one of them every day and I'd remember them. I'd say, "I remember you . . February 18, 1947 . . or August 8, 1954."

JESSE

Emmy . . ?

EMMY

And I'd never cross a day out. And once I became upset because some were red and most only black. So I found a red crayon in a tin box and went around and made them all the same. And when it was done, I was so happy that I started to cry and dance . .

JESSE

Cry . . and *dance* . . ?

EMMY

At the same time! And that was when my father made me take my calendars down. He brought me an electric picture of Jesus, that when you plugged it in the halo revolved. Only it was AC and we were DC . . so it never worked. And Daddy got mad and smashed the picture and went out back with a quart of beer and a Sears, Roebuck catalogue and wouldn't talk to nobody for five hours. Ever since then my walls were bare. And that is what I thought of during the ceremony.

JESSE

(*confused, not quite knowing what to make of his new bride*) Uhh . .

153

let me tell you this, Emmy. If you want to hang calendars . . it's perfectly okay with me.

EMMY

(*thoughtfully*) No . .

JESSE

I mean, when we settle down . . you can hang them all over. (*an after-thought*) Even in my den!

EMMY

No . . really. (*pause*) I thought about you too. All during the ceremony. It's really remarkable how it seems I'm able to think of two things at once. (*He kisses her.*)

JESSE

Like a frightened, new little star.

EMMY

Or a garden . . (*We hear a gentle note of music from Carrousel's guitar as he appears from the shadows.*) Goodness . .

JESSE

(*looking around*) What happened to the party?

CARROUSEL

It ended hours ago.

EMMY

Hours?

CARROUSEL

Everybody else kissed today goodbye and went to sleep.

JESSE

(*swallowing hard*) I guess we'd better . . eh . . turn in. Uhh . . for the night . . ya know? I mean . .

CARROUSEL

They all found themselves nooks and crannies downstairs. They want you two to have the upstairs tonight.

JESSE

Well . . that's . . beautiful . . or something. (*He picks Emmy up and starts toward the threshold. He's about to carry her through, when he stops — worried.*) Now . . you won't cry . . or . . *dance* . . or anything?

EMMY

Good night, Carrousel . .

(*He carries her inside. Carrousel strums his guitar gently. The only light on stage now is a dim moonbeam which catches the lonely pathetic little shape of Roger, sitting resolutely on the rail, alone for the first time. The*

154

light slowly fades, and soon the stage is in complete darkness. It stays dark for a few seconds, then another spotlight comes up slowly on Carrousel far downstage. He wears a sad expression. He slowly strums his guitar and sings the "Git-Away" song in a much slower tempo.)

CARROUSEL

> The time has gone by
>> Slowly day after day.
> We've almost accomplished
>> Our Great Git-Away.
> But the word from the mainland
>> Is hard to endure.
> For the word from the world
>> Is the world is at war.
>
> Yes the world is at war, folks,
>> Of that there's no doubt.
> And some of our crew
>> Feel a might bit put out.
> The ties to the mainland
>> Are hard to undo.
> The mem'ries of dear things
>> And yesterdays too.

(Carrousel continues to strum. The lights come up on the full stage and suggest bitter winter weather. The house is covered with long icicles. Everyone is wearing a heavy coat or is wrapped in a blanket. There is the sound of a mournful wind in the background.)

MAX

(sarcastic) Man, this is delightful! So *this* is the Happy Happy Hunting Grounds.

MARTHA

No . . not yet. We're waiting for the entrance to thaw like my friend, the whale, promised.

SARAH

(hopefully, perhaps losing some faith) He promised that the Hunting Grounds would be right behind those fields of ice. He promised!

MAX

The South Pole. I could be in Vegas.

HENRY

Ain't no more Las Vegas. News just came over this radio.

155

EMMY

Las Vegas gone too? Ain't nothing going to be left if we ever want to go back.

JESSE

Don't you fuss, Emmy.

MAX

Go back?! We're never going back. We're jammed in this ice pack for good.

EMMY

But that can't be . .

JESSE

(*to Max*) Please . .

MAX

Listen to that radio. Half the world's under water . . and the other half's all blown up!

EMMY

(*holding stomach*) But my baby? Where's he gonna go to school and church and college? Where's he gonna meet a nice girl? Where's he gonna get a job? Where's he gonna meet other nice, young married couples to come over and play cards and . .

MAX

I'd wait till he's born!

CARROUSEL

Infinity, when's Big Rainbow say that river will unthaw? (*Infinity gestures.*) Any time now?

MAX

Hah! A twenty-five-ton con man.

HERMAN

(*who is sitting with his arm around Gwen, glares at Max, then turns to Emmy*) Don't worry, Emmy. I'll teach your child everything there is to know. (*Gwen looks up to him and smiles.*)

EMMY

But if there is no world, what'll there be to teach?

HERMAN

(*after a moment*) Noble memories. Traditions. Emmy, one thing you can be certain of . . No matter what happens, world or no world, even if the sun burns itself out . . eight times six will still be forty-eight.

MAX

Huh?

HERMAN

(*puzzled*) What I mean is . . something keeps going! I'm sure! That is
. . (*He looks to Gwen and puts his arm about her more tightly.*)

MAX

Ye gods! Don't you saps realize? The world is ending and we're missing it!

CARROUSEL

Would you suggest going back?

MAX

Sure. I ain't no draft dodger. I fought in two wars, and with my own two
hands I helped build up the world after both of them. Top that!

CARROUSEL

Set 'em up in the next alley, eh?

MAX

That's the way it goes. It's better than your way. Stay home and float
away. Boy, that's some philosophy.

CARROUSEL

Why not, son? Why must the rule always be "When someone snarls . .
snarl back"? Why must the crazy-quilt pattern always be "Try, build, explode, fail and try, build, explode, fail and try, build, explode and fail
again"? Why don't we attempt something new for a change? Abolish the
adrenal gland and relax and absorb and not give a damn. Let's adopt the
philosophy of . .

MAX

Boy oh boy! The revolt of the shnooks! Noodnicks of the world, unite.
Bunch of crap, mister, a bunch of crap! 'Cause no matter how you slice
it, it comes out you're a mob of yellow cowards. Now, let me tell you something . .

EMMY

(*suddenly gives a cry of pain and clutches her stomach*) Jesse . .

JESSE

Wha . .

EMMY

Jesse.

JESSE

Emmy?

EMMY

(*nods yes*) Every four minutes and forty-seven seconds on the dot!

JESSE

(*for a moment no words come out, then a tiny cry*) Help!

CARROUSEL

Just guide her in gentle, boy.

JESSE

Help!

LO

(*to Le*) Hot water ready?

LE

Six buckets. I get. (*Lo rushes out. Martha, Gwen, Sarah, and Le gather about Emmy and lead her to the house.*)

MARTHA

(*to Jesse*) You stay out here, boy.

JESSE

Help.

MARTHA

Nu, Doctor Infinity? You ready? (*Infinity nods his head and follows the women in. They all exit.*)

CARROUSEL

(*to Jesse*) Just take it easy, boy. Infinity's done this thousands of times.

JESSE

It's the first time for her. Help! (*Lo dashes through with a bucket of hot water.*)

CARROUSEL

Now take it easy!

JESSE

I ain't fit to be a father. I just ain't fit! (*brings out pocket mirror and looks at himself*) Just get a load of *that*! Terrible! Who could call that . . daddy!

CARROUSEL

Now, son . .

JESSE

I'm almost nothing. And what isn't nothing . . is highly forgettable! (*still looking in mirror*) Big deal. Public Enemy Number One. Public phony . . that's me. I had those wanted posters printed up myself!

CARROUSEL

I never would have guessed. Well, maybe it's just as well . . seein' as how you're a papa.

JESSE

P . . P . . P . . Papa? Me? (*very dramatic*) I oughta be shot. How could anybody do such a thing to a fine American citizen like Emmy!! (*a cry from the soul*) Help!

158

CARROUSEL

Son . . relax. If we'd all just relax. (*Henry interrupts.*)

HENRY

Carrousel, listen to this . . (*He turns up the radio.*)

RADIO VOICE

(*A cheerful M.C. talks as a band plays "No Business Like Show Business" in the background. It is almost like signing off after a great telethon.*) So, I guess this is it. I don't know who's still listening to me. But, I'm as high as I can go . . and the water's up to my neck. Ha-ha-ha. What isn't blasted is flooded! So . . I guess we've come to the end of our special program, folks. It's been a wonderful experience. And thanks for all the nice letters. We wish to thank the makers of Buick, Babo, Wheaties, Lux, Winston Cigarettes, and Serutan for relinquishing their time so that we might bring you the end of the world. Till the next time, then, keep a smile on your face . . and remember . . (*He begins to sing "There's No Business Like Show Business" in the best Bert Parks tradition. After a few bars we hear the sound of bubbles drowning him out. Then silence.*)

HENRY

Well, that's it. Blub . . blub . . blub . . It's gone. Like that.

CARROUSEL

And we're all that's left. (*to Jesse*) Hang on, boy. We need new blood.

JESSE

How's . . How's Emmy doing?

MAX

(*grim*) Civilization has been destroyed. It's over, finished, done!

JESSE

Yeah. But how's Emmy?

MAX

Over! Do you know what I had back there? Eight mines, twelve factories, three airlines, half a dozen railroads, four newspaper chains, and sixty-five hotels. Not to mention my home . . real estate . . cars . . boats . .

CARROUSEL

If you were back there . . you couldn't do anything.

MAX

I couldn't, huh? I'd a hung onto everything! I'd a bailed water with my own two hands. I'd a made my own bombs . . and I'd a blasted any S.O.B. that came near. I'd a fought, damnit . . I'd a fought. I'd a gone down with my ships. I'd a inspired men to go on . . and die for me! *Inspired?* Hell, I'd a *paid* 'em! I'd a slugged and beat and pushed and kneed and . .

CARROUSEL

And you'd a been obliterated.

MAX

But I'd a gone down slugging all the way! I'd a shown a little aggression! (*Lo runs through with more hot water.*)

JESSE

How's Emmy?

MAX

And now it's all gone. God Almighty, all gone . .

CARROUSEL

We're still here.

MAX

You! A half a dozen slobs that never git in to begin with? What . . are you gonna start all over again? Tell me! Hah! You're a bunch of pretty sad excuses for Adam and Even! (*furious*) And what *bugs* me is that I'm stuck with ya!! I didn't want no part of it from the beginning!! If the rest of the world . . the *real* world . . is ending, then, damnit, I want to end with everything else!

CARROUSEL

You don't know what you're saying!

MAX

I'm a taxpayer! I demand my rights! I want to blow up with the world like a normal human being!! And, as for this boat ride to nowhere . . I want out!!

CARROUSEL

Don't say that, son, you might get it.

MAX

I want out!!

CARROUSEL

Please, son . .

MAX

I WANT OUT!!

CARROUSEL

(*after a long pause shakes his head sadly*) Then . . you've got it. (*He strums a few chords. The lights dim for a second, then come up. Max is gone.*)

HENRY

Hey, where'd he go?

CARROUSEL

Who?

HENRY

Huh? I dunno . . There was a man standing . . I remember his name was . . was . . I mean . . right here . . he was standing . . (*He rushes over to where Max was.*) Ain't nobody here. I coulda sworn . . (*He sees something.*) Ain't nothing here . . but a bright, red apple. (*He picks up an apple.*)

CARROUSEL

(*rises and rushes to him*) And *this* time . . We ain't taking any chances! (*He grabs the apple and hurls it over the side. As he does this, we hear the sound of several slaps from inside the house. Then the vibrant, loud, piercing, wonderful cry of a baby. All stop dead. Jesse rises. He is almost in a state of shock. Another loud cry.*) Uhhh . . Jesse, recognize the voice?

JESSE

Is that a . . a . . a . . *baby*?

CARROUSEL

Damn well better be!

JESSE

(*terrified, starts to sing again, trembles*) "Me and my shadow . ."

CARROUSEL

(*trying to calm him down*) Take it easy . . easy. You ain't alone anymore. (*Infinity enters in a doctor's outfit. He wears a great good smile. He gestures.*) Yup . . it's a baby. (*Sarah comes out beaming. Jesse rushes to her.*)

JESSE

I gotta know. Is it a boy or a girl?

SARAH

Uh . . what else?

MARTHA

(*entering — the eternal midwife — and announcing glowingly*) IT'S A BOY!

JESSE

ROGER? FOR REAL? ROGER?

MARTHA

You were expecting Peter? Mama's doing fine!

LO

(*rushing on with another steaming pail*) MORE HOT WATER!!

JESSE

FORGET IT! ROGER FINALLY GOT HERE!!

LO

(*realizes, looks down at pail, shrugs*) What the hell. I make coffee.

161

JESSE

Where's my son! I want to see my boy! (*He rushes inside. The lights grow brighter and warmer. Music.*)

SARAH

Hey! What's happening?

MARTHA

Somebody turned on the heat finally?

CARROUSEL

I wonder . . (*Infinity starts to gesture excitedly.*) What? What's that you say?!! (*Infinity points. He looks out ahead.*) Well I'll be damned! Our Captain has informed us . . that the passage has finally thawed. Look! Full speed ahead! Full speed ahead, Big Rainbow! (*With a glorious yell, Henry leaps up to his old perch on the roof. Martha comes down beside Carrousel. Sarah follows Henry. Lo and Le are together. Herman stands by himself downstage. Gwen rushes on from the house — she points wildly at the heavens. She rushes to Herman.*)

GWEN

Is it?

HERMAN

I don't . . I don't know.

HENRY

Hey . . look at the sky!

MARTHA

Like Coney Island!

SARAH

What is it . . a missile?

LO

Fireworks?

MARTHA

A saucer?

HERMAN

(*holding Gwen*) It is . . it is . . it's *Echelmeyer's Comet*!! Back again. Herman, you are vindicated!

LE

It cuts the sky in half.

MARTHA

(*astounded*) Loop-de-loops!

CARROUSEL

In Technicolor!

HERMAN

What did I tell you, my dear, what did I tell you? (*He embraces Gwen. They kiss, deliriously happy.*)

MARTHA

(*near tears*) Such a glorious sight. What a shame nobody but us can see it.

HENRY

(*double-take*) Nobody but us . . *hell*! (*practically jumping out of his clothes, pointing front*) Looky what's behind it . . following it like it was a guiding star!

CARROUSEL

What, boy, what . . ?

HENRY

Another whale, and it's pulling a house . . just like this one.

CARROUSEL

WHAT!

HENRY

(*awed*) And behind that . . another . . and . . another . .

CARROUSEL

Gawd Almighty!

HERMAN

Look! Cottages and huts and chateaus and wigwams and castles and mosques and pagodas and . .

GWEN

Every type of dwelling from the four corners of . .

MARTHA

It's a living geography book.

HENRY

Stretched out as far as the eye can see!

CARROUSEL

All the way to the sunrise and back!

HERMAN

But why? Why? I thought the world was over.

CARROUSEL

I . . I . . guess there's been some others . . who've had the same idea we had. (*tears streaming down his face*) All kinds of crackpots to keep it going.

LO

Now we go to the HAPPY HAPPY HUNTING GROUNDS!

CARROUSEL

NOW WE GO!! (*The lights come up full. Everyone drops his coat or blanket. Jesse, with Emmy holding her new baby, comes to the door. Carrousel shouts forward.*) Hey, out there. We're coming. Get ready for us. Make way for the human race. The *human* race. God's kindly, mixed-up, misfit, half-assed, magnificent human beings!!! You just be all ya promised to be, and we'll take it from there! (*Infinity suddenly becomes vocal, and gives a loud yell. The others are startled, and become silent. They look to him in surprise.*)

INFINITY

Now I've got something to say. (*A rainbow appears in the sky.*) In the beginning there was the end! And somebody sez, "Let there be something." And by God, there *was* something. And it was damn near everything!! And then . . ? (*Everyone freezes in position. All action stops. Complete silence for several seconds.*)

THE CURTAIN FALLS

The Great Git-Away by Romeo Muller was presented May 26–28, 30, 31, June 1, 2, 10, 11, 13–18, 20–25, 27–30, July 1, 2, 29, 30, August 1–6, 22–27, 1966, on the University of Minnesota Centennial Showboat, Minneapolis. It was directed by Frank M Whiting.

Cast of Characters

CARROUSEL JONES	Robert Reynolds
HENRY	Robert Larsen
INFINITY	Raye Birk
MAX ELLIS	John R. Cranney
SARAH	Loni Anderson
EMMY PLEASANT	Linda Kelsey
JESSE DALTON DILLINGER JAMES	Merrill Lessley
MARTHA GOLDEN	Lynne Rubel
HIGGENS, of the American Red Cross	Travis Lockhart
A GENT WITH A RED BEARD	Travis Lockhart
HERMAN	Robert Skloot
LO	Stanton Coffin
LE	Adriane Despot
MISS UNIT (GWEN)	Molly Atwood

JOHN STRANACK

With Malice Aforethought

A LIVING-ROOM COMEDY IN THREE ACTS

for R. G. S.

Dramatis Personae

PHILANDER, a young man-about-town
CUFFLINK, his man
HEADWAY, a businessman
CLAMBER, another businessman
FETISH, a go-between
MERGER, a young tycoon
DODGE, a tax man

DORINDA, a young widow, sister to Headway
NORAH PIKESTAFF, her cousin and companion
MRS. HEADWAY
MRS. CLAMBER
BODICE, her maid

Time: The Present

WITH MALICE AFORETHOUGHT

ACT ONE

Scene 1

A room in Dorinda's apartment. Enter Dorinda, Mrs. Headway, and Norah.

DORINDA

It's no use trying to console me. Help me. I'm merely his sister, I have no powers of persuading him. But, being his wife, you must.

MRS. HEADWAY

Naturally, but on this subject he is adamant. He has his duty as your husband's executor.

DORINDA

To plague me with paupery? To reduce me to indigence with an allowance not even sufficient to keep Norah in nosedrops? To badger me with a budget, to subpoena my bills and hold an inquest over every canceled check? Is that his legal duty as executor?

MRS. HEADWAY

I'm sure he allows you any reasonable expense.

DORINDA

He means to beggar me. I'll end up rattling a tin cup and coaxing weird tunes out of an accordion.

MRS. HEADWAY

I didn't know you played the accordion.

NORAH

I'm sorry that my sinuses are such an expense.

DORINDA

Nonsense, Norah. I've grown very fond of your sinuses. I'm railing against my brother, not at you. Your companionship is my only consolation at this point.

MRS. HEADWAY

Your husband made the arrangement for your own sake, my dear, so you wouldn't fritter his money away or fall victim to some fortune hunter after he'd gone.

DORINDA

Oh, if only he were still alive. I'd divorce him!

MRS. HEADWAY

What a tragic accident it was!

DORINDA

Had he landed that sailfish, we'd never have heard the end of it!

NORAH

I think it was a lovely end, being dragged away from the boat into the setting sun.

DORINDA

Why didn't the idiot let go of his rod?

MRS. HEADWAY

You must give him credit for not giving up. (*The doorbell rings.*)

DORINDA

Oh, that will be Clamber. She said she'd be popping in. I hope you don't mind. I know you two are not on the best of terms.

MRS. HEADWAY

Whom did you say?

DORINDA

Mrs. Clamber.

MRS. HEADWAY

I'm not aware of her. She is a matter of complete indifference to me.

DORINDA

That's good, because I'm quite fond of her.

MRS. HEADWAY

Then you are unique in that respect. (*Enter Mrs. Clamber and Fetish.*)

MRS. CLAMBER

Dorinda, darling, let me give you a hug. You're looking ravishing.

FETISH

Quite lifelike, in fact. Do I get a hug too?

168

MRS. CLAMBER

Fetish insisted on coming with me, so now we must be careful what we say. Cucumber, I call him, because of the way he repeats!

FETISH

I'm discretion itself and, by the bye, you must remind me to tell you about old Mrs. Pendulous.

MRS. CLAMBER

Hullo, Norah darling. And who's your friend?

DORINDA

Clamber, you know Mrs. Headway, my sister-in-law.

MRS. CLAMBER

How do you do?

MRS. HEADWAY

We have met before.

MRS. CLAMBER

You know, I do believe you're right. Forgive me. I would never have recognized you.

MRS. HEADWAY

It was some time ago. You were just a pretty young thing — then.

MRS. CLAMBER

Heavens, ancient history! But time wreaks its havoc on us all. I only hope it will deal with me as kindly as it has with you.

MRS. HEADWAY

Why, I think you have matured very gracefully.

FETISH

Mercy, let's not talk about the passing years. I have a theory, you know. The same way that money isn't as valuable as it once was, I believe that time today isn't worth what it used to be. Don't you find yourself spending more and having less to show for it? It's a new kind of inflation. Pouf, a day goes by and suddenly already it's next month!

DORINDA

And a new season, and a new style. It's hard to keep up with it.

MRS. CLAMBER

You should try being in the lead. You have to run twice as fast to stay ahead.

MRS. HEADWAY

I can't agree with you. True elegance is no effort for those with taste.

MRS. CLAMBER

I beg your pardon. *I* was speaking from experience.

MRS. HEADWAY

Forgive me. I would never have imagined. But I must admire your courage in wearing the new line. Isn't is cruelly unflattering?

FETISH

Oh, no. It's terribly gay!

DORINDA

I'm madly taking up hems on everything.

MRS. HEADWAY

Ah, but you have the legs for it, and a small behind. Besides, at your age you wouldn't look like mutton dressed as lamb.

MRS. CLAMBER

Oh, I'd rather be dressed as lamb than as rump roast!

MRS. HEADWAY

One must admire your spirit of Do or Die.

MRS. CLAMBER

You aren't altogether indifferent to the trends. Look at your heavenly wig!

MRS. HEADWAY

Actually, it's growing, but I'll pass on the compliment to Mr. Fred.

MRS. CLAMBER

Ah, Mr. Fred. I've heard that he's a wizard with problem hair.

MRS. HEADWAY

You've nothing to lose. Why don't you give him a try? What were you going to say about Mrs. Pendulous, Fetish? Nothing unkind?

FETISH

No, compliments, compliments! You know that she was supposed to be off on a cruise. Well, she's back, looking seventeen. She's lost five of her seven chins and her bust's unrecognizable.

MRS. CLAMBER

Surgery, indeed! Complete reincarnation is what she needs.

MRS. HEADWAY

I believe in being charitable. The poor thing needed *something*. We all knew that. This way, at least she will be bearable. Though why she bothered with her bust, I'll never know.

FETISH

Who knows? She may have been tightened everywhere!

NORAH

I think it's dreadful to tamper with nature like that.

FETISH

Well, my dear, think of our friend Miss Dexamyl and thank heaven she does. Her whole personality is straight out of the medicine cabinet.

MRS. CLAMBER

She's a walking pharmacopoeia.

FETISH

Apropos her, it was she who made the divinely killing remark about you and Brian Basket at the Muscular Dystrophy Ball.

MRS. CLAMBER

The scorpion! We were *not* unzipping each other!

MRS. HEADWAY

I'm so glad there's no truth in the story. One had heard it everywhere.

MRS. CLAMBER

You know, I'd never noticed what pretty wrists you have. Look, Norah. Hasn't she the prettiest wrists?

NORAH

Yes, they are nice.

MRS. HEADWAY

I have never noticed them.

MRS. CLAMBER

Terribly pretty. Are they natural? Excuse me, girls, I have been dying to powder my nose. (*Exit Mrs. Clamber.*)

MRS. HEADWAY

I'm surprised she didn't announce it in the paper. Really, Dorinda and you too, Fetish. How you endure that woman is quite beyond me. She's totally without a redeeming quality. Who does she imagine she is? Or what? And yet it is pathetic, really, I suppose. I can't blame her as much as I blame the magazines. They put these ridiculous aspirations into women's heads. It's gotten so that anyone who can read imagines that she's With It. What the poor thing doesn't know is that that sort of being In is absolutely Out, at least among the people that *really* count; the lovely people, who do interesting things and lead beautiful lives. It really would be a kindness to disillusion her, but in the face of such pretentious vanity I fear it's a bootless task. If she thinks she's swinging in the thick, the more fool she. But she's not one of the lovely people, I can tell her that!

FETISH

Well, I think she's a camp and I admire her.

DORINDA

And so do I. She's always full of pzazz!

MRS. HEADWAY

You're too good-natured, Fetish. You can't be relied upon. You at least, Norah, will agree with me?

NORAH

I beg your pardon? I haven't been following.

MRS. HEADWAY

That girl, she lives in a world of her own! Knit, knit, knit.

NORAH

I'm not very good and I have to concentrate.

FETISH

Anyone would think you were expecting twins! Speaking of which, I hear that Virginia Vestal, who shall be nameless, is three months gone.

MRS. CLAMBER

(*re-entering*) By whom, my dear, by whom?

FETISH

You know how vague she is. She couldn't hope to remember her pills!

MRS. HEADWAY

Those who play with fire . . !

MRS. CLAMBER

Well, that should stop her singing in church for a while.

FETISH

And get her off Philander's neck. She was throwing herself at him in a shameless way. And to no avail.

DORINDA

Along with Carol Cleavage and the rest of them.

MRS. CLAMBER

Who is this man Philander one hears so much about?

MRS. HEADWAY

Some sudden upstart, who, because a few silly women lose their heads over his so-called charms, imagines now that the whole sex is in love with him.

DORINDA

I didn't know you knew him.

MRS. HEADWAY

I don't. One doesn't have to, with a man like that. That's what ears are for!

MRS. CLAMBER

I hear he's absolutely irresistible.

DORINDA

He's attractive, all right.

MRS. HEADWAY

Hmph! Well, I certainly envy you having nothing better to do but amuse yourselves with gossip all day long. But I've important things to attend to before my Zen class this afternoon.

MRS. CLAMBER

You seem to be keeping a very full schedule during your visit to our town.

MRS. HEADWAY

What do you mean, visit? I live here.

MRS. CLAMBER

Forgive me, it's so long since I've heard your name I imagined you'd moved.

MRS. HEADWAY

Oh dear me, no. I am very much around. But it's hardly likely that you would know friends of mine.

MRS. CLAMBER

Why, I believe I know both of them.

MRS. HEADWAY

Goodbye, Dorinda. Fetish, we can share a taxi if you're going my way.

FETISH

Grand, and remind me to tell you the hilarious thing that happened at the Mazeltoff's Bar Mitzvah the other day. Dorinda, love, it was heaven seeing you. *Hasta la vista*, all! (*Exeunt Mrs. Headway and Fetish.*)

MRS. CLAMBER

That woman! Aren't you going to give me full marks for restraint?

DORINDA

Oh, she's not so bad.

MRS. CLAMBER

Those preposterous airs. I detest the water she walks on! Zen indeed. I hope the lotus position gives her a double hernia! But far be it from me to malign your sister-in-law. There are so many others who are much better at it than I. Do let's talk about something pleasant for a change. Tell me you've found a man who's madly attractive and whom your brother will consider as husband material.

DORINDA

I'm on the lookout, but I doubt such a being exists.

MRS. CLAMBER

Don't I know it. Attractive, available men are rarer than phoenixes.

DORINDA

At least you always have Clamber to fall back on.

MRS. CLAMBER

Slim satisfaction in that. He's about as exciting as the Dead Sea Scrolls.

173

DORINDA

It's even more demoralizing without a husband, believe you me.

MRS. CLAMBER

You and Norah don't know how lucky you are.

NORAH

Heavens, I gave up any thought of a husband long ago.

DORINDA

And yet you shall have one, Norah. You are not to throw in the towel. It isn't feminine.

NORAH

It's no use fooling myself. No man would want to marry me.

MRS. CLAMBER

That has nothing to do with it. You must make a man have you, whether he wants to or not. There isn't a woman living who isn't more than some man deserves.

DORINDA

Norah would make a very serviceable wife.

MRS. CLAMBER

I've no doubt of it. Has she tried her hair at all in a bit of a twist? To make her look a little less like Joan of Arc. And perhaps just a touch of color on the cheeks.

NORAH

Oh, I couldn't breathe with cosmetics in my pores. I don't think it's right to tamper with nature like that.

MRS. CLAMBER

Dear life! Listen to the child. Live in the twentieth century and not tamper with nature! The Lord knows how much strontium ninety we all drink in our morning tea. We may tamper with a clear conscience if you ask me. If the fallout doesn't kill us, something will. Boredom, no doubt. My dear, I'm so vexed and frustrated I could die. I want to have the house redecorated and by no one less than the fashionable Mr. Bauble himself.

DORINDA

I've heard he's all the rage.

MRS. CLAMBER

He's an epidemic.

NORAH

But your home is so nice. Why do you want it changed?

MRS. CLAMBER

Sweet child. She inhabits another world. In this world, at least, there are forces beyond our control, and if one's to live at all it's in a house that Bauble has decorated. It's as simple as that. The only snag is he's so besieged he won't take another client before Doomsday at the earliest. Didn't you use him once? Can't you intercede for me?

DORINDA

I asked his advice, which was so preposterous I decided to cope myself.

MRS. CLAMBER

But you have an eye for these things; and besides, your lives are not so elaborate. You can do as you please. I'm a martyr to fashion. It's practically killing me. Anyway, Dodge, my tax man, does Bauble's accounts and he's promised to persuade him if it's humanly possible.

DORINDA

There's nothing that Dodge isn't able to arrange.

MRS. CLAMBER

Isn't he a genius? Anyway, my dears, much as I adore you, I have a thousand-and-one-and-a-half things I must do . . before my *Rosicrootsian* meeting this afternoon. Let me see. I must try and find some gloves in that new fungus shade, and a yard and a half of ribbon that will match, and a pair of shoes that are not too clever, but just clever enough, not to mention lunch with young Mrs. Honeymoon. She phoned in a great state and wants to ask my advice on a very personal matter. Can't wait to find out what it is. Naturally I'll let you know all when I see you next. Now I must rush. Goodbye, my dears. It's been simply lovely hearing all your news. (*Exit Mrs. Clamber.*)

DORINDA

What a gay life they lead, always rushing about. And look at us.

NORAH

I don't believe a word of what they say and pretend to do. It's just a way of talking, that's all it is.

DORINDA

At least it sounds exciting.

NORAH

It isn't any way I'd want to live. They make fun of their husbands and malign their friends. Anything important they pooh-pooh. They're only serious about things of no consequence.

DORINDA

Not everyone's as saintly as you are, Norah dear.

NORAH

I'm not a saint. I'm very ordinary and quite content.

DORINDA

Contentment is a trap. It's as bad as despair. It makes you give up the struggle.

NORAH

The struggle for what? I'm not a competitor.

DORINDA

Well, I'm not resigned to my lot, I can tell you that. A single woman is such an albatross.

NORAH

You didn't seem to regret being rid of your Ancient Mariner.

DORINDA

Oh, sly one! You can make a funny when you try.

NORAH

What I meant to say was, at least you've been married once.

DORINDA

Don't apologize. You too could be a bitch if you wanted to.

NORAH

Dorinda, you know I would never . .

DORINDA

Don't be silly. A touch of bitchiness is essential to being feminine.

NORAH

It's not part of my makeup. Maybe that's what's wrong with me.

DORINDA

The trouble with us is, Norah, we're far too nice. And look what happens to us. Nothing. Nothing at all. Here we sit, like two Christmas cakes that were ordered and not called for, while the world scurries by.

Scene 2

A street. Enter Mrs. Headway and Fetish.

MRS. HEADWAY

Detestable woman!

FETISH

Which one?

MRS. HEADWAY

Clamber, of course. Dorinda is my sister-in-law and it's very déclassé to disparage one's relatives; though how she can stand that Clamber woman is quite beyond me. She's such a vulgarian, such an arrant arriviste. Her social aspirations are a standing joke.

FETISH

You can't blame her for trying to improve herself.

MRS. HEADWAY

I don't despise her for that. But she imagines that she's In. I ask you, a parvenu like Clamber? I refuse to dwell on the subject anymore. I've quite enough vexations as it is. I spoke to Bauble's secretary on the phone and there isn't the slightest hope of his doing my house. You must persuade him for me.

FETISH

Bauble and I have had a falling out. I'm not speaking to him.

MRS. HEADWAY

Really, you and your tiresome feuds. You're no use at all.

FETISH

Bauble's a bitch. I've crossed him off my list.

MRS. HEADWAY

Fortunately Dodge, my tax man, is going to intercede with him on my behalf.

FETISH

If Bauble is busy, why not use somebody else?

MRS. HEADWAY

I despair of you. If Bauble's the man this year, one doesn't live in a house by anybody else.

FETISH

(*suddenly*) There's a pumpkin!

MRS. HEADWAY

Run and catch him before the fat woman does! (*exeunt*)

Scene 3

Philander's lodgings. Enter Philander, in a dressing gown, and Dodge.

PHILANDER

It is very good of you, Mr. Dodge, but I have such an infernal hangover it is difficult for me to concentrate. (*calling*) Cuff! Mix me a tombstone!

DODGE

A tombstone? What is that?

PHILANDER

A desperate remedy: Bromo-Seltzer, curry powder, a raw egg, and vodka. I'm afraid I haven't been able to follow one word of your scheme. To save taxes I should turn myself into a company, is that it?

177

DODGE

Let me explain it, slowly, once again. You incorporate yourself not as one company, but two.

PHILANDER

I'm with you so far.

DODGE

Then you negotiate with one company to buy the other out. You quote yourself a price much bigger than you're worth, haggle a bit for the sake of appearances, then clinch the deal.

PHILANDER

So now I have acquired both halves of myself.

DODGE

Exactly. Now you amalgamate, owing yourself the buying price. Therefore you raise a loan from yourself which in due course you fail to meet, whereupon you foreclose and take possession of the company, which by this time has run itself handsomely into debt. All of which is deductible from your income tax.

PHILANDER

It sounds too straightforward. There must be a snag in it.

DODGE

Not a one. Why, I've got clients who are indebted to themselves for thousands all over town and others who are taking control of themselves every day of the week. I have some who have even forced themselves into involuntary liquidation, and then others who have made quite a nice thing by going into partnership with themselves. (*The telephone rings, off.*)

PHILANDER

The way you outline it, it sounds quite promising.

DODGE

If you let me handle your affairs, you'll get more money back from the government than you've given them. (*Enter Cufflink.*)

CUFFLINK

It's Miss Vestal on the phone again. What shall I say this time?

PHILANDER

Tell her I've been arrested.

CUFFLINK

What shall I tell her you've been arrested for?

PHILANDER

Indecent exposure. (*Exit Cufflink.*) I apologize, Mr. Dodge. Now, where were we?

DODGE

I have another item I've been working on. It's a scheme to avoid paying rent, but it's still in the experimental stage. You make yourself your own subtenant with a lease; then, with the lease as collateral you raise a mortgage on the premises, with which you pay the rent.

PHILANDER

But what happens when the mortgage eventually comes due?

DODGE

Then you have to evict yourself, but I'm working on that part now. (*The telephone rings, off.*)

PHILANDER

I see.

DODGE

It shouldn't cost you a penny in the end.

PHILANDER

That's what makes it so attractive. (*Enter Cufflink, with the pick-me-up.*)

CUFFLINK

That was Miss Manslaughter on the phone, so I said you had gone for your penicillin shots. She wanted to know what was wrong with you and I said it was something I didn't think a lady ought to hear.

PHILANDER

Good work, Cuff. If that doesn't shake her off, nothing will.

CUFFLINK

I hope I haven't touched off a panic among your lady friends. (*Exit Cufflink.*)

PHILANDER

Anyway, Mr. Dodge, though I'm sure your services are excellent, at the moment my resources are purely hypothetical.

DODGE

I was told that your finances could do with some straightening out.

PHILANDER

Report spoke true, but, as ever, somewhat behind the times. My finances, when I had them, could have done with some straightening out. But, alas, dear doctor, the patient whose life, without doubt, your science could have much prolonged, expired last night when I pressed my last piaster on the kind taxi man who deposited this nerveless form outside its own front door. I am insolvent. In a word, broke!

DODGE

Broke? Well . . well . . well . . well . . well. There's a thing, isn't it?

179

PHILANDER

You see how it is. I am grateful for your interest, and rest assured that, should my prospects become brighter, I shan't hesitate to call you in. But in the meantime . .

DODGE

I understand. Hmmm. Broke, you say?

PHILANDER

Through my own folly and improvidence, and I am prepared to suffer for it like a man. (*Enter Cufflink.*)

CUFFLINK

Well I'm not going to suffer, I can tell you that. You can have my notice.

PHILANDER

Cufflink. Eavesdropping? I'm surprised at you. Consider yourself dismissed.

CUFFLINK

Oh no you don't. I don't get dismissed without six months' back wages in my pocket.

PHILANDER

You can't be serious.

CUFFLINK

Six months, two weeks, five days this very day. I paid myself out of your pants pocket last May the seventeenth.

PHILANDER

How do you remember that?

CUFFLINK

I wanted to get Bodice a birthday present, that's how I know. You can go ahead and suffer all you want, but I'm giving notice. (*to Dodge*) And you're a witness.

PHILANDER

You can pack your bags and clear out at once.

CUFFLINK

Not till I get my money. (*to Dodge*) Go on, give him a loan. Just until his dividends are due.

PHILANDER

I wouldn't think of it.

CUFFLINK

Go on. How about it, Dodge?

DODGE

A loan is out of the question. Too poor a risk. Besides, at the moment I happen to be a little strapped myself.

CUFFLINK

Too bad. Seems we're all in the same boat.

DODGE

But there is a certain proposition that might interest you. It's a delicate undertaking which, if handled with flair, could bring in quite a tidy little sum for all concerned.

PHILANDER

First, I suppose, we form three companies?

DODGE

No, nothing like that. Come with me and I'll explain it as we go. There is in this town a much sought-after interior decorator by the name of Bauble, and two society ladies, clients of mine, who are arch-enemies . . (*exeunt*)

Scene 4

A locker room. Headway and Clamber, discovered.

HEADWAY

Don't know what was wrong with me today. Couldn't play worth a damn.

CLAMBER

Don't worry, Headway. We all have our off days. A few sessions with the pro and you'll be back in form.

HEADWAY

Don't gloat, Clamber. You know I beat the spots off you as a rule. It's this damned bursitis . .

CLAMBER

Nothing wrong with your stroke. That one divot went at least two hundred yards.

HEADWAY

I replaced it!

CLAMBER

It's that slice of yours you've got to watch.

HEADWAY

Fairways are nothing. The only challenge in golf is recovering from the rough.

CLAMBER

You were challenged, all right. Half the time all I saw was the top of your hat in the shrubbery.

HEADWAY

Glad you're amused. Put you in a good humor, winning for once.

CLAMBER

I look forward to the drink you're buying me.

HEADWAY

Welcome. Lord knows you've had to buy me enough.

CLAMBER

You're a great guy, Headway, even if you play lousy golf. You know it's odd, when we get along so well, that our wives don't see eye to eye.

HEADWAY

Strange. But you know how women are. The devil knows what gets into them. Take Minerva. We have a comfortable house, but damnit if she doesn't decide that it isn't fashionable. Got to be all redecorated from stem to stern.

CLAMBER

Now that's a coincidence! Eunice insists that our house be done over too.

HEADWAY

The unholy expense! It's enough to give a man a coronary.

CLAMBER

It's all very well for you. Your wife's squandering her own money. But think of me. It's my hard-earned living my wife is splashing about.

HEADWAY

Look here, Clamber, I don't care for your inference. Let me tell you, being married to a woman with money is a serious responsibility. It's a business like any other, except that you live under the same roof with the majority stockholder, and that's no bed of roses, believe you me!

CLAMBER

No offense. At least your old girl knows what she's worth. Mine thinks I'm made of money and spends it accordingly.

HEADWAY

Crack the whip, man! Crack the whip!

CLAMBER

I've tried, my friend, I've tried. Rows, sulks, tantrums I can do without. I have one ulcer at the office. I don't need another at home.

HEADWAY

Speaking of which, tell me, these decorator guys . . They'll be hanging around the house when we're not there. Not that I don't trust Minerva, but can we trust these men?

CLAMBER

Good heavens, Headway, don't you know about male milliners, interior decorators, and other gentlemen of that ilk? They're all what-you-may-call-'ems.

HEADWAY

Is that so? Well, that's a relief. Only mentioned it because . . You heard about old Antler, I suppose?

CLAMBER

No.

HEADWAY

Came home from the office a bit early one afternoon and found his wife stripped for action and the television repairman taking a shower.

CLAMBER

Antler's own fault. I always said she was too young for him. (*Enter Merger.*)

HEADWAY

Why there's young Merger. Haven't seen you in a while.

MERGER

Hullo there. How are you? Bullish I hope. Don't let me interrupt.

HEADWAY

We weren't talking shop.

MERGER

Pity.

HEADWAY

You know my friend Clamber here?

MERGER

Amalgamated Transcontinental Industries. Of course I do. Good to see you again.

CLAMBER

Have you been playing today?

MERGER

Playing — heavens no! I'm hard at work. People talk much more freely when they're out of their business suits. At the bar I heard of a very low dividend. In the showers I learned of a possible proxy fight. And I just overheard a stock that's going to split three ways — in the john.

HEADWAY

This boy's on the job!

CLAMBER

I'll see you presently in the steamroom, gentlemen. (*Exit Clamber.*)

HEADWAY

I admire a bright young fellow like yourself. Most people work for money but a few smart ones use their wits. Make money work for them.

MERGER

That truth struck me when I was a little boy. On my paper route I delivered only the *Wall Street Journal*. Believe me I have such stratagems! Let company chairmen tremble in their seats. I'll tell you in the strictest confidence that, as of now, I command twenty-five percent of the voting stock of Consolidated Tube, Flue, and Duct, the acknowledged leader in the hot-air industry.

HEADWAY

You don't say!

MERGER

It's destined to become a colossus, you mark my words!

HEADWAY

Very interesting. Twenty-five percent of the stock, you say. And I know how you could come by a further twenty-six percent.

MERGER

Indeed? This is one of my better days.

HEADWAY

I have a widowed sister and she owns a considerable block of Consolidated shares.

MERGER

Twenty-six percent. With my twenty-five, a controlling interest!

HEADWAY

A possibility occurs to me.

MERGER

Widowed? . . I think I catch your drift.

HEADWAY

An eligible bachelor.

MERGER

There's no denying it. An older or a younger sister, may I ask?

HEADWAY

Younger by far. Baby of the family.

MERGER

Not that it matters, of course, where so much is involved. But how could I repay you if this came about?

HEADWAY

Let's say a seat on the board? How does that strike you?

MERGER

Very businesslike. I have delayed getting married for just an occasion like this.

HEADWAY

Good boy. The only remaining obstacle is my sister herself. I don't imagine she'll prove insurmountable to a purposeful young fellow like yourself.

MERGER

I'm not without my attractive qualities.

HEADWAY

I'll arrange for her to meet you without delay. Put your proposal to her and I'll back you up. The thing's as good as done. We'll join Clamber in the steamroom. Mum's the word?

MERGER

Mum's the word. I never spoil a good thing by passing it on! (*exeunt*)

Scene 5

A street. Enter Philander, Dodge, and Cufflink.

PHILANDER

It's outrageous. Utterly reprehensible! The very model of deceit, imposture, and chicanery.

DODGE

You are too generous.

PHILANDER

It's nothing but a clandestine conspiracy to bamboozle; a contemptible collusion to defraud. No one but a scoundrel would have any part of it. It's unthinkable. Yet . . it's not without possibilities.

DODGE

I knew it would appeal to you.

PHILANDER

It is fraught with risk and difficulty, of course.

DODGE

No risk at all, barring the unexpected.

CUFFLINK

The money's worth whatever risks we run.

PHILANDER

There is truth in that.

DODGE

Fifty percent for you for bringing it off and fifty percent for me for thinking it up.

PHILANDER

It's villainous, but I'll do it.

DODGE

That's my boy. I'll undertake the preliminaries. The ladies have set their hearts on having Mr. Bauble do their houses and we will provide him, or a reasonable facsimile.

PHILANDER

There's no chance of Bauble changing his mind?

DODGE

None whatever. He's booked ahead for years.

PHILANDER

I wonder if I can carry off the part?

DODGE

Don't worry. I'll coach you. But are you sure that you have never met either of the ladies before?

PHILANDER

Never laid eyes on them.

CUFFLINK

Bodice will recognize me right off the bat, but I'll think of something to put her off the scent.

DODGE

We may as well run over preliminaries now.

PHILANDER

The sooner the better.

CUFFLINK

I've got to wait here for Bodice. She has a welfare parcel she's bringing me.

DODGE

Then join us as soon as you can. (*Exeunt Philander and Dodge. Enter Bodice, pushing a perambulator, from the other side.*)

CUFFLINK

Hullo, beautiful. On time for a change.

BODICE

That's enough of your lip. I've brought you what I could, and I've got to get back. If she finds out I'm gone, old Clamber will have a fit.

CUFFLINK

All contributions gratefully received.

BODICE

(*handing them over*) Here's a ham, a tin of plums, a box of coconut, some cornflakes, and I don't know what this is. Oh, it's Drano.

CUFFLINK

It will come in handy anyway. I feel like the wolf that waylaid Red Riding-hood. How about a kiss along with the loot?

BODICE

In broad daylight? What do you think I am?

CUFFLINK

Go on, be a good girl!

BODICE

In front of the child! There's a good show playing at the Princess this week.

CUFFLINK

For a whole year now that's all we ever do . . smooch in the dark.

BODICE

What more do you expect, I'd like to know? You'd have my all in no time, give you half a chance.

CUFFLINK

Why won't you marry me? I've asked you a hundred times.

BODICE

Sex, that's all you ever think about! When are you going to get a real job? Everytime we go to the movies I have to pay. How will you ever support me . . and our family? Anyway, meet me here tonight, and don't be late.

CUFFLINK

Thanks for the CARE package.

BODICE

Thank old Mrs. Clamber, don't thank me. (*They exeunt, severally.*)

Scene 6

A room in Mrs. Clamber's house. Mrs. Clamber, discovered.

MRS. CLAMBER

(*on the telephone*) Hello. Can I speak to Mrs. Bedstead? . . Tell her this is the Bureau of Internal Revenue. Thank you . . Hello, Betty darling, this is me. Ha-ha! Yes, I thought that would give you a hot flash. My dear, I called for nothing more than to tell you I was at Mrs. Multitude's last night and you didn't miss a thing by not being asked. Your name only came up twice, but with nothing that I hadn't heard before. They're not an inventive set . . Oh, the usual crowd. Sarah Bellum was there. If you ask me she is even queerer now than before her analysis. And have you noticed how earnest Susan Sacrilege has become all of a sudden. She's taken

187

to being quite maddeningly serene and has dyed her hair a very devout shade of pink. It's that Science of Religion cult that she's taken up. They practice Group Psychic Reactivation . . No, not the faintest but it sounds rather lewd to me . . No, my dear, nothing new. I just sit quietly waiting for the Change of Life. I'm sorry we haven't time for a proper natter now. We must arrange it soon. Tomorrow week is perfect; I'll write it down. Bless you for phoning, Betty my sweet. Goodbye. (*She hangs up. Calls.*) Bodice! Where is that wretched girl? She's never here. Bodice!

BODICE

(*off*) All right, all right! I'm coming. You don't have to shout the place down. (*Enter Bodice.*) Okay, what is it? What do you want?

MRS. CLAMBER

A little civility. It would make a pleasant change.

BODICE

(*sarcastically*) Yes, madam. What is it madam wants?

MRS. CLAMBER

What have you been doing to your hair?

BODICE

I gave myself a permanent. Tried that new rinse of yours. I don't think it's much good, if you ask me.

MRS. CLAMBER

Oh, don't you. Is that all you have to think about this afternoon? Have you fixed that hem that I gave you to do?

BODICE

Oh, come on. Don't be such a Simon Legree.

MRS. CLAMBER

Have you unpicked the bows yet on the purple dress?

BODICE

I've only got one pair of hands. I can't do everything at once.

MRS. CLAMBER

And as I think of it, I must object to your using my cologne as liberally as if it were household disinfectant. I notice half a bottle gone and can only presume that you have been drenching yourself.

BODICE

Well, if I'd known you were saving it, I wouldn't have touched a drop.

MRS. CLAMBER

And while I think of it, though I never stop ordering food, Cook tells me there's scarcely a thing in the pantry left to eat. Have you any idea what might have become of it?

BODICE

So that's it. You think I'm a thief. Just because I borrow a bit of scent, you call me a criminal and accuse me of stealing you blind. Oh, Lord, I dread the day when you mislay a brooch. You'll turn the police on me and say you knew all along that I was the thieving kind. Go on, search me then! Ransack my room! You'll find no meat under my mattress or cheese in my chest of drawers. I am innocent!

MRS. CLAMBER

I didn't accuse you of anything. I'm simply mystified.

BODICE

Perhaps it's mice.

MRS. CLAMBER

They'd have to be sturdy mice to carry off a large smoked ham.

BODICE

Well, if you have nothing else to accuse me of, I've got things to do.

MRS. CLAMBER

I have the decorator coming this afternoon. I want you to make yourself useful while he's here. And my friend Dorinda is coming in for tea, so tell Cook to make a plate of . . (*The telephone rings.*) Answer it and say I'm out.

BODICE

Hello, the Clamber residence. Oh, Mrs. Cummerbund. No, I'm sorry but the Madam is out for the afternoon. (*to Mrs. Clamber*) She says to ask you what you are wearing to Mrs. Casserole's tonight. She wants to synchronize wardrobes with you.

MRS. CLAMBER

I haven't thought yet.

BODICE

(*on the telephone*) She says she hasn't thought yet. All right, cheeribye. (*to Mrs. Clamber*) She is wearing strumpet pink crepe de chine and she begs you to avoid wearing anything that will clash.

MRS. CLAMBER

You can press my flame-colored sheath with the lavender overskirt. That will do perfectly. Casserole is sure to be wearing that new orange bombe of hers, and between the two of us Cummerbund will look as if she is in her underclothes. (*The doorbell rings.*) That will be Mr. Bauble now.

BODICE

Scuttle can let him in.

MRS. CLAMBER

How thrilling that he's here at last. (*Enter Philander and Cufflink with rolls of wallpaper, swatches of fabric, etc.*) Mr. Bauble, welcome. How glad I am you've come. I am eternally grateful to dear Dodge for prevailing on you.

PHILANDER

Dear Mrs. Clamber, the pleasure is entirely ours. This is Mr. Tassle, our assistant decorateur.

MRS. CLAMBER

How do you do.

CUFFLINK

Charmed, I'm sure.

BODICE

Cufflink, what are you doing here? You look like a flippin' fruit.

MRS. CLAMBER

Bodice. Have you quite lost your mind?

BODICE

That's Cufflink. I'd know him anywhere.

MRS. CLAMBER

I'm sure the gentleman knows who he is much better than you.

CUFFLINK

Cufflink? How very curious. I'm afraid you are mistaken, but what a droll coincidence. This young lady has mistaken me for Cufflink, my twin brother, whom I haven't seen for years.

BODICE

He never told me he had a twin brother.

CUFFLINK

I daresay not. Whatever became of him? The last I knew he was very come down in the world. Working as a valet, I believe.

BODICE

And he still does.

MRS. CLAMBER

There, you see what a fool you are, stupid girl. (*to Philander*) Now, I put myself entirely in your hands. Feel absolutely free to do what you like. I hope, however, you'll be able to leave most things just as they are.

PHILANDER

Mrs. Clamber, I presume that all this was thrown in when you took the house, so I can safely tell you that in the course of my entire life I have never clapped eyes on such a collection of monstrosities under one roof. The contents of this magpie's nest must be carted away without more ado.

MRS. CLAMBER

But I could never part with this. It is Louis Quatorze.

PHILANDER

If that is Louis Quatorze, I am Madame de Montespan. It is more likely middle-period General de Gaulle.

MRS. CLAMBER

But the dealer told me . .

PHILANDER

I tremble at your gullibility. Thank heavens I'm here.

MRS. CLAMBER

Nothing will make me part with that rosewood settee.

PHILANDER

Ah, Grand Rapids' finest hour . . thirty years ago! We are going to be cool, streamlined, contemporary. Out it goes! With any luck the Salvation Army might . . but I don't know. We'd better take a look at the rest of the house. Tassle, you start here by measuring up the room. This place was furnished by Edgar Allan Poe! (*Exit Philander.*)

MRS. CLAMBER

Bodice, you stay and give this gentleman a hand. (*Exit Mrs. Clamber.*)

CUFFLINK

Perhaps you would be so good as to hold the end of my tape. (*Bodice does so.*) That's very kind of you. (*measuring*) It looks like twenty-three and three-quarters to here. How curious that you should know my brother.

BODICE

Yes, isn't it. We know each other really quite well, him and me.

CUFFLINK

You don't say. I'm afraid he was the black sheep of our family.

BODICE

I didn't know.

CUFFLINK

Oh, yes. A real letdown he was. Could you just hold it a little higher? That's it, thank you. Yes, a real prodigal. In a couple of years he had run through all his inheritance.

BODICE

Inheritance? He never told me any of this. I thought his mother was a cleaning lady and his father a merchant seaman.

CUFFLINK

Ha-ha. If only Mama could hear that, she'd bust a gut. But I expect he didn't want to admit to you how far he has fallen in the world.

BODICE

I guess.

191

CUFFLINK

But then again we've got to give the devil his due. My brother had a lot of good points about him too. He always had a good heart, was kind, thoughtful and affectionate, generous to a fault, honest, loyal, even-tempered, handy, and strong. He'd make some lucky woman a wonderful husband, I always said. And a marvelously handsome fellow, by far the better looking of we two.

BODICE

Now that I know you better I can see you're not really alike at all. It's hard to believe you're twins.

CUFFLINK

We're not identical. Is he still a bachelor?

BODICE

I'll say he is. He's been trying to get me to marry him for a year.

CUFFLINK

What a fool I've been, giving away his secrets and ruining his chances with such a lovely girl. Promise you won't hold anything I've said against him. You're just the girl to reform him for life. Lucky brother! Just think. If you marry him you and me will be relatives! I'm your brother-in-law to be. A kiss to celebrate! (*He seizes and kisses Bodice. Enter Philander and Mrs. Clamber.*)

PHILANDER	MRS. CLAMBER
Tassle!	Bodice!
Stop manhandling her!	

CUFFLINK

It turns out that we're relations.

MRS. CLAMBER

It looked as if you were about to have them.

PHILANDER

Now go and measure the guest bedroom like a good chap.

MRS. CLAMBER

Bodice, go and show him where it is. (*Exeunt Cufflink and Bodice.*)

MRS. CLAMBER

Mr. Bauble, surely you will spare my Biedermeier commode. It's solid mahogany.

PHILANDER

I don't care if it's a piece of the true cross. Out it goes, and with it the chiffonieres, the jardinieres, the muffineers, and the fusiliers.

MRS. CLAMBER

Oh, you are too hard.

PHILANDER

Taste is tyrannical.

MRS. CLAMBER

But what will you give me instead? What have you in mind for here?

PHILANDER

Why, in this room . . In this room we shall have only things that begin with a "P." Such as pillows, poufs, paintings, and pilasters; a piano, some plants, plaques, a plinth, and a great deal of plastering.

MRS. CLAMBER

It sounds divine, but I know that my husband would simply never stand for it. You must try to be a bit more conventional.

PHILANDER

Conventional! That word is obscene.

MRS. CLAMBER

All I want is a gracious home that has Good Taste written all over it.

PHILANDER

Just leave it to me. The Bauble touch! That's what you'll have.

MRS. CLAMBER

But nothing out of the ordinary, you understand. If I didn't have a husband to consider, I'd be only too happy to let you do whatever you pleased.

PHILANDER

Yes, that is a pity. They're such un-understanding things.

MRS. CLAMBER

But don't let the thought of him limit your imagination in any way.

PHILANDER

Oh no, I shan't let it do that, by any means.

MRS. CLAMBER

After all, it is I who have to spend so much time here, all alone. Sometimes I think of doing something quite wild to relieve the monotony.

PHILANDER

I'm sure you must.

MRS. CLAMBER

Something unscrupulous and irresponsible.

PHILANDER

I know, like fuchsia chiffon drapery in swathes, or a crazy beaded curtain hung with bells.

MRS. CLAMBER

Not exactly like that.

193

PHILANDER

A leopard-covered sofa with a fringe, or an antique-mirrored bathroom trimmed with fur?

MRS. CLAMBER

I meant something much more wicked than that.

PHILANDER

There *is* nothing more wicked than an antique-mirrored bathroom trimmed with fur.

MRS. CLAMBER

Isn't there? We haven't discussed how you will treat the bedroom yet. Come in here and tell me what you think. (*Exit Philander and Mrs. Clamber. The door closes. Enter Bodice and Cufflink.*)

BODICE

Mr. Tassle, you should be ashamed of yourself. I thought you were a gentleman.

CUFFLINK

A thousand apologies. All my life I have had these dizzy spells. I suddenly felt myself falling and grabbed hold of you. It's lucky the bed was there or I might have pulled you over on the floor.

BODICE

You do look a bit queer.

CUFFLINK

When I'm in these fits I must be humored, or I get quite violent.

BODICE

You should see a doctor.

CUFFLINK

There's no way they can help. It's to do with the heart. One of these times, it will be the end.

BODICE

You poor thing.

CUFFLINK

Would anyone mind if I laid down on the chaise longue? I seem to have lost my strength.

BODICE

Go right ahead.

CUFFLINK

It's very bright. Could you close the drapes? (*Bodice does so.*) That's nice. Can you tell if my forehead is feverish?

BODICE

(*feeling it*) It's rather cold and clammy, if you ask me.

194

CUFFLINK

Ah, just as I feared. That's the worst sign. Give me your hand, my dear. I feel one of my spells coming on. This could be the end. There's a strange sensation creeping up my leg.

BODICE

Oh Lord, it's one of his fits again.

CUFFLINK

How cold I am.

BODICE

I'll get you a blanket.

CUFFLINK

Don't leave, for pity's sake. Don't let me die alone.

BODICE

Oh mercy. You must stay warm.

CUFFLINK

Hold me.

BODICE

He's got a desperate chill.

CUFFLINK

I'm sinking fast.

BODICE

He's in a spasm. He's got a grip like iron.

CUFFLINK

Kiss me goodbye. You're nearly my next of kin. (*Enter Mr. Clamber.*)

CLAMBER

Good God, what's going on? The curtains drawn at four in the afternoon and flagrant carnage taking place in the sitting room. Who is this man, Bodice? Don't tell me he's here to fix the washing machine.

BODICE

Oh sir, I didn't expect you home so soon.

CLAMBER

Evidently not.

BODICE

This is Mr. Tassle. He had a sudden turn and had to lay down. (*Enter Dorinda.*)

DORINDA

Hullo, everyone. I'm dying for tea!

CLAMBER

(*to Bodice*) Where's Mrs. Clamber?

BODICE

She's in the bedroom with Mr. Bauble.

CLAMBER

In the bedroom. What the devil is she doing in there? (*Enter Mrs. Clamber and Philander.*)

MRS. CLAMBER

Hullo, dear. Back so soon?

CLAMBER

My appearance seemed to catch the household by surprise.

MRS. CLAMBER

Dorinda darling, it's lovely to see you. (*to Clamber*) This is Mr. Bauble, our decorator.

PHILANDER

How do you do. I'm a terrible fright. We've been shifting the furniture. (*produces a compact and looks in the mirror*) My wig is standing on end.

MRS. CLAMBER

He has wonderful plans for the house.

PHILANDER

Come on, Tassle dear. Pull yourself together. Look how late it's got. Mrs. Clamber, you're not to worry about a thing. The house will be exquisite. I can feel it in my bones.

CLAMBER

I wouldn't have suspected that he had any.

DORINDA

So this is the gentleman.

MRS. CLAMBER

I thought you two had met before.

DORINDA

I remember Mr. Bauble, but I doubt he remembers me.

PHILANDER

Why, of course. Could I forget? Forgive me, my memory is like a sieve.

DORINDA

A word in your ear, Mr. Bauble, if I may.

PHILANDER

Dear lady, I'd be delighted, but at this instant I am *tellement pressé*.

DORINDA

(*sotto voce*) Shall I expose you here and now, Philander?

PHILANDER

Good heavens, no! That would never do. Nile green with mauve piping! You mustn't think of it.

196

DORINDA

(*handing him a card*) Then you will call on me later to give me your advice.

PHILANDER

Certainly I will, and in the meantime, don't do a thing until you hear from me. Have you got everything, Tassle? We must fly. *Arrivederci, tout le monde!* (*Exit Philander and Cufflink.*)

CLAMBER

What a howl. That fellow's as good as a play. Bodice, have Scuttle bring drinks to the library. (*Exit Clamber.*)

DORINDA

Now, my dear, what has been going on? I need to hear everything! (*exit*)

MRS. CLAMBER

(*adjusting her bra*) My pet, if you don't know the Bauble touch, you haven't lived!

CURTAIN

ACT TWO

Scene 1

A room in Dorinda's apartment. Enter Dorinda and Norah, knitting.

DORINDA

Well, Norah, it was very curious. I went there for tea and who should I find but Philander, got up like Titania and carrying on like the Queen of the May.

NORAH

Are you sure it was he?

DORINDA

Silly, how could I mistake him? I'd know him anywhere.

NORAH

But why was he pretending to be decorator?

DORINDA

I intend to find out.

NORAH

Oughtn't you to have told Mrs. Clamber she was being imposed upon? She is your friend.

DORINDA

And let him slip through my fingers? Not a chance. That would tax friendship too far. (*The doorbell rings.*) That will be my odious brother. Oh to be left in such fraternal care! (*Enter Headway.*) Hullo, brother. What have I done to deserve this visit?

HEADWAY

'Lo, Dorinda. 'Lo, Norah. Glad to find you both looking in the pink.

DORINDA

Norah is a martyr to her sinuses today and I have a splitting headache . . that just began.

HEADWAY

Sorry to hear it. Well, we have a few business matters to discuss, haven't we?

DORINDA

Your idea of discussion is a dreary homily.

NORAH

You will excuse me, but it's almost time for my inhalation now.

HEADWAY

That's right. You go and have a good steam up while I chat with Dorinda here.

DORINDA

And don't parboil yourself. (*to Headway*) She's hyperconscientious, that girl. (*Exit Norah.*)

HEADWAY

(*opening his briefcase*) Now, picked up your bills and bank statement for this month and thought you might like to go over them with me.

DORINDA

What a curious idea of recreation you have. I'd as soon have a tooth extracted without novocain.

HEADWAY

Here is a check made out to Gundelfinger, Incorporated, for twenty-six dollars and forty-seven cents. What was it for?

DORINDA

Gundelfinger? Never heard of them. Did I write that? It seems like such an odd sum, doesn't it? The twenty-six dollars could have been for anything, but the forty-seven cents is a mystery to me.

HEADWAY

Come. Think hard. You can't forget so casually what you did with twenty-six dollars and forty-seven cents.

DORINDA

You know perfectly well that I spent them at Gundelfinger's, so what are you worrying about?

HEADWAY

What did you spend it on? There's no explanation on the stub.

DORINDA

Perhaps even at the time I didn't know. Perhaps I never will. And who cares? It's such a stupid sum for a grown-up person to get worked up about.

HEADWAY

It's the principle. You should care. You've no more money sense than an Eskimo. You'd have reduced yourself to penury if you didn't have me to look after things.

DORINDA

What is the difference? You've virtually reduced me to penury anyway.

HEADWAY

I don't consider it penury when you can squander twenty-six dollars and forty-seven cents without being any the wiser where it went.

DORINDA

My God, a man of your age, obsessed with a little thing like that! Look, to set the whole matter straight, I'll *give* you twenty-six dollars and forty-seven cents out of my handbag now, and that will settle everything once and for all.

HEADWAY

Not only have you not the slightest notion of money, but not the faintest conception of arithmetic.

DORINDA

What makes you think that you have more than an elder brother's share of the intelligence in our family? You yourself have made me only too painfully aware of the value of money, and as for arithmetic, I can still recite my nine-times table . . Nine ones are nine, nine twos are eighteen, nine threes are twenty-one, nine fours are . . Well, anyway, ask old Miss Abacus if I wasn't third in her math class at Radclyffe Hall. So I don't know what you're talking about!

HEADWAY

Shan't argue with you.

DORINDA

I'll say not. I don't have to listen to your homilies. Just you let me have what is rightfully mine. And, what's more, I'm sick of your trying to marry

199

me off to spooks like Portfolio. I don't care what kind of figure he cuts at Muddle, Flinch, Purge, Flutter, and Split.

HEADWAY

He is one of the ablest young men on the street.

DORINDA

Able at nothing I'm likely to require, that's for sure.

HEADWAY

I would be happy to hand over your affairs to someone we both find suitable, but until then, I am bound by your husband's will.

DORINDA

In that case I remain a widow all my life.

HEADWAY

That isn't necessary.

DORINDA

No man can possibly satisfy us both.

HEADWAY

I know one that might.

DORINDA

I wouldn't marry Portfolio if he were sole survivor of the human race.

HEADWAY

I don't mean Portfolio, but someone else whom I think you'll take kindly to.

DORINDA

Impossible, if he's another jewel of yours.

HEADWAY

Be reasonable. I advise you to consider this proposal very carefully. I've broached it to young Merger and he's mighty interested. Seems to me to be all you could hope for in a husband: able, ambitious, good family, well liked, plenty of get-up-and-go, bright future, and sound business head.

DORINDA

The answer to Sylvia Porter's prayer. The only snag, I suppose, is that he's two feet high.

HEADWAY

There's nothing wrong with him at all.

DORINDA

Except the fact of your recommending him.

HEADWAY

And what is more, he owns twenty-five percent of Consolidated Tube, Flue, and Duct.

DORINDA

So that's it, my pimping brother! If you think I'm going to be part of a package deal, you can think again. You can take your Mr. Merger and shove him up the Tube, Flue, and Duct.

HEADWAY

You're making a great mistake. Listen to me.

DORINDA

Listen I must, unless I stuff my ears, but speak to you I'm not obliged to do. I shan't address another word to you. (*calling*) Norah! Norah, come here!

HEADWAY

This is no time to be ridiculous. Your tantrums won't put me off. I promised Merger you'd see him, and I insist that you do. Remember this. If you marry him, you would be free of my guardianship at once and as much your own mistress as any married woman ever is. (*Enter Norah, with a towel over her head.*)

NORAH

What is it?

DORINDA

Norah, tell this man . .

NORAH

What!?

DORINDA

Don't argue. Tell this man that I'll accept his ugly proposition, if only to get rid of him. I will meet this Merger creature and nothing more.

NORAH

She says that she accepts your ugly . .

HEADWAY

That's all I wanted to hear. Remember, if you decide on him, the estate is yours. And now I'm off. I'll bring Merger 'round later. You'll have got over your snit by then. (*Exit Headway.*)

DORINDA

Snit! The fury of Medea was mere petulance compared to my violent rage. I loathe him. I never want to set eyes on the brute again. Oh, Norah, you should have heard him. Oh, was any woman more abused than I? Tormented past all endurance? So put upon?

NORAH

Why, what did he say?

DORINDA

Why have you got that thing on your head like Lawrence of Arabia?

NORAH

I was having my inhalation when you called.

DORINDA

He accused me of being a moron, of squandering money and not under-standing arithmetic. The man's a stark-raving lunatic! And, to add insult to injury, he's trying to marry me off to some slack-jawed, watery-eyed, knock-kneed, midget financier who is prepared to have me, sight unseen, shackled to him for life in return for my shares in some stupid corpora-tion. As far as he's concerned, I could be the homeliest fright in Christen-dom . . Norah, look at me! I've had an idea. A stroke of genius! I sud-denly know how Madame Curie must have felt when she discovered ra-dio. The most brilliant idea is forming in my mind and you, my dear, are to be the star attraction.

NORAH

Me?

DORINDA

Yes, Norah, you. Come with me, and I shall pour all into your little cock-leshell. (*exeunt*)

Scene 2

The same. Enter Dorinda and Norah.

NORAH

Oh, I couldn't do it, Dorinda. It would be a terrible thing.

DORINDA

Just an innocent deception, and such a favor to me. You won't be break-ing even one of the Ten Commandments.

NORAH

It would be like bearing false witness.

DORINDA

Was that in the movie? I don't remember it. My brother has been so hate-ful. You will help me be revenged on him. You're such a darling, Norah, and you've always helped me out when I needed you. To show you how appreciative I am I want you to have my little stone-marten stole.

NORAH

Oh, I couldn't accept that.

DORINDA

Of course you could. It isn't a bribe.

NORAH

Oh, Dorinda, it's too kind of you. I don't know what to say.

DORINDA

It's yours. Don't say a word. I had thought you might like that enormous opal dinner-ring of mine, but I remembered that some people think opals are unlucky.

NORAH

Oh, not your opal dinner-ring! I think that's a very silly superstition, don't you?

DORINDA

I'm so glad. Then I can give it to you without fear of wishing you bad luck.

NORAH

Oh, I couldn't. Not your opal dinner-ring. I've always thought how beautiful it was. I'd never be able to thank you.

DORINDA

You're not to try. Just be as sweet and helpful as you always are.

NORAH

Oh, Dorinda, you are too generous.

DORINDA

I know you'll humor me. It's really a very innocent little scheme.

NORAH

I don't know how to thank you, I really don't. (*She sobs.*) You are too good. Nothing like this has happened to me before.

DORINDA

Pull yourself together, or you'll have me crying too and that'll be the end of my mascara.

NORAH

I don't know what to say. You've been too kind.

DORINDA

Stop sniffling. Think of your sinuses. (*The doorbell rings.*) Who can that be?

NORAH

I'll answer it. (*Exit Norah.*)

DORINDA

I know very well. My heart just did a double somersault. What do I look like? My God, the wreck of the Hesperus! I must be calm. This was sheer madness. How should he find me? In a chair, on the sofa, or the floor? No, at the window. There's always a scene where he comes in and she is silhouetted against the twilight with her eyes half-closed and a provocative,

203

faintly amused expression as if to say, Really, wasn't it rather rash of you to come? (*Enter Philander and Norah.*)

PHILANDER

I hope not. But you did insist.

DORINDA

Oh, it's you.

PHILANDER

Punctual and obedient.

DORINDA

Norah, why not go into the kitchen? You can have a good cry in there to your heart's content. If you hear me scream, you're to rush in with a carving knife, understand?

PHILANDER

It doesn't sound as if you trust me.

NORAH

A fur stole and a dinner-ring. I don't know what to say . . (*Exit Norah, sobbing.*)

PHILANDER

What's up? Has someone stolen a dinner-ring?

DORINDA

You wouldn't understand. It's you who have the explaining to do, you fraud.

PHILANDER

You know all there is to know. I'm masquerading as Bauble and decorating Mrs. Clamber's house and I might as well tell you I'll be doing Mrs. Headway's next.

DORINDA

Who put you up to this?

PHILANDER

It was Dodge's idea.

DORINDA

Another of his harebrained schemes.

PHILANDER

For which he's snagging fifty percent of the take.

DORINDA

It's a scandal.

PHILANDER

I agree. Twenty percent would have been more reasonable.

DORINDA

That's not what I meant. It's villainous of you to impose on two poor, senseless women like my friends. You shan't get away with it.

PHILANDER

I don't see why not.

DORINDA

Your plans have come unstuck already, haven't they? I have found you out and I can think of no reason why I shouldn't disabuse Clamber and Headway at once.

PHILANDER

I disagree with you. I think you have a reason or you would have done so already. Now it's my turn to ask you a question. Why didn't you give me away as soon as you found me out?

DORINDA

That's simple enough. I wanted to hear what explanation you had to offer, and, since you have none, I shall not hesitate to tell them that you are a cheat and an imposter. What do you know about decorating? You should be ashamed.

PHILANDER

You're right. I see it now. In a weak moment I was tempted. Can you forgive me? Is there some way I can redeem myself? Here, take this phone and put an end to my shame. Tell Clamber who I am and let her be revenged any way she will.

DORINDA

Wait a minute. Don't get carried away. Let's not rush into this.

PHILANDER

The sooner I've made a clean breast of it the better I'll feel.

DORINDA

Don't be impatient. Once you've started a thing, I feel it's only honorable to go through with it.

PHILANDER

That's very true.

DORINDA

If Clamber thinks you're Bauble, what harm is in that? And I'm sure she's mad to have you finish what you've just begun!

PHILANDER

Do you really think so? She'd waste her money on him; she might just as well on me.

DORINDA

Then it isn't nearly as bad as I thought at first.

PHILANDER

I'm so glad.

DORINDA

One has an obligation to protect one's friends, but if they're perfectly content to make fools of themselves, who is one to interfere?

PHILANDER

You're absolutely right. I must go through with it. I hadn't realized, it's quite a fun profession, this decorating thing.

DORINDA

I must say it was a strange disguise to find you in.

PHILANDER

Tell me. How did you know who I was?

DORINDA

Oh, you're quite a common sight, and one can't avoid hearing about you, it seems.

PHILANDER

Oh dear, was it that bad?

DORINDA

It isn't fair. The same reputation that ruins a woman is flattering to a man.

PHILANDER

Who cares about gossip? You know, I suppose, of the rumor that you're cold?

DORINDA

Frigid, is that what you've heard?

PHILANDER

And that you and your girl friend there, well . .

DORINDA

Me and Norah! What a grizzly thought! I can see how it might appear, though. Living alone together. It isn't by choice. There simply are not enough men to go around.

PHILANDER

It probably won't appeal to you, but how about the two of us seeing more of each other?

DORINDA

It's kind of you, but you aren't obliged to every single female in the world. You'll wear yourself out.

PHILANDER

I'd be yours exclusively. And I'm far from worn out.

DORINDA

You look in fairly good shape, I grant you that.

PHILANDER

I haven't thought of another woman since seeing you.

DORINDA

About an hour ago. I'm overwhelmed! You don't know it, but I first saw you at the Dystrophy Ball.

PHILANDER

I didn't know you were there.

DORINDA

At the risk of giving you a permanently swollen head, I'll tell you that I asked Norah to find out who you were.

PHILANDER

I wish we had met.

DORINDA

You had that dreadful Vestal girl draped on your arm.

PHILANDER

Oh, Virginia.

DORINDA

I've heard she's insatiable. Is it true?

PHILANDER

I wouldn't be so ungallant . . Yes, she is. It's an awful bore.

DORINDA

You left with her.

PHILANDER

She'd bought the tickets and I am a gentleman.

DORINDA

You see, I had Norah, like a bloodhound, sleuthing after you.

PHILANDER

I wish I'd known. Are you sure that you and she aren't . . ?

DORINDA

To tell you the honest truth, she smokes foul cigars, wears boots to bed, and beats me unmercifully, which, of course, I adore.

PHILANDER

I think you're adorable.

DORINDA

You're just saying that because I have you in my power.

PHILANDER

You'd be very unwise to trust me otherwise. You're much too desirable.

DORINDA

Oh, don't do that. I get goose pimples when a man talks through his teeth.

PHILANDER

That's a very good sign.

DORINDA

Of what? I should phone Clamber this instant. I was a fool not to have done it hours ago.

PHILANDER

Do, and tell her the joyful news.

DORINDA

I should have had more strength of character.

PHILANDER

Are you sure your girl friend's all right in there?

DORINDA

She's probably trying on her furs and having a good cry. I don't know what's come over me. I shouldn't trust you an inch. (*She lies back on the couch.*) Ouch! (*She shrieks.*) It's Norah's bloody knitting. (*Enter Norah, in a fur stole and brandishing a carving knife.*)

NORAH

(*attacking Philander*) Ah, lecher!

DORINDA

No, Norah! Down! Off! Back! He wasn't attacking me.

NORAH

I heard your cry.

DORINDA

I jabbed myself on your blasted knitting, that's all. I can't think why you leave it all over the place. It could cause a nasty accident. And put away that knife. You look like Nanook of the North.

PHILANDER

She's as loyal as a Doberman pinscher.

NORAH

Oh, the stole is lovely, Dorinda. I can't ever thank you enough. They're beautiful, with all their little feet and everything. I don't know what to say. (*She sobs.*) You are too kind, too kind . .

DORINDA

Now don't start that again. You've caused enough disturbance for one day. Tell Fidget to bring some ice out onto the terrace. We all badly need a drink. (*Exit Norah. To Philander.*) I think that something cool would do you good. (*exeunt*)

Scene 3

A street. Enter Mrs. Headway and Fetish.

FETISH

My dear, did you ever see anything like it in your whole put together? *Epouvantable!*

MRS. HEADWAY

A dreadful film about dreadful, common people.

FETISH

I can't think what the critics were talking about.

MRS. HEADWAY

Everyone was poor and each more unattractive than the next. I don't know why everything ugly is considered artistic these days.

FETISH

I nearly had hysterics when the mine caved in. From the minute I saw the coal pit, I knew it was going to collapse.

MRS. HEADWAY

It's not what I call entertainment at all. Give me the old *vague*, any day.

FETISH

I had the giggles the whole way through. (*Enter Philander, on the other side.*) Look who is over there. The very person we were talking about.

MRS. HEADWAY

Who is it? Without my glasses I can't see a thing.

FETISH

(*greeting him*) Philander, *mon ange*, what a pleasant *rencontre.*

MRS. HEADWAY

Philander?

FETISH

Your name came up only this morning; but I stuck up for you. You two don't know each other. (*to Mrs. Headway*) This is my friend, Philander. We were in the Navy together, in the days of sailing ships. If you think he's attractive now, you should have seen him in uniform.

MRS. HEADWAY

So this is the man. No woman with a reputation to lose can afford to be seen with him.

PHILANDER

If her reputation were no better deserved than mine. I hope not otherwise.

FETISH

(*to Philander*) This is Mrs. Headway.

PHILANDER

Oh, no! Not *the* Mrs. Headway!

FETISH

In flesh and blood.

PHILANDER

You caught me off guard. Forgive me. I've heard so much about you and at last we meet.

FETISH

What had you heard! Do tell!

PHILANDER

Nothing but compliments.

FETISH

How dull.

MRS. HEADWAY

Your friend is charming, Fetish. You should have brought him round. We must see more of him. You will come, I hope, to my little housewarming ball. Everyone who exists will be there.

PHILANDER

I'm glad I'm included. I would love to come.

MRS. HEADWAY

Are you coming, Fetish? I must go. I have my decorator coming to the house.

FETISH

No, I must now away to my masseur; a merciless brute but does wonders for the soul. Philander, love, I long to see you soon.

MRS. HEADWAY

At my ball. Now don't forget.

FETISH

She does a mean watusi.

PHILANDER

I have no doubt. It was a pleasure meeting you. Goodbye. (*Exit Mrs. Headway and Fetish.*) Of all the confounded people in the world! That's ruined everything. Now what can we do? (*Enter Cufflink on the other side.*)

CUFFLINK

I saw you talking to Mr. Fetish, so I waited till they'd gone.

PHILANDER

Cuff, the game is up.

CUFFLINK

What do you mean?

PHILANDER

That woman you saw was *the* Mrs. Headway herself.

CUFFLINK

What rotten luck. Where do we go from here?

PHILANDER

We have to use her to complete our scheme.

CUFFLINK

I don't see how we can. She knows who you are.

PHILANDER

Wait a minute. I've got an idea. Yes, of course. She may know that I'm not Bauble, but she doesn't know that you're not.

CUFFLINK

What, me? Oh, no you don't. I could never do it!

PHILANDER

Of course you can. And, anyway, you must. We're in too deep now to get out of it.

CUFFLINK

But I don't know the first friggin' thing about decorating.

PHILANDER

Neither does she. That's how Bauble makes his livelihood. It's very simple. I'll tell you a few technical terms and you throw them into the conversation whenever you can. You can memorize them on the way there. Let's go through some of the styles. There's Chippendale and Sheraton, Queen Anne, Adam and Regency, Provincial, Empire, Hepplewhite, Biedermeier, and Louis Quatorze . . (*exeunt*)

Scene 4

A room in Dorinda's apartment. Dorinda and Norah, discovered.

DORINDA

Norah, you're an angel. And you're not to have any scruples.

NORAH

I'll try, but I've never told an untruth in my life.

DORINDA

Once you start, you'll soon get the hang of it. Now, let's drink a small martini to your success.

NORAH

Oh, no, I couldn't. Strong drink is a slow killer.

DORINDA

Well, we aren't in any hurry. Here. (*handing Norah a martini*) Try this.

NORAH

Oh, I don't know if I can.

DORINDA

(*raising her glass*) You'll carry it off superbly. I know you will.

NORAH

Just this once then. Chin-chin. (*She drains her glass.*)

DORINDA

My dear. You didn't have to drain it at a draught. Savor it.

NORAH

It isn't nearly as bad as I thought it would be.

DORINDA

I'd dawdle over the other half. Hold out your glass.

NORAH

A martini tastes like tears, doesn't it?

DORINDA

It hadn't occurred to me.

NORAH

Like frozen orphan's tears.

DORINDA

Depressing thought.

NORAH

Isn't it getting warm? Has the steam heat come on? (*The doorbell rings.*) Ting-a-ling-a-ling. Come in, come in whoever you are.

DORINDA

That will be Philander. (*Enter Philander.*)

PHILANDER

Hullo, at the bottle already. Norah, I'm surprised.

DORINDA

We're getting the campaign off to a proper start. Now Norah is just off to take her bubble bath.

NORAH

All right. I know. You want me out of the way. I know very well. It's Norah come here, when I'm needed, and it's Norah buzz off when I'm not. Don't think I haven't noticed. But I don't mind. I have a funny feeling in my nose. It seems to have gone to sleep. (*Exit Norah.*)

PHILANDER

You've got her primed for this evening, I see.

DORINDA

I've coached her in the part and if I'm not mistaken, a star will be born tonight.

PHILANDER

My plans nearly came unstuck this afternoon. Who should I run into on the street but Fetish with Mrs. Headway.

DORINDA

How awful. What did you do?

PHILANDER

I sent Cufflink instead. Let's pray he carries it off. Our plans are rapidly coming to a head.

DORINDA

I shall never trust you after what you have done to Clamber and my sister-in-law.

PHILANDER

Nor I you, after what you're doing to poor Merger and your brother. We're two of a kind. But perhaps a little mutual distrust is healthy in a relationship.

DORINDA

A relationship . . is that what we're having? It sounds so technical.

PHILANDER

With your permission, we could happily make it an affair.

DORINDA

No, that's something a woman has with her husband's best friend.

PHILANDER

Or her best friend's husband.

DORINDA

Yes, in the afternoon and usually on the floor. But what is the word for the free association of two intelligent people who are mad about each other?

PHILANDER

Wedlock.

DORINDA

You forget. That Chinese water-torture I've been through before.

PHILANDER

Why did you marry him?

DORINDA

The dear departed? I suppose because he was a solid citizen and families approve of that, you know; and because he could give me pretty things.

PHILANDER

I haven't much to offer in that line.

DORINDA

You? Heaven knows why you should attract me. It's contrary to sense.

PHILANDER

But I do, a bit, don't I? Give me a break. Because, you know, a thought had occurred to me.

DORINDA

How exhausting for you.

PHILANDER

Be serious for two seconds. If you can.

DORINDA

I'll be all Norah. (*putting on Norah's glasses*)

PHILANDER

We make a pretty sensational couple . .

DORINDA

What my brother would call "a team."

PHILANDER

And my suggestion is that we make it permanent.

DORINDA

Oughtn't you to be on one knee?

PHILANDER

Heartless. I mean it.

DORINDA

This time, he says.

PHILANDER

Honestly, what do you think?

DORINDA

I think it has distinct possibilities. But remember, once bitten, twice extremely shy.

PHILANDER

This time it will be different, I promise you.

DORINDA

Could be, could be. But before plunging headlong into the maelstrom of nuptial bliss, it's only fair to warn you that I'm very peculiar.

PHILANDER

I guess each of us has his idiosyncrasies.

DORINDA

And unless you put up with mine we shall be violently incompatible.

PHILANDER

You're bearing in mind that tolerance works both ways?

DORINDA

Not necessarily! Horses. I get violent hay fever if you even mention them.

PHILANDER

I promise not to. Sailing. I'm abysmally seasick on anything that floats.

DORINDA

I thought you were in the Navy?

PHILANDER

That's how I know.

DORINDA

I detest the violin. It sets my teeth on edge.

PHILANDER

I loathe practical jokes of absolutely every sort. I get very mad.

DORINDA

I abhor all clubs that send you anything of-the-month.

PHILANDER

Plastic flowers. I'll throw them out of the house.

DORINDA

Chamber music. It depresses me mortally.

PHILANDER

You can't mean that.

DORINDA

I certainly do.

PHILANDER

You're essentially frivolous.

DORINDA

If that's how I strike you, I'm glad to know it now.

PHILANDER

But so far we have only discussed the important things. How about the trivialities? Who did you vote for?

DORINDA

The man and not the party. You'll never know. Too many husbands agree to pair with their wives and then sneak off to the polls behind their backs. Are you very ecclesiastical?

PHILANDER

Only weddings when I've known the bride.

DORINDA

In the biblical sense.

PHILANDER

And occasional christenings that I have been responsible for.

DORINDA

How sentimental of you.

PHILANDER

Are you modern?

DORINDA

If that means going to bed with two people at once and swapping husbands, no I'm not. You're not suggesting that already, are you?

PHILANDER

Not particularly.

DORINDA

I trust you're not an exhibitionist.

PHILANDER

Only around the house. Not to extremes.

DORINDA

That's reassuring. If we go on like this much longer we'll have no surprises left.

PHILANDER

That would be a shame. There's only one thing more that I insist. If the occasion to make love with someone else should prove irresistible, be gallant enough never to let me be aware of it.

DORINDA

If that unlikely eventuality should arise, you shall know nothing of it. However, should you find yourself in a similar situation, you must know that I shall demand to know everything and I mean *everything*! But the subject, I hope, is a totally academic one.

PHILANDER

For the time being, at least. Well, I suppose that one way and another we might come to terms.

DORINDA

The obstacles do not appear insurmountable.

PHILANDER

You are delicious.

DORINDA

Talking through your teeth won't do you any good.

PHILANDER

But you do like me, a bit.

DORINDA

That's beside the point. After all, I'm essentially frivolous, don't forget.

PHILANDER

That's right. You have a point.

DORINDA

An impasse. I simply can't decide. (*Enter Norah.*)

NORAH

I'm immaculate. Hope I'm not disturbing anything.

DORINDA

Norah, you make up my mind for me. Shall I have him, or shan't I?

NORAH

Why not? There's no harm in giving it a bash. Any more of that martini going begging? My bath had a rather devitalizing effect.

DORINDA

You've had enough. They'll be here any minute now. Come and let me help you dress. (*The doorbell rings.*) My God! There they are now. We'd better get out of here. Fidget can let them in.

PHILANDER

I'd better scoot.

DORINDA

No, you must stay here. We may need your protection if anything goes hideously wrong. (*Exeunt Dorinda, Philander, and Norah. Enter Headway and Merger.*)

MERGER

. . so I take an option to "put" at the high price and an option to "call" at the low so I'm sitting pretty whichever way the market goes. If it rises I use my option to buy in, and if it falls I exercise my option to sell out.

HEADWAY

It takes a real gift to think of a gimmick like that.

MERGER

This is going to be a great day for Consolidated Tube, Flue, and Duct.

HEADWAY

I spoke to my sister and put it to her straight.

MERGER

I don't know of anything about me she could find objectionable.

HEADWAY

Of course not. She was a bit petulant at first, but she'll have calmed down by now.

MERGER

And she's attractive, you say? Of course, it's not important, but it would be nice.

HEADWAY

Stunning, if I say it myself.

MERGER

Good, good. Won't the directors of Consolidated Tube be in for a surprise!

HEADWAY

Where is Dorinda? What could be keeping them?

MERGER

Them? Why, who else is here?

HEADWAY

Oh, Norah; cousin of ours who keeps Dorinda company and helps out with the house. Dear girl, really, but hasn't a penny to bless herself with and not exactly what you might call an oil painting either. (*calling*) Dorinda. Where are you? I've brought Mr. Merger here.

DORINDA

(*off*) Norah, tell my brother I do not intend to see or speak to him.

NORAH

(*off*) She says she doesn't intend . .

HEADWAY

I heard what she said and I think she's being damned rude. Mr. Merger has come here as my guest.

DORINDA

(*off*) Tell him I have nothing against Mr. Merger, but I do not intend to meet him as long as my brother is in my living room.

NORAH

(*off*) She says she has nothing against . .

HEADWAY

Damnit, Dorinda, you're carrying this game too far.

DORINDA

(*off*) Kindly ask my brother not to curse. I am not his wife.

NORAH

(*off*) She says . .

HEADWAY

I heard. Normally, you understand, Merger, I wouldn't stand for this, but, as there's so much at stake, perhaps we should humor her.

MERGER

Is she often like this?

HEADWAY

Not in the least. Gentle as a lamb. Would it seem odd if I left you two alone?

MERGER

Not a bit.

HEADWAY

Very well then, I'll be on my way.

DORINDA

(*off*) Norah, look through the keyhole and tell me if he's gone.

NORAH

(*off*) He's at the door.

HEADWAY

(*to Merger*) Remember. Lay it on the line. I'll be expecting to hear from you. (*Exit Headway, slamming the door.*)

DORINDA

(*off*) He's gone.

NORAH

(*off*) Hallelujah! See if the coast is clear. (*Enter Dorinda, dressed as Norah.*)

DORINDA

(*to Merger*) Good evening. (*She crosses the stage and looks out of the other door.*)

MERGER

Good evening. (*to himself*) The companion. Poor girl. She is on the homely side.

DORINDA

All clear, Dorinda. (*Enter Norah, beautifully dressed.*)

NORAH

Mr. Merger, how do you do. I hope you will forgive our little family game.

MERGER

Good heavens, are you Dorinda?

NORAH

You seem surprised.

MERGER

Your brother said you were stunning, and he was right.

NORAH

(*to Dorinda*) Mr. Merger and I have certain matters to discuss, Dora dear. You can occupy the time very usefully.

DORINDA

If you don't need me I'll go and read a few chapters of *Science and Health*. But do ring, Norah, if there's anything I can do. I hope Mr. Merger will excuse me.

MERGER

By all means. (*Exit Dorinda.*)

MERGER

I'm afraid I'm a bit confused. Did she call you Norah?

NORAH

Yes, of course she did.

MERGER

Oh. I thought your brother said your cousin's name was Norah.

NORAH

No, her name is Dora. They sound very alike.

MERGER

But he calls you Dorinda.

NORAH

We have our family jokes. We call each other endless pet names.

MERGER

I see.

NORAH

You mustn't take us seriously. We really dote on one another, he and I, but there's always some little game going on between us.

MERGER

That accounts for it.

NORAH

You know, you are really much nicer than I imagined you.

MERGER

I'm told I have my good points.

NORAH

I thought you were going to be some dreadful person with a sinister ulterior motive for meeting me.

MERGER

I hope you don't think that still.

NORAH

Now that we've met, I can see you are a gentleman. Since we are both adults, Mr. Merger, let's be perfectly frank. We each know why you are here, so why don't we take it from there?

MERGER

I'm agreeable, I admire a woman who can be businesslike.

NORAH

Now, I understand that you're available.

MERGER

Well, let us say I was considering . .

NORAH

That's good enough. And you were told that I was available. Heaven knows that's true. But Headway mentioned something about some shares, and that's where I drew the line. I don't want some man who is only interested in monkeying around with my portfolio. He's got to be interested in me, M.E., exclusively, or it's no dice.

MERGER

Naturally I quite agree with you.

NORAH

I've said my piece. Now over to you, Mr. Merger, roger and out.

MERGER

Of course I appreciate your point of view. A woman in your financial position must be careful about whom she encourages.

NORAH

Forget my financial position. Just supposing I had nothing in the world. That's what I want to know.

MERGER

Of course it's wrong to marry on account of money alone.

NORAH

It's pretty crass to marry even partly on that account.

MERGER

When you put it that way, there's no denying it.

NORAH

That's good to hear. Let us behave as if we were the poorest people in the world with only the warmth of an honest affection to recommend themselves.

MERGER

I see you have a whimsical turn of mind.

NORAH

It runs in the family.

MERGER

I'm grateful to your brother for introducing us.

NORAH

Are you? Why?

MERGER

He has a very charming sister.

NORAH

Is that all?

MERGER

I find her fascinating company.

NORAH

How fascinating?

MERGER

Had I not met you so recently, I'd be tempted to say perhaps more than I should.

NORAH

Well, don't feel shy. Let me fix you a drink. I'm as dry as the Sahara.

MERGER

A drink would help, now that you mention it.

NORAH

(*mixing a cocktail*) A little of this . . and a little of that . . and a dash of this should do the trick. (*Using a shaker as maracas, she dances the "Habanera" from Carmen.*) "L'amour est une oiseau rebelle, tralalalala la, la, la — Si tu ne m'aime pas, je t'aime, si je t'aime, prends garde a toi!" Cha-cha-cha. (*pouring*) How's that look?

MERGER

Excellent. You're a splendid hostess.

NORAH

(*toasting*) Oh, you pick it up. Well, here's looking up your old address!

MERGER

And yours. (*draining his glass*) That was very tasty, whatever it was.

NORAH

From here on you must help yourself. To anything. (*She stretches herself out on the couch.*) This is Liberty Hall. (*Merger clears his throat.*) Well, Merge, out with it. There's something on your mind.

MERGER

Since we've dispensed with ceremony . .

NORAH

Make yourself at home. Take off your shoes.

MERGER

And have spoken quite candidly . .

NORAH

Man to man.

MERGER

Would you think me bold . .

NORAH

Be as bold as you wish.

MERGER

It seems to have got very warm.

NORAH

Perhaps you have a fever. Let me feel. Maybe you should take off your coat and tie.

MERGER

No, no, that isn't necessary.

NORAH

Sure you wouldn't like to lie down for a bit?

MERGER

Maybe I ought to take a breath of fresh air . .

NORAH

Mustn't risk a chill. Besides, we still have a lot to talk about. We haven't settled anything at all.

MERGER

On such a brief acquaintance, I wouldn't presume . .

NORAH

You don't presume enough. That's what's wrong with you. There's nothing to stop us coming to an agreement right here and now.

MERGER

I suppose not.

NORAH

As you are the man, it's up to you to speak first.

MERGER

That would be the best way, wouldn't it?

NORAH

Well, then, to put the matter in a nutshell . .

MERGER

In a nutshell . .

NORAH

You are asking me to become Mrs. Merger, is that it?

MERGER

Yes, I suppose it is.

NORAH

Well, now. I'll have to have time to think about that.

MERGER

Yes, by all means. One shouldn't rush into these things. Take as much time as you like and in the meanwhile I'll be in touch with your brother . .

NORAH

No need to do that. I've made up my mind already. My answer is yes! Oh, Merge, I am so happy that it's all decided now, aren't you?

MERGER

Why, yes. It's all happened so suddenly . .

NORAH

Aren't you going to kiss the bride?

MERGER

That is the usual procedure, isn't it? Do you mind?

NORAH

I am all yours!

MERGER

So you are.

NORAH

There's only one condition. We must be married at once. You must elope with me tonight.

MERGER

But surely we must get your brother's consent.

NORAH

He has as good as given it, but I have a whim to be married before it comes. I want to do this one thing on my own initiative.

MERGER

Always playing games, but, I suppose, if you insist . .

NORAH

I do, I do. (*calling*) Dora! Dora, dear. I have wonderful news. Come here at once. (*Enter Dorinda.*)

DORINDA

What is it, Norah dear?

NORAH

Mr. Merger has asked me to be his wife. Haven't you, dear?

MERGER

Yes. It's all happened so suddenly.

NORAH

And I've accepted him. We are going to be married at once. I will just go and throw a few things into a bag. (*Exit Norah.*)

DORINDA

Oh, I'm so happy. So happy for you both. Congratulations, Mr. Merger. You're a lucky man. You must be a fast worker to have swept her off her feet. (*Exit Dorinda.*)

MERGER

I surprised myself. I guess I'm more irresistible than I thought. She is certainly no cover girl; an incipient alcoholic, I suspect, with nympho-maniacal tendencies as well. But with twenty-six percent of Tube, Flue, and Duct, she is Helen of Troy as far as I am concerned. (*Re-enter Norah and Dorinda.*)

NORAH

(*waving a bottle of champagne*) I keep one on the ice for emergencies.

Dora, be an angel and take down a note while I pour us each a glass to celebrate.

DORINDA

I'm ready.

NORAH

(*dictating*) My dearest brother, comma, I don't know how to thank you for bringing Mr. Merger into my life. He has made me the most happy woman by his choice. I hope you are as delighted with this news as I am. I have decided to get married immediately. Please send me your consent by return but do not come yourself as we are leaving at once. Look forward to seeing you soon with the latest member of our family at my side. Your devoted and affectionate sister, Dorinda. I think that covers everything. See that Fidget takes it round to him at once.

DORINDA

I will. (*toasting*) A long and happy marriage for both of you.

NORAH

First things first. Let's drink to our honeymoon.

MERGER

For richer, for poorer and all that sort of thing. Ha, ha, ha. (*They all laugh.*)

NORAH

Now, young Lochinvar, you may carry me off in your crimson Jaguar. But let me take one for the road. (*She puts a bottle of whiskey in her bag.*) Stay out of mischief, Dora, and take good care of yourself. Beware of strange men at the door.

DORINDA

Goodbye, Mr. Merger. Take good care of her. Goodbye and good luck, both of you. (*Exeunt Norah and Merger. Enter Philander, on the other side.*)

PHILANDER

How can you be such a hypocrite.

DORINDA

(*dabbing her eyes*) Other people's weddings always make me cry a bit.

PHILANDER

I must say Norah's being a brick to go through with it.

DORINDA

She's a trouper, that girl. True blue. You know, I think she really quite likes him, in a way. Holy motel rooms! There'll be some swinging from the chandeliers tonight!

PHILANDER

Come on, let's finish the champagne. Shall we drink to what is foremost in our minds? (*They do so and, coming together in the center of the stage, they kiss.*)

DORINDA

Hey, do you realize? We just lost our chaperone!

CURTAIN

ACT THREE

Scene 1

A room in Mrs. Headway's house. Enter Headway and Mrs. Headway.

HEADWAY

Believe me, young Merger is the perfect match for Dorinda. She should consider herself lucky he's interested.

MRS. HEADWAY

I'll be surprised if she accepts him, all the same. She was quite vehement the last time I spoke to her.

HEADWAY

I put the situation to her bluntly this time. I think she'll see the light.

MRS. HEADWAY

I'll be glad to hear it. The sooner she's settled the better for all concerned.

HEADWAY

I'm going now. Promised I'd meet Clamber at the Club.

MRS. HEADWAY

You two live in each other's pockets. I can't think what you see in him if he's anything like that dreadful wife of his.

HEADWAY

I've invited them both to come to our ball tonight.

MRS. HEADWAY

That woman! Over my dead body.

HEADWAY

If necessary. (*Exit Headway.*)

MRS. HEADWAY

Comedian! (*The telephone rings.*) All right, Drudge, I'll take it in here. (*answering the phone*) Oh, hello, Hussey dear. How did it go at Casserole's last night? . . Not that unspeakable Clamber woman. Well, she wouldn't have dared to say it to my face, I can tell you that. No, just a

226

quiet evening at home; a few people in. Did you happen to notice if there was anything in the paper today? . . No, I never do either. People like us don't have to, because we were there. The society page is meant for those who weren't . . No, I was just curious. We were thirty-six for dinner and the press were so sweetly inquisitive. Of course I always send them a decent tip or they spell the names wrong. Well, now you mention it, I did catch a glimpse. Do you see the paragraph that begins "That gracious and charming hostess . ." and "in the tradition of the great salons"? . . Aren't you a dear to say it. I must admit it was one of our better affairs. Well, that's your fault for accepting Casserole's. Incidentally, apropos disasters, you must see that new foreign film. I was never so moved by anything in my life. Especially the climax where the mine caves in. Soul-stirring! (*The doorbell rings.*) My decorator is at the door, dear, I must fly. Yes, *the* Mr. Bauble himself. Aren't I a lucky girl? . . And a big wet kiss to you, pet. 'Bye for now. (*She goes to meet Cufflink at the door.*) Mr. Bauble, I can't tell you how thrilled I am that you have agreed to take me on. I am so grateful to Dodge for pleading my case.

CUFFLINK

(*entering*) What a dump! I've seen better furnishing in a barrack's dayroom.

MRS. HEADWAY

I know of your exquisite taste. This house cries out for a touch of your genius.

CUFFLINK

It's crying out for something, that's for sure. Just look at this! Heppendale and Chipplewhite all mixed up with an Audubon rug and bits of the British Empire. I ask you. I can see you don't know your Adams from your escritoire! Here's a bit of Louis Swartz with a pair of Queen Anne's drawers on Queen Victoria's legs.

MRS. HEADWAY

I'm sure you will find the drawers are of the period.

CUFFLINK

With ladies, I know better than to discuss drawers or the you-know-what! And what you got growing here? Marijuana? The places for plants is in the jardin and not the maison.

MRS. HEADWAY

But indoor plants are all the rage. I thought . . ?

CUFFLINK

Lady, it's me who decides what's the dernier crise, not you. What's this supposed to be? (*pointing to a painting*)

227

MRS. HEADWAY

It's a non-objective painting.

CUFFLINK

Well, *I* object to it. I can see I've got my work cut out for me. The first thing we do is get rid of all this junk.

MRS. HEADWAY

Oh, but I intend to keep everything that's here. I just want you to rearrange our rooms and create a new color scheme.

CUFFLINK

The only way to rearrange these rooms is with an axe. This all goes, or I do. How can you stand to be around such stuff, a lady of your taste, your looks, your intelligence, and your build?

MRS. HEADWAY

But some of these things are priceless.

CUFFLINK

Priceless. I'll say. They're a frigging scream. Now, no more argument. I'll have a van come truck it all away.

MRS. HEADWAY

Well, I don't know what my husband will have to say.

CUFFLINK

A big girl like you! If he's got anything to say, you just pop him in the snoot. (*opening the door*) And what have we in here? The bedroom. Quite a nifty little boudoir you've got there.

MRS. HEADWAY

Oh heavens, the dreariest room in the house. I'm sure a great deal can be done with it.

CUFFLINK

Let's go in and see. The two of us can work out something interesting.

MRS. HEADWAY

I've always felt it needed livening up.

CUFFLINK

The Bauble touch. I've something in mind that might do the trick. (*They go into the bedroom.*)

Scene 2

A street. Enter Headway and Clamber.

HEADWAY

Just got a note from Dorinda. All went merry as a marriage bell.

CLAMBER

That's wonderful news.

HEADWAY

One look and she fell for him. Couldn't wait to get married. They're already on their honeymoon.

CLAMBER

That's quick work. Merger must be more of a Casanova than I gave him credit for.

HEADWAY

I sent them a cordial note giving my consent.

CLAMBER

You're quite the matchmaker.

HEADWAY

They were meant for each other. It was more than coincidence that they hold shares in the same company. The next thing I intend to do is get your wife and mine to see eye to eye. You're bringing her, I hope, tonight.

CLAMBER

I doubt it will work as we hope, but I'll make her come with me.

HEADWAY

I hope to hell the place will be finished in time. The decorator's thrown out every stick of furniture we own.

CLAMBER

The same with us. Have you run into this Bauble fellow yet?

HEADWAY

No.

CLAMBER

You wait. You'll get a good laugh out of him. The biggest what-you-may-call-it you ever saw.

HEADWAY

So much the better. At least that way we know the women are safe.

CLAMBER

Not like poor old Horner's wife, at least. He came home from a business trip unexpectedly and caught her in the act with the exterminator man.

HEADWAY

You don't say. Shocking thing!

CLAMBER

You can't trust anyone anymore.

HEADWAY

Disgrace. Why, Horner paid a fortune for that place. What was it, termites or mice?

CLAMBER

Never thought to ask.

HEADWAY

That's the trouble with old buildings. Never know what's underneath the floor. Termites, I expect. Usually is. (*Exeunt. Enter Dodge and Cufflink, wearing a tailcoat.*)

DODGE

Here it is. A beautiful buy; seven eighths of a carat at least.

CUFFLINK

It's beautiful, but doesn't it have a bit of an orange tint?

DODGE

Slightly off-color stone, that's why the bargain price. Any girl would give her you-know-what for a ring like that. You could corrupt a mother superior with that center stone.

CUFFLINK

I'll take it.

DODGE

You won't regret it. Now tell me, how's the decorating business coming along?

CUFFLINK

So far, so good. But the strain is getting me down. I'll be grateful when it's all over and done with tonight.

DODGE

It's gone off without a hitch, like I told you it would. Then we'll be seeing each other at the ball.

CUFFLINK

Will you be there?

DODGE

Naturally. Mrs. Headway is very grateful to me. Besides, I still haven't given her the bill. (*Enter Bodice.*)

CUFFLINK

Hullo, beautiful.

BODICE

(*stopping*) Who are you? You, or that brother of yours?

CUFFLINK

It's me, Cufflink.

DODGE

I'll vouch for that.

CUFFLINK

Mr. Dodge, have you met my fiancée?

DODGE

Delighted, I'm sure. I hope the young lady will excuse me, but I have to see a man about a dog. Farewell, you lucky boy. (*Exit Dodge.*)

BODICE

What are you got up like that for?

CUFFLINK

Come over here. I don't want to have to shout.

BODICE

If you're your brother, I warn you, if you lay a hand on me I'll scream bloody murder, and I just passed a cop.

CUFFLINK

I'm not going to do anything to you.

BODICE

You're as bad as each other. Sex maniacs!

CUFFLINK

Bodice, I'm afraid I can't keep our date tonight.

BODICE

Oh, no? Why?

CUFFLINK

I've got to buttle for Mrs. Headway. She's giving a reception and she's short of help.

BODICE

What am I supposed to do, swing the bag?

CUFFLINK

Why don't you come with me? You could help out and we could go on someplace afterwards.

BODICE

Work on my night off! A fat chance.

CUFFLINK

By the way, I've got a surprise for you.

BODICE

What sort of surprise? Knowing you . .

CUFFLINK

(*holding out the ring box*) Take a look at this.

BODICE

What is it? Well, now, I say . .

CUFFLINK

An engagement ring.

BODICE

What kind of stone is it?

CUFFLINK

A diamond.

BODICE

I've never heard of an orange diamond.

CUFFLINK

They're very rare.

BODICE

Where did you get the money to pay for it?

CUFFLINK

Never you mind. It's worth what it cost if you say you'll marry me.

BODICE

This is so sudden. Well, I don't suppose there's any harm in being engaged.

CUFFLINK

We've been as good as engaged for the past year. Now I want you to marry me right away.

BODICE

You are the impatient one.

CUFFLINK

We've waited long enough. A man can stand just so much. It's seven or eight carats at least, Dodge said.

BODICE

All right then, if that's what you want.

CUFFLINK

You mean you'll marry me?

BODICE

Well, I didn't say I was going to take the veil.

CUFFLINK

Oh, Bodice, you've made me the happiest man in the world! (*He seizes her in his arms.*)

BODICE

Hey! Cut that out. You and your brother. Rapists, that's what you are! (*exeunt*)

Scene 3

A room in Mrs. Headway's house. Headway, Mrs. Headway, and Dodge, discovered.

HEADWAY

House is a great success, Minerva. I congratulate you.

MRS. HEADWAY

It gives one such assurance to know that everything in it is the acme of good taste. When one relies on one's own judgment one can never be sure. I am so grateful, Mr. Dodge.

DODGE

It was my pleasure to do what I could. (*Enter Cufflink.*)

MRS. HEADWAY

And here is the man of the hour, the hero himself. Welcome, Maestro. You have done magnificently. I have had nothing but compliments. (*to Headway*) My dear, this is Mr. Bauble.

CUFFLINK

Pleased to meet you, sir. Your wife is a charming lady. I found her very cooperative. Yes, this is one of my better efforts, I'll confess. I'm glad that Dodge put me up to doing it.

DODGE

And I'm glad that you were able to pull it off so satisfactorily.

MRS. HEADWAY

Now you two must go and mingle and enjoy yourselves.

HEADWAY

Don't let the food and liquor go to waste. (*Exeunt Cufflink and Dodge.*)

MRS. HEADWAY

Bauble is such a cultivated man. We must have him here more often. He's obviously *de bonne famille*.

HEADWAY

I'm surprised that Dorinda and Merger haven't shown up yet. (*Enter Dorinda.*)

MRS. HEADWAY

Here she is now. Congratulations, Dorinda, dear. I'm so happy for you. You're looking radiant.

DORINDA

Hullo, darling. Hullo, brother. Everything is forgiven and forgotten, I hope?

HEADWAY

'Course, Dorinda. Congratulations, my dear. Where's the lucky man?

DORINDA

He will be here in a moment. He's parking the car.

MRS. HEADWAY

How does it feel to be a married woman again?

DORINDA

Wonderful. I've never been so happy.

HEADWAY

Off the shelf at last. You can't say I didn't do you a good turn.

DORINDA

And I'm very grateful, too.

HEADWAY

Well, I'm relieved to see you settled down at last. I can hand over the estate to your husband and you with confidence.

DORINDA

It must have been a burden to you, I'm sure.

MRS. HEADWAY

Anyway, it has all turned out for the best in the end.

DORINDA

It has indeed.

HEADWAY

No hard feelings. Let bygones be bygones. (*Enter Philander.*)

MRS. HEADWAY

Ah, here you are. (*to Headway*) I don't think you have met Philander, dear. (*to Philander*) This is my husband, Mr. Headway.

HEADWAY

I don't know the gentleman, but certainly I've heard of him.

PHILANDER

How do you do.

MRS. HEADWAY

(*to Dorinda*) You two, I think, have met each other before?

DORINDA

We have indeed.

PHILANDER

You look even lovelier than when I saw you last.

HEADWAY

I would take care, if I were you. You are paying compliments to a recently married woman.

PHILANDER

That accounts for her extraordinary radiance tonight. She is in love.

DORINDA

You are right. Is it so obvious?

PHILANDER

It surrounds you like an aura. Nothing becomes a woman more than being in love.

HEADWAY

And nothing less becomes a gentleman than to flirt with another man's wife.

MRS. HEADWAY

Headway!

PHILANDER

Madam, your husband is perfectly right. I have been at fault in that particular from time to time. But the women, I find, take less exception to it than the men. (*Enter Merger and Norah.*)

HEADWAY

Ah, here is Merger now, and none too soon. (*to Philander*) This is the husband, sir, and he would take some exception I am sure.

MRS. HEADWAY

And here's dear Norah, looking much improved. How nice to see you.

NORAH

Hullo, everyone.

HEADWAY

Merger, boy, let me congratulate you. Welcome to the family. This is Mrs. Headway, my wife.

MRS. HEADWAY

How do you do. I'm so happy for you both.

HEADWAY

Know everyone else?

MERGER

I think we've all met before.

HEADWAY

Good, good. Now, why don't you bring the blushing bride. I want to introduce you to the guests.

MERGER

Very well. (*to Norah*) Come with us, my dear.

HEADWAY

No, Norah. You stay here for the minute. I'll first take the bride and groom.

NORAH

This is the point at which I need a drink.

HEADWAY

(*to Merger*) After this you and I will have some business to talk about. Dorinda, coming?

MERGER

I was bringing her, but you just told her to stay.

HEADWAY

I told Norah to stay.

MERGER

That's what I said. I asked her to come and then you told her not to.

HEADWAY

What are you talking about? I asked Norah to stay.

MERGER

Did you say Norah or Dora?

HEADWAY

Norah. (*pointing*) I want Dorinda, your wife, to come with us.

MERGER

This is Dorinda.

HEADWAY

That's Norah.

MERGER

I know that, but you call her Dorinda, don't you?

HEADWAY

I certainly do not. That is Dorinda.

MERGER

She's Dora, isn't she?

HEADWAY

No, this is Norah.

MERGER

Of course I know that. She's my wife.

HEADWAY

Your what!?!

MERGER

My wife. Well, whatever you call her, she's your sister, isn't she?

HEADWAY

No, she is not!

DORINDA

Brother, I think you ought to sit down. You too, Mr. Merger. There is something I have to explain.

MRS. HEADWAY

I had my suspicions all along.

NORAH

I need a drink.

PHILANDER

Let me get you one.

HEADWAY

Stay where you are. No one's leaving this room till we have got to the bottom of this affair.

DORINDA

That won't take long. It's very simple, really. Mr. Merger here proposed to Norah and she accepted him and they got married. That is all there is to it.

HEADWAY

Oh, no, it's not. Why did Merger propose to Norah instead of you?

DORINDA

He preferred her, I suppose, or perhaps he thought she was me.

HEADWAY

Why should he think that?

MERGER

(to Headway) She told me she was your sister.

NORAH

Oh no, Mr. Merger, I never did. You assumed I was. I admit it was unfair to let you marry me thinking I was an heiress. But never mind. I won't hold you to it. You can divorce me as soon as you wish, and I won't ask for any settlement. Nothing could make me richer than you already have. You gave me something I might otherwise never have had, a wedding and a honeymoon. I'll remember that all my life and be grateful to you. I'm sorry I haven't any shares to give you in return.

HEADWAY

I'm sorry too, Merger, to let you get taken in like this. It was a shabby trick. I should have known better than to trust this treacherous sister of mine.

MERGER

This has come as a great shock and surprise. I don't know what to think. (to Norah) I'm still not quite sure who you really are but if you weren't unhappy on our honeymoon, I might as well admit that neither was I. Since we are man and wife, if you have no objections, I'm perfectly agreeable to leaving the situation that way.

NORAH

Oh Merge, what a very sweet thing to say. In a short while, you know, I've grown very fond of you.

MERGER

And I can say the same.

237

HEADWAY

Well, at least that settles that. And you (*to Dorinda*) it seems, are back where you were before; my responsibility.

DORINDA

Not exactly. I have conferred that onerous burden upon this gentleman.

MRS. HEADWAY

Philander!

HEADWAY

What do you mean by that?

DORINDA

He is my lawfully wedded spouse as of a few hours ago.

HEADWAY

Well, well, well. Then that settles that matter too.

DORINDA

Welcome your new brother-in-law into the family.

HEADWAY

Welcome, by all means, and thank you for taking Dorinda off my hands. I just hope you have the means to support her extravagance. You didn't marry an heiress, you know.

DORINDA

Oh yes, he did. Now I can come into my estate.

HEADWAY

If I've explained it to you once, I've explained it a hundred times. Under the terms of the will you forfeit the inheritance if you marry without my consent.

DORINDA

But I have your consent.

HEADWAY

To marry this gentleman? No, you certainly do not.

DORINDA

Do you have my letter?

HEADWAY

(*producing it*) Right here. You said you were going to marry Merger. That I consented to.

DORINDA

Very well then, read it to me.

HEADWAY

(*doing so*) "My dearest brother . ."

DORINDA

Yes, I admit that was stretching it a bit.

HEADWAY

"I don't know how to thank you enough for bringing Mr. Merger into my life."

DORINDA

Yes, so that I could get you out of it and a husband for Norah.

HEADWAY

"He has made me the most happy woman by his choice."

DORINDA

Of Norah, not me.

HEADWAY

"I hope you are as delighted with this news as I am."

DORINDA

Apparently you aren't, but I can't help that.

HEADWAY

"I have decided to get married immediately. Please send me your consent by return but do not come yourself . ."

DORINDA

I should think not.

HEADWAY

". . as we are leaving at once. Look forward to seeing you soon with the latest member of our family at my side."

DORINDA

And here he is.

HEADWAY

"Your devoted and affectionate sister."

DORINDA

And that I am. Now let me read your consent. "I thoroughly approve your choice. Congratulations on the sound decision you have made. You have my permission for and my blessing on the match. All best wishes for your future happiness. Fondest brotherly love." Could anything be clearer than that?

MRS. HEADWAY

Even I must admit that there's no doubt about it at all.

HEADWAY

Who asked for an opinion from the bench? I must think this over.

DORINDA

There's nothing to think about. My lawyers will be in touch with you in the morning.

HEADWAY

A damned conspiracy, an underhanded trick! (*Exit Headway.*)

NORAH

Let's go and get some liquid refreshment, Merge. I feel a little parched. (*Exeunt Norah and Merger. Enter Fetish.*)

FETISH

Bon soir, tout le monde. Headway, my dear, you look breathtaking to-night.

DORINDA

(*to Philander*) If Fetish takes a close look around, he could ruin every-thing.

PHILANDER

I'll get him out of the way before he notices anything.

FETISH

(*to Mrs. Headway*) So many pretty people you have here. Is that my chum Philander over there? (*crossing to him*) *Âme de mon âme,* how are you dearest thing? Dorinda, my love.

PHILANDER

Fetish, I want you to be the first to know. Dorinda and I got married this afternoon.

FETISH

To whom, to whom? Do tell me all.

PHILANDER

Excuse us, Dorinda. If you have a minute, Fetish, I want to ask you some-thing outside.

FETISH

Anything, my dear, anything. (*Exeunt Philander and Fetish.*)

HEADWAY

(*entering*) Minerva, Clamber and his wife have just arrived.

MRS. HEADWAY

In my house! Never! I am not at home!

HEADWAY

I forbid you to make a scene. (*Enter Clamber and Mrs. Clamber.*) Clam-ber, old boy, glad you two could come. (*to Mrs. Headway*) You know Mrs. Clamber, dear.

MRS. HEADWAY

By sight, of course yes, everybody does.

MRS. CLAMBER

What a charming house. I understand you are having it redecorated soon.

MRS. HEADWAY

It has just been redecorated.

MRS. CLAMBER

How clever. You should have used my man Bauble. He did our house and it's perfectly divine.

MRS. HEADWAY

Bauble has just finished doing this house of ours.

MRS. CLAMBER

Indeed? I would never have guessed.

HEADWAY

(*to Clamber*) Come with me. Got to ask your advice.

CLAMBER

Nice place.

HEADWAY

Suits us.

CLAMBER

Sort of reminds me of our old house. (*Exeunt Headway and Clamber.*)

MRS. CLAMBER

And so it should. It has suddenly dawned on me!

MRS. HEADWAY

(*to Mrs. Clamber*) You will excuse me. I must see that my dear friends are taken care of properly. (*Exit Mrs. Headway.*)

MRS. CLAMBER

Dorinda, do you realize what Bauble has done? He's palmed off all my old junk on Headway. Don't you see? Everything here was mine.

DORINDA

Oh, are you sure? It can't be true.

MRS. CLAMBER

I swear. Do you see that stain? That's where Mrs. Distemper's poodle was incontinent. This is the most delicious piece of mischief in the world. Headway would have a seizure if she knew.

DORINDA

You must be mistaken.

MRS. CLAMBER

No question about it. This has absolutely made my day. I can't wait to tell Fetish and then the whole world will know. (*Enter Mrs. Headway and Norah.*)

MRS. HEADWAY

He chose nothing but antique pieces, and each contributes its traces of the past.

MRS. CLAMBER

(*to Dorinda*) Mrs. Distemper's antique poodle, my dear.

241

NORAH

Yes, I notice a great change.

MRS. HEADWAY

It's almost difficult to remember what this room was like before. There was the hideous abstract painting over there.

NORAH

I was never very fond of it.

MRS. CLAMBER

It takes a rather highly cultivated taste to appreciate non-objective painting. As a matter of fact Bauble discovered a sensational one for me. Terribly profound.

MRS. HEADWAY

And here was the enormous tropical plant that wouldn't bloom.

DORINDA

Oh, everyone has one of those nowadays.

MRS. HEADWAY

Used to have. They have gone quite Out now, you know. Nothing is being grown indoors anymore.

MRS. CLAMBER

I can't agree with you. Bauble brought me the most superb plant himself. It's from Australia. Blooms once every seventy years.

MRS. HEADWAY

Bauble insisted that I get rid of mine.

DORINDA

I dare say the fashions change.

MRS. HEADWAY

And over there I had that tapestry settee, with those rather rude satyrs . .

MRS. CLAMBER

Pursuing some half-dressed nymphs?

DORINDA

Tapestry is always the same. Weavers have a one-track mind.

MRS. CLAMBER

The curtains?

MRS. HEADWAY

Were beige brocade . .

MRS. CLAMBER

With bands of embroidered braid. The rug?

MRS. HEADWAY

Was oriental with a design of pea . .

MRS. CLAMBER

. . cocks and pomegranates.

MRS. HEADWAY

Yes, and everything went to the dump.

MRS. CLAMBER

(*with a roar*) Bauble. Where is that monster? Just wait until I get my hands on him.

MRS. HEADWAY

What has come over her?

MRS. CLAMBER

Vengeance! How could he have done this thing to me?

MRS. HEADWAY

What, what has he done?

MRS. CLAMBER

You don't know the half of it. He's going to pay for this. I'll have his blood. The thief, the sneak, the rat, the snake in the grass.

MRS. HEADWAY

She's unhinged. I'd better call Bauble in to humor her. (*Exit Mrs. Headway.*)

MRS. CLAMBER

The wretch! The treacherous cur! To make a fool of her is one thing, but to make a fool of me . . ! The dump indeed! Wait till I get ahold of him.

DORINDA

Now, you mustn't let yourself get carried away.

MRS. CLAMBER

I'm apoplectic. I'll murder him. How dare he do this to me! (*Enter Mrs. Headway and Cufflink.*)

MRS. HEADWAY

This lady wants to have a word with you.

CUFFLINK

Mrs. Clamber!

MRS. CLAMBER

I won't vent my spleen on the miserable minion. I want the blood of Mr. Bauble himself. (*Enter Philander.*) There is the man I want!

PHILANDER

Good God, Clamber.

MRS. CLAMBER

Yes, Clamber, you worm. The chips are down. The cat is out of the bag. (*Enter Bodice with a tray of drinks.*)

243

NORAH

Bless you, my dear. We all need a little refreshment here.

MRS. CLAMBER

Bauble, the jig is up. I am undeceived. My retribution will be terrible and swift. No one trifles with me with impunity.

MRS. HEADWAY

She's taken leave of her senses. (*to Mrs. Clamber*) That isn't Bauble. That is Philander.

MRS. CLAMBER

Philander?

MRS. HEADWAY

This is Mr. Bauble here. (*pointing to Cufflink*)

BODICE

No he's not. That's Cufflink, my fiancé. Or if you're that brother of yours
. .

CUFFLINK

No, it's me, Cufflink, I promise you.

MRS. HEADWAY

(*to Cufflink*) Do you mean to tell me you are not Mr. Bauble?

CUFFLINK

No, ma'am.

MRS. HEADWAY

Then who are you?

CUFFLINK

I am this gentleman's gentleman.

MRS. HEADWAY

Then it must be me that has gone mad. (*to Bodice*) Would you please fetch Mr. Dodge from the other room. He is the only one who can sort this out. (*Exit Bodice.*)

MRS. CLAMBER

(*to Philander*) You mean you are not Mr. Bauble, the eminent decorator?

PHILANDER

No, I'm afraid I am not.

DORINDA

And I must forbid you to lay hands on him, my dear, because he is my husband. If you do I shall have no alternative but to blacken both your eyes.

MRS. CLAMBER

This is preposterous. But you don't deny that you supervised the removal of all my old furniture and installed it in this woman's house?

MRS. HEADWAY

What! All your old furniture?

MRS. CLAMBER

Yes, dear.

MRS. HEADWAY

The scoundrel. And what happened to all of mine?

MRS. CLAMBER

I have it, nymphs, pomegranates, the lot. (*Enter Bodice and Dodge.*)

MRS. HEADWAY

Dodge, come here at once.

DODGE

Oh, Holy Moses, Mrs. Clamber here.

PHILANDER

Yes, Dodge, the game is up.

DODGE

I knew from the beginning we were running a risk.

MRS. HEADWAY

Now what is all this? I asked you to get Bauble to do my house.

MRS. CLAMBER

And so did I.

DODGE

Well, ladies, since Mr. Bauble was unavailable I thought I'd oblige by providing the next best thing, with the aid of Mr. Philander here. Now, if you two had continued to be proper arch-enemies, there's no reason why you should ever have found otherwise. But now that you've got together, you've gone and spoiled everything.

MRS. HEADWAY

It seems to me that if we'd got together a good deal sooner, we'd have saved ourselves from being hoodwinked like this.

MRS. CLAMBER

You never said a truer word, my dear. (*to Dodge*) Now, what do you intend to do? If ever this gets out we'll be a laughingstock. You'd better arrange to have all this taken back to my house and Mrs. Headway's furniture returned to her.

DODGE

Now, ladies, let's be sensible. (*to Mrs. Headway*) Before you found out that all this here was hers, you were perfectly satisfied, weren't you? (*to Mrs. Clamber*) And before you found out that all your furniture came from here, you thought likewise, didn't you?

MRS. HEADWAY

That's true.

DODGE

Well then, why don't we leave it like that? Your houses have been redecorated like you wanted and nobody but the people in this room are any the wiser how it came about.

MRS. CLAMBER

There is some sense in that. Clamber would have a fit if he found out.

MRS. HEADWAY

Headway would never let me hear the end of it.

DODGE

There you are then. We'll all keep it under our hats. (*to Mrs. Clamber*) When you get nostalgic about your old home, you can come and visit here. (*to Mrs. Headway*) And when you feel like a glimpse of your old things, you can visit her.

MRS. CLAMBER

Of course, you will be welcome whenever you wish.

DODGE

Then only one slight formality remains. The bill. (*handing Mrs. Headway and Mrs. Clamber envelopes*) Now if we all keep mum, no one need ever know. (*Enter Fetish.*)

FETISH

Oh, here you all are. It's most extraordinary, you know, but I've such a queer feeling that I've seen these things before. It's all strangely familiar.

MRS. HEADWAY

Nonsense. It's your imagination.

MRS. CLAMBER

What on earth makes you say a thing like that?

FETISH

Well, maybe I'm wrong. (*Enter Headway, Clamber, and Merger.*)

HEADWAY

How's the party going in here? (*to Mrs. Headway*) You and Mrs. Clamber getting along?

MRS. HEADWAY

We find we have a lot in common.

HEADWAY

Knew you would think so.

CLAMBER

I must compliment you, Mrs. Headway, on a charming house. From the moment I walked in, I have felt at home.

MRS. CLAMBER

Yes, so have I.

FETISH

That's it. (*to Mrs. Clamber*) Now I know where I've seen these things before. They used to be in your house, Clamber, my dear.

MRS. CLAMBER

Good heavens, our house was never as nice as this.

CLAMBER

No, not a bit like our old stuff. You can see that this has been done by a decorator.

FETISH

I must be mistaken then. I would have sworn . .

HEADWAY

Well, Dorinda, I had a long talk with my friend Clamber, and I've decided to take his advice, that is, to concede to you gracefully. Hope you will accept my warmest wishes, both of you.

DORINDA

Very gratefully, and what's more I think Philander and Merger will have a lot to talk over soon about the future of Consolidated Tube, Flue, and Duct, and I'm sure they'll be needing another director on the board.

HEADWAY

Wonderful. Come on now, everyone. This is a ball, but nobody's dancing. (*They all take partners.*)

FETISH

Well, Mr. Dodge, do you lead? I could make a fair shift of following if I tried.

DORINDA

You see, if we leave them alone, things have an extraordinary way of working out for the best; for

> Who shrewd and prudent most themselves believe
> Are, at all odds, the easiest to deceive.

(*Music. Everyone dances and the curtain falls.*)

THE END

With Malice Aforethought by John Stranack was presented on June 30, July 1, 2, 7–9, 1966, at Scott Hall Auditorium, University of Minnesota, Minneapolis. It was directed by Maxine Klein.

Cast of Characters

DORINDA	Janet Howard
MRS. HEADWAY	Lorraine Steiner
NORAH	Susan Pearson
MRS. CLAMBER	Paulette James
FETISH	Martin Bowman
PHILANDER	Richard Ramos
DODGE	Michael McManus
CUFFLINK	John Sylwester
MR. HEADWAY	Ivan Dusek
MR. CLAMBER	Thomas Houde
MERGER	Mark Stromwall
BODICE	Bonnie Pfaffenbach

PHILIP BARBER

I, Elizabeth Otis, Being of Sound Mind

to Mac Harris and the cast and staff
of Theatre in the Round, Minneapolis

Cast of Characters

MRS. COOMS	STEVEN OTIS
ELIZABETH OTIS	NANCY OTIS
MARY CAMPBELL	YOUNG STEVEN
BENJAMIN CAMPBELL	GEORGE OTIS
HOLLAWAY	REV. ZEDIAH JORDAN
BET CAMPBELL	HENRIETTA CLAPP
FRANK CAMPBELL	LEONARD CLAPP
MAMIE	MAYOR JORDAN

CONGREGATION and PALLBEARERS

The Setting

PLACE: The mind of Elizabeth Otis, a spirited woman in her eighties, at home in the town of Boue City, Iowa.

TIME: Two days in June, not very long ago, and also the preceding seventy-five years of Mrs. Otis' life.

SCENE: The living room in Mrs. Otis' Victorian house and, at the left, part of the yard. At the right two steps lead through a broad arch to a higher level which is a hall. This hall gives access to the front door and front porch, off down right, and to stairs, the kitchen, and the other downstairs rooms of the house, off up right. A French door, well left of center, leads to the yard. There are exits up left and down left. Furnishings of the living room include a handsome old leather sofa with raised end, up left center, in front of which is a sturdy coffee table and a hassock. Down center is an armchair with side table, down right a side chair, right a circular library table, with three chairs set about it, and up right a bench. Extreme right, in the hall, is a hall table with a mirror over it and chairs on either side. In the yard, at the extreme left, is a garden bench. On the side table, next to the armchair, is Mrs. Otis' "necessary basket," in which she keeps the essentials of her life — her pills, checkbook, letters and pictures from her son, writing materials, etc. There is a phone on the side table.

I, ELIZABETH OTIS, BEING OF SOUND MIND

ACT ONE

At rise, Mrs. Otis is sitting in her throne chair. Mrs. Cooms, the house-keeper, a sharp-featured woman in her seventies, wearing a large apron over a nondescript dress, is pushing a dustmop about, right. Up left, Mary Campbell, the mother of Mrs. Otis, is hoeing an imaginary garden. But Mary is as Mrs. Otis remembers her seventy-five years ago, a vigorous woman in her forties, in a gray gingham dress and sunbonnet, with black gloves on her hands. Mrs. Otis is watching her.

MRS. COOMS
When I'm dead, I'll be dead.

MRS. OTIS
No heaven?

MRS. COOMS
Can you see me playing a harp? I only ask to rest quiet in a decent, well-tended grave — that I don't have to take care of.

MRS. OTIS
We're only dead when we're forgotten.

MRS. COOMS
You say. *You* got this house full of your ancestors, you think. What's your mother doing right now?

MRS. OTIS
Hoeing the garden.

MRS. COOMS

Funny I don't see her. Know why? Because she isn't there. She's in your head.

MRS. OTIS

Everything is in my head. (*Benjamin Campbell, Mrs. Otis' father, as he was in the 1870's, a big, strong man with red hair and beard, in rough woolen trousers and a plaid shirt, strides in from down left. He has a struggling chicken hanging by the legs from one hand and carries an axe in the other. Mary stops him, feels the chicken, gives grudging approval. Benjamin crosses and exits up left.*) Father's going to kill a chicken.

MRS. COOMS

I hope he picked a fat one. Pity you don't dream this house clean and save me a day's work.

MRS. OTIS

You've cleaned our chicken?

MRS. COOMS

Look in your head and find the answer!

MRS. OTIS

I do — and I see that you've put no seasoning in the dressing.

MRS. COOMS

In *my* head I see you coming out in the kitchen and seasoning it yourself, no matter what I do. Thank the Lord I wasn't born with brains that have to keep wiggling and worrying! When Mr. Cooms died I heaved a sigh and forgot him. If I had to keep bringing him back and listen to his sharp tongue! There's real pleasure in being a widow. (*Mary Campbell exits down left with her hoe.*)

MRS. OTIS

Last night when I couldn't sleep I lay awake counting widows. Fifty in this town that I know of. Yet when I was a little girl it seemed as though the women died first. A vigorous man would use up two or three wives in a lifetime.

MRS. COOMS

That's true.

MRS. OTIS

Though mother was too much for father.

MRS. COOMS

Well, this is as clean as it's going to be. Did you order eggs?

MRS. OTIS

Egg money was all the women used to have for their own. Now the widows have got it all.

252

MRS. COOMS

(*sharply*) Don't wander. Did you order eggs?

MRS. OTIS

(*sorry for herself*) I wish you wouldn't scold me.

MRS. COOMS

Pick up that phone and order eggs! Unless you don't want your son to have eggs for breakfast tomorrow. I'm sure I don't care.

MRS. OTIS

(*picking up the receiver*) Please go. I'll order the eggs. Find something to do in the kitchen. You wear me out. (*into the phone*) Eight-nine-two-five, please.

MRS. COOMS

(*carefully picking up the mop, holding it in front of her like a lance, so that none of the dust will fall from it, going up right, into the hall*) I'd give notice if I thought you'd find anyone else to work for you, but I can't go off and let you die — though it's a temptation! (*She exits up right.*)

MRS. OTIS

(*into the phone*) This is Mrs. Otis — is this Roger? . . Roger, my son and his wife are coming for a visit and I'd like a dozen of your choicest brown eggs . . Today please . . Thank you. (*As she hangs up, the front doorbell rings. Confused, Mrs. Otis picks up the phone again.*) Hello? (*The doorbell rings again. This time she recognizes it as the door. She puts the receiver back, rises rather stiffly, but then walks briskly toward the front door down right.*) Good morning, Mr. Hollaway.

HOLLAWAY

(*outside*) May I come in?

MRS. OTIS

What on earth? (*Hollaway, a brisk young man in his late twenties, in sport coat and flannels, enters. He is carrying two gaily colored gingham dresses and two sunbonnets, of the style we've just seen on Mary Campbell, but these are bright and new. Over his other arm he has a man's frock coat and on the back of his head a "stovepipe" hat.*)

HOLLAWAY

Your dress!

MRS. OTIS

(*Curiously taking a sunbonnet from him and trying it on, she makes a face, slips it off, and hands it back to Hollaway.*) I'm not in the pageant, thank goodness.

HOLLAWAY

Oh, but you are! Everybody in town's dressing up! (*putting the dresses*

253

over the back of a chair near the library table, the sunbonnets on another chair) Don't forget, the pageant's really about you. I got the background from you, didn't I? Don't forget those afternoons we spent. Your name's right in there below mine.

MRS. OTIS

(*as Hollaway holds up the frock coat, before putting it over the back of another chair*) Father wore something like that.

HOLLAWAY

For your son. (*He puts the hat on the seat of the chair.*) When does he get in?

MRS. OTIS

They're coming by the afternoon plane.

HOLLAWAY

That's cutting it short — I've got to rehearse him for his part in the prologue. You wrote him he was in it, didn't you?

MRS. OTIS

(*ignoring the question, sitting on the sofa*) I won't be able to see the parade. Doctor McEwen said, "either the parade or the pageant," and I want to see Steven in the prologue.

HOLLAWAY

I know — you told me. But I've got news! You're going to see the parade tomorrow. We've rerouted it to come past this house! You can sit right out there on your own front porch and you'll see it all!

MRS. OTIS

That's quite an honor — and an aggravation. I'll have to have Mrs. Cooms put chairs out. I suppose I'll have to offer them cake. (*Worrying, she rises.*)

HOLLAWAY

Not a thing! And no chairs. I've ordered folding chairs from the funeral parlor.

MRS. OTIS

Who's dead? (*Holloway laughs heartily but he's not sure what she means.*) The past? You're burying the past. Just as well, perhaps. It wasn't very nice. Dirt and stench. You didn't use much of what I told you, but people don't want to be reminded of what's unpleasant. You didn't use about our neighbor got caught in the blizzard? (*Holloway shakes his head. He is pacing about restlessly.*) Killed his horse and cut the innards out. Crawled in to try to keep warm. We found him in the spring when the thaw came. Not a hundred yards from our door.

HOLLAWAY

I know. Look, I'll come back later. I want to interview your son for to-morrow's Centennial Edition.

MRS. OTIS

Did you ever chop off the head of a chicken? (*She looks left where Benjamin carried the chicken.*) Stump of a neck spouting blood, flapping around in circles.

HOLLAWAY

(*crossing right, eager to be gone*) No — no, I didn't.

MRS. OTIS

That was a chicken dinner. Now if you wanted a roast beef — hit the steer on the head with the sledge — big brown eyes looking up so helpless — then cut the throat to bleed it. Put that in your pageant!

(*The lights dim in the room, except on Mrs. Otis' face, and come up in the yard, as Benjamin Campbell strides on from the right. He is wearing a black frock coat, the mate of the one Hollaway brought; on his head a rakishly placed stovepipe hat. He is carrying a Navy Colt cap-and-ball revolver. Running along just behind him is Bet Campbell — this is Mrs. Otis at eight years old. She is barefooted, her red hair down her back. She wears a gray gingham dress and a sunbonnet of the same material, which hangs down her back by its string. She is carrying a rag doll in her arms.*)

BENJAMIN

Hey — I spy an Injun!

HOLLAWAY

(*at the door*) Goodbye for now. (*But Mrs. Otis is watching Benjamin and does not answer. Benjamin motions Bet to stand aside, she wide-eyed and fearful. He raises the pistol and fires, apparently at Hollaway, who exits abruptly, closing the door. There is a yell and Frank Campbell comes running in, past Hollaway. He runs across the room, out into the yard. He is a handsome boy of nineteen, with goatee and long hair in the fashion of General Custer. At the moment, he is hatless, wearing a gay plaid shirt and boots like his father.*)

BENJAMIN

(*jovially*) What's the matter, Frank? I scare you?

FRANK

You could of hit me!

BENJAMIN

(*laughs*) Like hell. I aimed to miss you, son. You're just a fraidy-cat. What are you following us around for anyhow? Look — you go get the parcel from the front seat of the buckboard. (*Grumbling, Frank goes off*

up left. Bet, clutching her doll, is frowning at her father. He goes down on one knee, puts an arm about Bet.) Posie — don't you frown like that. Suppose it come on to freeze and your face was to get frozen like that? Why, you'd scare the horses . . make the cattle stampede and the chickens roost in the trees. (*Bet relaxes into a reluctant, fleeting smile.*) That's better. Want me to say you a poem?

BET

(*eagerly*) Yes! Yes! "To a Mousie"?

BENJAMIN

(*He takes her by the hand, and leads her to the bench, left. Sitting, he pats the bench beside him. Bet sits, her doll in her arms, looking up at her father. He begins to recite with dramatic feeling. Mrs. Otis sits in her chair, watching.*)

> "Wee, sleekit, cow'rin', tim'rous beastie
> O what a panic's in thy breastie!
> Thou need na start awa sae hasty,
>   Wi' bickering brattle!
> I wad be laith to rin an' chase thee . . .
>
> Thy wee bit housie, too, in ruin!
> Its silly wa's the win's are strewing!
> An' naething, now, to big a new ane,
>   O'foggage green!"

(*Mock sorrow on Benjamin's face, mirrored in Bet's. He laughs and Bet giggles in happiness. Frank comes on right, holding a doll, wrapped in a large bandanna handkerchief.*)

FRANK

Here's what you sent me for.

BENJAMIN

(*Rising, he extends his hand, his other arm around Bet.*) Give it to me. (*Frank gives it to him. Benjamin gives it to Bet.*) Open it. I'll hold your dolly. (*Benjamin takes the rag doll, as Bet unwraps the parcel to disclose a fine, new, china-headed store doll. Benjamin looks with amusement at the rag doll, holds it up by the cornsilk hair, then jerks off the cornsilk and tosses the rag doll onto the ground. Bet doesn't notice.*)

BET

(*clutching her new doll*) Oh! What's her name?

BENJAMIN

The Duchess of Argyll. You can call her Meg. (*Benjamin puts the bandanna in his pocket.*)

256

I, ELIZABETH OTIS, BEING OF SOUND MIND

FRANK

(*crosses to the rag doll, picks it up, sees the hair and picks it up*) Hey —
what happened to Annie Laurie?

BET

(*with a cry of distress, running to take her rag doll from Frank*) Annie
Laurie!

BENJAMIN

(*with mock solemnity, taking the hair from Frank*) By God, she was
scalped by the Injuns. Don't matter. You got a new one, now. (*He strides
off up left. Bet is crooning over the rag doll — but still holding her new
china doll.*)

FRANK

Never you mind. I'll stick her hair on again. It's just cornsilk.

BET

Oh will you? Now.

FRANK

Wait. I been trying to catch you alone all morning. I got a secret.

BET

About me?

FRANK

No, me. I ain't going off to study law like Mother wants.

BET

Goody.

FRANK

There's better'n that.

BET

Tell me!

FRANK

Maybe I'm getting married. (*Bet's eyes grow round with the awfulness of
this news.*) Ask me who to.

BET

Who to?

FRANK

Guess.

BET

There isn't nobody in six miles hasn't got a husband.

FRANK

You're not trying. Don't act stupid. Guess.

BET

I won't.

FRANK

I'll tell you.

BET

No! (*She starts away.*)

FRANK

It's Mamie! (*Bet puts her fingers in her ears and runs off right, past Frank who catches her by the arm. Mrs. Otis has echoed Bet's action, put her hands over her ears.*) Say something.

BET

(*near tears*) She's just our hired girl.

FRANK

Don't be so hoity-toity. She's pretty, that she is. Ain't she?

BET

She's an old woman. She's twenty-five and I'm going to run away and never see you again. (*She pulls loose and runs off down left.*)

FRANK

(*calling after her as he follows her off, down left*) Bet! Damnit to hell! When you're getting married folks are supposed to be glad! (*Mrs. Otis rises, walks about in distress of memory. From up left Mary Campbell enters carrying a rush clothes basket and calls.*)

MARY

Bet! Bet!

BET

Yes, Mother. (*Entering from down left. Mrs. Otis watches.*)

MARY

(*puts down basket*) Help me wring out these sheets. (*She takes a sheet from the basket. Bet puts her doll on the bench.*)

BET

Why — why do people get married?

MARY

To raise a family. (*She hands an end to Bet, who doesn't take it immediately.*)

BET

But why do you marry the person you do?

MARY

The flesh, I suppose. Take this end! (*Bet takes the end of the sheet extended to her.*) The flesh draws you — twist. (*They twist the sheet.*)

BET

Like horses draw a wagon?

I, ELIZABETH OTIS, BEING OF SOUND MIND

MARY

Like you throw a ball up and the earth draws it down.

BET

Grav-ity. Does it hurt to be drawed?

MARY

At the beginning and at the end. (*She takes the sheet, puts it back in the basket, and takes out another.*)

BET

I want to marry Frank.

MARY

Sisters don't marry brothers.

BET

Why?

MARY

They don't want to. Twist.

BET

I do.

MARY

(*stops twisting*) What started you on this?

BET

It's a secret.

MARY

Tell me what you know! (*She twists the sheet so violently that Bet drops her end.*) Oh, plague you! Now it's got to be washed all over again! (*Mary Campbell thrusts the sheet into the basket, picks up the basket, and strides off up left as Mamie, the hired girl, a buxom, frowzy girl of twenty-five, enters, passing her. Mary gives Mamie a sharp look and Mamie gives her an impudent smile in return. Mamie is barefooted, wearing a too-tight gingham dress, strained over her full breasts. She carries two wooden pails. Bet has picked up her doll, backs warily out of Mamie's path.*)

MAMIE

Hey, Carrot-top!

BET

What?

MAMIE

Stir your shanks and help me pump water. (*Mamie sets down the pails. Bet shakes her head.*) Lazy, huh? (*Mamie has taken a snuffbox from her pocket, opens it.*) Want some snuff? (*Bet steps forward, looks at the snuff, shakes her head, and steps back. Mamie takes a pinch.*) You don't know what's good. Hey — cat got your tongue? (*Bet shakes her head.*) What

you down in the mouth about? Some boy you sweet on give you the mit-
ten? (*Bet shakes her head violently.*) Well, now, you don't need boys to
have fun. Ever see a bull take on a cow? (*Bet shakes her head.*) Don't
your head work but one way? (*Mamie sits on the bench.*) Now, look. You
and me can have some fun tomorrer afternoon. I know where there's a
bust board in the barn, see? (*Bet nods.*) You and me is going to hide in
there, where we can see good — right into the bull pen. How about that?

BET

See what?

MAMIE

(*Rising, she takes Bet's arm and leads her a little down, glancing back up
left to make sure they are not overheard. She speaks intensely, into Bet's
ear.*) Hain't you heard? Old Man Wells is bringing a cow over to get it
from your pappy's black bull — and when they get together . . (*She
looks warily again up left, then whispers into Bet's ear. Bet listens a moment, then pulling away hits at Mamie.*) Why you — (*Mamie slaps at
Bet repeatedly, moving after her as Bet backs away. Mary comes running
on from up left.*)

MARY

Stop that!

MAMIE

She hit *me*!

MARY

(*to Bet*) Did you hit her? (*Looking at her toe, Bet nods.*) Why? (*Bet
looks at Mamie with deep inner fury.*)

MAMIE

(*hastily*) Oh, it don't matter, I shouldn't of, anyhow. I guess I was teasing
her a little.

BET

She said Old Man Wells was bringing his cow over tomorrow afternoon
and there was a bust board by the bull pen —

MARY

(*Silencing Bet with a hand over her mouth, she steps toward Mamie.*)
You can get inside and pack up your things. I'll see you're paid and driven
into town.

MAMIE

(*speaking as though she were cursing Mary*) That's-fine-with-me . . I
was going to tell you I was quitting.

MARY

Then go!

I, ELIZABETH OTIS, BEING OF SOUND MIND

MAMIE

Don't you want to know why I was quitting?

MARY

No!

MAMIE

(*proudly*) But I don't know as I'll quit right now. Maybe in a week. When I feel like it. When I get married to —

MARY

(*interrupting her*) You'll go now!

MAMIE

Mr. Campbell hired me, not you. I'll go when he says to go, not you. (*Mary abruptly turns and hurries off down left. Mamie calls after her.*) Don't you want to know who I'm marrying? (*Mamie, believing in her triumph, turns to Bet.*) I'll get you for telling on me! You're a little snotnose. I never had no use for you. I got a mind to wallop you now. (*She takes a step toward Bet who steps back.*) Tattletale! Stinking little sneak! (*Mary re-enters from the left, a black-snake whip in her hand, and advances on Mamie. Bet gasps at her mother. Mamie turns and screams, backs away knocking over a pail as Mary strikes at her. She raises the whip again and walks after her as Benjamin enters right, shouting.*)

BENJAMIN

Mary! (*Benjamin runs forward so he is between Mamie and Mary. He snatches the whip from Mary.*) What in hell, Mary! You lost your mind?

MARY

I'm sending her away. Give her a week's pay.

BENJAMIN

Why?

MARY

I don't choose to say.

BENJAMIN

(*to Mamie*) Go on in the house. (*Mamie goes slowly toward up left, pauses.*) What's going on here? Good God Almighty!

MARY

Take those pails in. (*Mamie hesitates, looks from Benjamin to Mary.*)

BENJAMIN

Do as she says. (*Mamie picks up the pails and sullenly goes off up left. Bet retreats down left, watching her mother and father.*)

BENJAMIN

(*looking at the whip*) I never saw you raise your hand to man or animal.

261

MARY

I lost my temper. Do you know about her marrying?

BENJAMIN

Frank. I didn't take it serious.

MARY

You'd better.

BENJAMIN

You'll get nowhere going at it like that! That's how your folks did when you wanted to marry me, so we just ran off and did it. So will they.

MARY

What do you say to do?

BENJAMIN

Talk to Frank. Reason with him. I tell you — the two of you drive into town. Time you was buying groceries for next month, anyhow. I'll hitch up the good buggy and — here's a yellow-back. You can have dinner in town. You talk to him. Reason. You want to get him to back out.

MARY

He was to be a lawyer.

BENJAMIN

(*putting his arms comfortingly about Mary*) You poor sweetheart, you. (*Bet goes quietly off down left, looking back.*) Darling of my life. It breaks my heart to see you looking like that, the sorrow in your face. Damn her — I'd fire her in two minutes if I thought that was how to do it. Heavenly day, you lovely, gentle dove, you precious balm of heaven and the peace of my life. Now, you'll talk Frank out of this. Give me a little smile now, don't you know I can't stand to see you unhappy?

MARY

Go 'way. (*But she is comforted.*)

BENJAMIN

(*taking one hand from Mary to place it on his heart*) Oh the beating of my heart when I hold you in my arms! The trembling in my breast at the touch of you. Give me a smile — don't you know when you look sweet at me I feel the blessed coolness of a holy spring, and I quench my thirst in its beauty.

MARY

You! (*She tries to pull away but now Benjamin puts both arms about her and kisses her with searching hunger, and they sink down on the bench in a fierce embrace. When he lets her go, his face yearning and tender, she pretends to be angry. She puts her sunbonnet straight.*) Don't act such a fool. I'll take Frank to town. Maybe I can talk to him.

BENJAMIN

Come on now, you Balm of Gilead, get yourself ready. (*They walk off up left, Benjamin a little behind, a satisfied smile on his face. He picks up the whip. Mrs. Otis stumbles to a chair — it is the one on which Benjamin's frock coat is draped. She pushes it onto the floor and sits.*)

MRS. OTIS

I'm going to leave this house. I'll go to New York and live with Steven and Nancy. I'll put every bit of the past out of my mind if it kills me. I'll live in New York. I'll do things, I'll meet new people. I'll go to the opera . . (*The lights fade, take on a silvery quality, as Mrs. Otis sits rubbing her forehead with the tips of her fingers. Then, in a ray of silver moonlight, Bet enters. She is holding her china doll, Meg, in her arms.*)

BET

(*singing softly, cradling her doll, looking up at the moon*)
"Flow gently, sweet Afton, among thy green braes,
Flow gently, I'll sing thee a song in thy praise . ."
(*She exits into the shadows, right. A few moments later Mamie enters from down left, stealthily, looking back over her shoulder. She crosses toward the right. Benjamin comes from up right of the stage to intercept her.*)

BENJAMIN

Mamie.

MAMIE

Oh. (*Benjamin puts his arms about her, loosely, his hands moving over her body.*)

MAMIE

Somebody'll see. (*She pretends to back away. Benjamin pulls her close.*)
Where's Bet?

BENJAMIN

Sleeping. And Frank and Mary won't be back for hours. They never got away till five o'clock. (*He embraces her closer, more fiercely.*)

MAMIE

Not here! I guess we won't be doing this much longer.

BENJAMIN

Don't talk. Get along. In the hayloft.
(*He leads her off, left. Mrs. Otis is staring after them, her face bitter. Benjamin, following Mamie, gives her a half-slap, half-caress, on the behind. Mrs. Otis buries her face in her hands and the lights go down on Benjamin and Mamie as they exit down left. Slowly Mrs. Otis takes her hands from her face. And slowly Bet comes from the right, an anguished look on her*)

face, the doll held loosely in her arms. She walks slowly on for a few steps, looks at the doll, then smashes the doll's pretty china head on the ground. Darkness follows, except on Mrs. Otis' face. In the background, above, red and yellow lights swirl and mix and go away. Now we hear the music of a wheezy pump organ, playing the Wedding March. A moment later Frank, in frock coat, and Mamie, in her "best" dress, enter from down right. Behind them come Benjamin and Mary — Mary in a black dress. Bet follows her mother. Mrs. Otis rises, moves left.)

MRS. OTIS

(*turning toward them*) Do you take this man and so forth to love and obey and do you take this woman to cherish until the mercy of death provides an escape for one or both, and is there any honest soul among the several who know absolutely, certainly, and surely that they should not be joined in holy wedlock, is there one who will shout out the terrible truth why these two should not be coupled? Who loves Frank enough to speak and save him the misery of his life to come? Who does?

BET

(*cries out, runs toward her mother*) Mother!

MARY

Sssh. (*Benjamin takes her up in his arms. Frank looks uneasily back at her. Bet beats at her father's face. He carries her toward the right, past Mrs. Otis. Mamie tugs at Frank, motions off left, and they go off, up left, Frank to the end looking unhappily back at Bet.*) Give her to me.

BENJAMIN

Now quit your crying, Posie. What got into you? (*But he hands Bet over to her mother, who takes her only to put her down with a shake.*)

MARY

Now stop crying. I'm ashamed of you. Only babies cry.

MRS. OTIS

Let her cry! Pick her up! Hold her! Don't you know how to give comfort? Oh, what a mother I could have been to myself! (*Benjamin and Mary go off down left. Bet follows, wiping her eyes. The front doorbell rings and a moment later the door is opened and Steven Otis enters. Steven is a well-preserved man in his fifties, tall, with a touch of gray in his plentiful hair. He is wearing a gray — not flannel — summer suit, a blue shirt and bow tie and is hatless. He is carrying two suitcases.*)

STEVEN

(*to his mother, Mrs. Otis*) We're here! (*Turning back to his wife, Nancy, who is behind him and whom we have not yet seen, he speaks with some asperity.*) Well, hurry it up, darling! All the flies in town are getting in ahead of you.

NANCY

(*enters wearing a smart dress and hat, carrying a makeup box*) I told you to take one of my tranquilizers. (*Meanwhile Mrs. Otis has slowly switched her attention from her memories to the here and now and has absorbed the fact of Steven's presence. She rises to her feet. Steven puts down his suitcases and goes to her.*)

MRS. OTIS

(*her face working — she is having a hard time controlling her tears*) Son! (*She puts out her arms to her son. They embrace, a short awkward hug, during which they peck a kiss. Then their arms drop and Steven steps back, grinning with a self-conscious cheeriness at his mother.*) You got here too soon! I'm so glad.

STEVEN

We caught an earlier plane.

MRS. OTIS

Nancy! (*Nancy steps forward with a smile, her hand outstretched. But Mrs. Otis puts her arms out and Nancy accepts her embrace, her makeup kit still in her hand. They kiss warmly.*) I'll have to sit down and get used to this. (*But for a moment the three stand with self-conscious amiability. Mrs. Otis is absorbing the two of them with her eyes. Nancy finds herself unexpectedly touched and pleased to see her mother-in-law. Steven's grin masks a self-conscious wariness.*)

STEVEN

How are you?

MRS. OTIS

Oh, I'm all right. You look *thin*. You both do.

NANCY

Thank you.

STEVEN

Last time you thought I was overweight.

MRS. OTIS

Never mind. We'll feed you up. I don't think you've been getting enough sleep.

STEVEN

Maybe not. It's good to see you.

MRS. OTIS

What are we all standing up for? Put those things anywhere.

STEVEN

(*crossing to the nearby chair and picking up a gingham dress and a sun-bonnet*) What's this?

MRS. OTIS

Horrible, gingham dresses. Nancy — they thought they were going to get you and me into those — with sunbonnets! For the Centennial. (*She sits, indicates the hassock to Nancy.*) I want to hear all about everything. How are the children?

STEVEN

(*Who has found the frock coat and top hat. He puts the top hat on, puts the dresses down, and holds up the frock coat.*) How about this? Grand-pa's?

NANCY

(*sitting*) They're both just fine. Jimbo was on the Dean's list again.

MRS. OTIS

(*to Steven, bristling*) It's not his but he wore one like it. What's wrong with it?

STEVEN

I like it. (*Steven, amused, takes the frock coat, dresses, and sunbonnets to an upstage chair, drapes them over it. He adjusts the stovepipe hat to a jaunty angle.*)

NANCY

Steven, how silly. Take it off.

MRS. OTIS

(*forgetting she has asked before*) How are the children? How could you leave them?

NANCY

Steven, suppose *you* tell her about Jimbo.

STEVEN

(*crossing to his mother*) He's on a six-week sailing cruise. Fifty-foot schooner. San Salvador and other points Columbus touched.

MRS. OTIS

Oh, dear.

NANCY

I felt the same way. But through a friend in Washington, I've had the Coast Guard alerted to keep an eye — or the Navy, or whoever it is that watches over silly people who do things like that.

STEVEN

Dirty trick. You could have let him be on his own, for once.

I, ELIZABETH OTIS, BEING OF SOUND MIND

NANCY

(*to Mrs. Otis*) At least it's better than being in Mississippi for the summer — that was his first idea. Patricia's off to France with a group. She'll bicycle through the chateau country and Brittany, end up in Paris.

STEVEN

Have you got NATO checking on her? By special arrangement with de Gaulle?

MRS. OTIS

Isn't she a little young?

NANCY

I don't think so. She's not one to make a fool of herself over boys — or men.

STEVEN

You don't know her, for heaven's sake. She's not the cool, clever reflection of you that you think she is.

MRS. OTIS

Mothers know best. They have to make the decisions about children.

STEVEN

Like chickens — once the egg's fertilized, the hen does the rest. Roosters aren't even good to eat — unless they've been caponized.

MRS. OTIS

(*a little puzzled — then to Steven*) We're having capon for dinner . . Now Steven, don't be cross. You've been drinking too much coffee. Come here, son. (*Steven obediently crosses to his mother.*) Take that hat off. (*He obeys. Mrs. Otis takes his wrist, gives him a playful shake.*) You're not smoking cigarettes again?

STEVEN

No. (*to Nancy*) Suppose we go up and wash?

MRS. OTIS

Why don't you go first? (*to Nancy*) There's only one bathroom, as perhaps you remember. (*to Steven*) Nancy and I will keep each other company. (*Steven is silent. He looks at Nancy, who is amused at his unease.*)

STEVEN

All right. (*He goes over to pick up the suitcases, crosses toward the stairs up right, the women watching him. He hesitates, turns back.*) I don't want to miss anything.

NANCY

(*with mock humility*) May I tell her about my new job? (*Steven glares at her.*)

267

MRS. OTIS

What are you two — what new job?

STEVEN

Nancy's been made a vice president.

MRS. OTIS

How wonderful! Congratulations! (*to Steven*) Didn't they make you a vice president too?

STEVEN

(*annoyed*) It's a different company! One has nothing to do with the other! (*Steven exits, up right. They both watch until he is out of sight.*)

MRS. OTIS

So that's why he's cross.

NANCY

I'm afraid that's ordinary, everyday Steven.

MRS. OTIS

(*after a quick look at Nancy, deciding to change the subject*) You must be extra happy about your new job.

NANCY

(*with a warm, happy smile*) Oh, yes!

MRS. OTIS

You must be very good at it. Like Negroes, a woman has to be twice as good to get equal recognition.

NANCY

There *was* a man in the running. The executive VP, Mr. Hertzbaum, made the decision. He'd asked us both for plans to reorganize the buying services. (*Nancy sparkles as she tells the story.*) Well. Mr. Johansen, the *man* who was after the job, is a big genial Norwegian — oh — six feet three — but he has a high, squeaky voice. He's really a very good merchandiser, but he's *terrified* of Hertzie. I think he's embarrassed because he's so big and Hertzie's such a tiny man. Well. There's been gossip going around that Johansen's a fruit — you know, a sissy — so when he gets in to see Hertzie to present his plan, he wants to make clear he's a *he-man*, so he starts showing him pictures of fish he'd caught up in Maine, or somewhere.

MRS. OTIS

Pictures of fish?

NANCY

Men do that. Well, Hertzie looked at them, then at Johansen, and said, "Mr. Johansen, I don't even like gefüllte fish." (*Nancy laughs, expects Mrs. Otis to, but she doesn't so Nancy goes on.*) Anyhow — Johansen

blushed. He blushes like a girl, knows he does, too, and then he giggles —
he has a nervous, high giggle —

MRS. OTIS

Mercy!

NANCY

You can imagine what a mess he made of his presentation after that!

MRS. OTIS

How did you know? Were you there?

NANCY

Oh, no. Maude, Hertzie's secretary, was there and she tells me everything.
I made friends with her in the very beginning. So, when I came in I felt
pretty sure of myself — and I guess I did a good job.

MRS. OTIS

I'm sure you did. Is that all that's wrong between you and Steven?

NANCY

(*frowns, gives Mrs. Otis a quick glance*) He's — not well.

MRS. OTIS

(*alarmed*) His heart?

NANCY

His mind!

MRS. OTIS

I'm relieved.

NANCY

Mother Otis! It's terrible! Now don't joke. You've got to do something.
He won't listen to me.

MRS. OTIS

He's your husband.

NANCY

He was your son first.

MRS. OTIS

I did what I could while I had him. Now he's yours.

NANCY

Did you know then that he was mentally disturbed?

MRS. OTIS

Nonsense. It's the nature of men to be wild. They've got a force in them
that has to be tamed.

NANCY

I don't fancy myself as a lion tamer, thank you.

MRS. OTIS

It's more like breaking a horse — use a curb bit and keep an apple handy. Steven toed the line while I had him.

NANCY

It made him hate you.

MRS. OTIS

Steven said that?

NANCY

I thought you knew . . I'm so sorry.

MRS. OTIS

I guess I didn't want to know. But then, I hated my father. I thought I did.

NANCY

The point is, he needs help.

MRS. OTIS

Explain that.

NANCY

A psychiatrist. (*Mrs. Otis is silent.*) Or better — if you could persuade him to go into an institution — (*Startled, Mrs. Otis gives Nancy a sharp look.*) An open one, of course.

MRS. OTIS

How silly!

NANCY

He's potentially paranoic!

MRS. OTIS

Peculiarity runs in the family. Perhaps I should have been put away, too.

NANCY

You! Why, you're the sanest, hardest-headed woman I know. You take care of all your business —

MRS. OTIS

(*interrupting*) What would be the point of this — institution? Since you aren't suggesting he be locked up the rest of his life.

NANCY

They delve into the past. Steven had an unhappy childhood, and —

MRS. OTIS

Who didn't?

NANCY

Please listen. By going into the past they would make it possible for Steven to understand himself, and so get free of these compulsions.

MRS. OTIS

You didn't say anything about compulsions.

I, ELIZABETH OTIS, BEING OF SOUND MIND

NANCY

I could talk for hours —

MRS. OTIS

I'm sure you could, but I reject your premise.

NANCY

But Mother Otis —

MRS. OTIS

(*rising in indignation, turning away from Nancy*) As though human beings could be pulled apart like paper dolls and remade, if only teacher will supply the paste!

NANCY

You're not taking the problem seriously!

MRS. OTIS

I don't take anyone's opinions very seriously. I'm used to looking for the facts.

NANCY

(*rising, following Mrs. Otis*) Facts! What do you call turning up at the Country Club formal in a sports jacket?

MRS. OTIS

(*dryly*) How dreadful.

NANCY

It's his antisocial compulsion! And that's just one of a hundred "facts." One night when we were entertaining *very important* business associates of mine, he insisted he had to drive downtown to get the correct wine for the fish — and he didn't come back till the next night! And not just things designed to hurt *me*! He took over a Scout troop for an afternoon —

MRS. OTIS

Surely that was a good thing.

NANCY

It was? They collected water snakes in the swamp and put them in the Club swimming pool! The only reason we weren't dropped from the Club was that so many of the boys had important parents!

MRS. OTIS

(*Mrs. Otis is laughing over the episode; she represses her mirth.*) Where did you say you grew up?

NANCY

Montclair, New Jersey. What's that got to do with it?

MRS. OTIS

We're tougher in Boue City.

271

NANCY

Or less civilized? Do you consider police action amusing?

MRS. OTIS

(*sobered, indeed*) Police?

NANCY

Twenty times I've had to talk and bribe and cajole the police to keep him out of jail for some of his happy inspirations.

MRS. OTIS

Oh, dear!

NANCY

He had an idea he'd revive dueling as a way to settle arguments — he challenged the head of the American Legion to fight a duel with Army forty-fives, and I got there with the police just in time.

MRS. OTIS

No!

NANCY

Yes. And the pack of hounds he kept — sending clear to Arkansas for them, and testing their voices as though they were opera singers! Those hounds could be heard clear down to the railroad station! When the town made him get rid of them — he started breeding Irish wolfhounds. Did you ever see an Irish wolfhound?

MRS. OTIS

No.

NANCY

They're the size of ponies, and his favorite, he called Shaughnessy, he liked to have in the house. It was a friendly dog and wagged his tail a good deal. With every wag he could sweep a coffee table clear of *objets d'art*.

MRS. OTIS

Steven must have had something in mind —

NANCY

Destruction! He's an anarchist!

MRS. OTIS

But he never really destroyed anything.

NANCY

He cracked up a racing car at Watkins Glen!

MRS. OTIS

No, no!

NANCY

He'd bought a Lotus and competed locally — unfortunately he usually won. Got delusions of grandeur and went on to Watkins Glen. Demolished the Lotus — it turned over and burned, but Steven was thrown clear — and walked away. If his racing wasn't suicidal — a death wish — what was it? That's why I say paranoic! And women — I grant you sex is a disease of advertising men, their promiscuity is like a nervous tic, but at least I can demand discretion. Listen to *this* —

MRS. OTIS

Stop! I don't like tattletales. If you want to tell me, you'll tell me in front of Steven! Please go upstairs, now. I've had enough. Go.

NANCY

(*picking up her vanity case*) You simply aren't living in the modern world. (*She crosses to up right, exits.*)

MRS. OTIS

Thank goodness! (*Mrs. Otis watches Nancy out of sight, sits a moment, then rises with some difficulty, straightens herself, and walks about, with increasing nervousness. Then she crosses to up right and calls.*) Steven! Steven! Come down! (*Young Steven, at the age of thirteen, comes down the stairs. He is wearing knickerbockers, coatless, but with a tie. He is apprehensive, his face a stolid mask.*) What were you doing upstairs?

YOUNG STEVEN

Nothing.

MRS. OTIS

Have you thought over what I told you? (*Young Steven looks desperately about, then nods.*) About ending in an asylum? (*He hangs his head.*) Now I want to know where you got those dirty pictures. (*He doesn't answer, digs his toe at the floor.*) You want a whipping? (*He shakes his head. From down right George Otis, Mrs. Otis' husband as he was in his forties, comes forward. He has a youthful bounce to his walk, a lively, nervous air about him. He is carrying a newspaper.*)

GEORGE

Hello, son! (*He crosses to Mrs. Otis and pecks her on the cheek, looks at her, looks at Young Steven, then speaks.*) You're all as quiet as mice. What's the matter?

MRS. OTIS

Steven — go into the kitchen. I want to talk to your father.

GEORGE

(*As Young Steven passes him on his way up right George slaps him affectionately on the shoulder.*) Cheer up. The Giants won. (*Young Steven gives his father the ghost of a smile — more anguish than smile — and exits. George walks to a chair, pulls it to a new position, and sits, opening the*

273

paper.) I'm tuckered out. Been running from morning to night. (*He opens the paper*.) I forgot to pick up that loaf of bread.

MRS. OTIS

Put the paper away, please. I want your attention. (*George lowers it*.)

GEORGE

Now suppose your face should freeze looking like that? There's no tax on a smile.

MRS. OTIS

(*paying no attention*) When I made Steven's bed this morning — I found a spot, a nasty spot, on the sheet. (*George makes business of turning a page of the paper, folding it, slapping it even, etc., staring at it, pretending to read*.) Under his bed was a copy of the *Ladies' Home Journal*!

GEORGE

Shouldn't think he'd find much to read in there.

MRS. OTIS

Don't pretend. You know. I've seen you going through it, looking at the corset ads, pretending you weren't!

GEORGE

I never! Well, I never did, particularly. (*shouting to cover his embarrassment, putting paper down*) What you trying to make out of that? You don't want him to see it, cancel your subscription!

MRS. OTIS

(*without raising her voice*) I want you to talk to him.

GEORGE

Sure I'll talk to him. But not about that. No, sir. I'm not making a fool of myself.

MRS. OTIS

There's worse. I knew that with that smoke there must be fire. I searched his things. There in a bottom drawer, underneath his old teddy bear and baseball mitt I found pictures of naked women.

GEORGE

I don't believe it. Let me see them.

MRS. OTIS

(*with a dry laugh*) I certainly will not. Anyhow, I burned them. *Now* will you talk to him? I want to know where he got them and he won't tell me.

GEORGE

Then he won't tell me!

MRS. OTIS

You can frighten him into it.

GEORGE

How?

MRS. OTIS

(*exasperated*) Tell him the danger of self-abuse! That it'll give him softening of the brain!

GEORGE

(*after a pause*) Who knows if it does? I don't believe it.

MRS. OTIS

How can you say that?

GEORGE

(*Uncomfortable, but stubborn, not daring to look at his wife, but doggedly resisting. He rises, crosses away from her.*) Because it don't! That's why! I say it don't — not necessarily!

MRS. OTIS

(*after a sharp, speculative look at George*) I see. Well, perhaps it doesn't in a grown man, but —

GEORGE

(*shouting*) You make me sick and tired!

MRS. OTIS

(*When George shouts she becomes more quiet.*) You're his father. What do you want for your son?

GEORGE

(*crossing to face Mrs. Otis*) Would you rather he got mixed up with bad girls? I don't want *that*! You think it's easy to be a boy? It's so doggone unfair! You women with your silk stockings and smell of talcum and dresses that show your arms and chests — to try and drive boys crazy and then we get blamed! It's not fair! I'd rather die than go through being young again!

MRS. OTIS

I should have known I couldn't count on you, but I never give up hope. All right. You get out. Go for a walk. First send Steven in to me. If you're hungry, there's food on the stove. Feed yourself. Go on.

GEORGE

(*crushing the paper in his hands*) I'd like to go on and on and never come back! (*He rushes off up right toward the kitchen.*) Never! Never! (*Mrs. Otis puts her head in her hands. A moment later Young Steven enters from up right slowly, in despair.*)

MRS. OTIS

(*looking up, turning toward Young Steven*) Come here. (*He comes closer to her.*) Sit there. (*She points to the hassock. Young Steven sits, head*

275

down, abject, on the hassock. Mrs. Otis speaks gently.) I'm sorry for you, Steven. (*He looks up, a tiny hope in his face.*) I want to help you. Do you realize how much we love you? (*He bobs his head "yes," and looks down.*) I want you to grow up to be a fine, strong, good man. (*He is silent, waiting for his doom.*) Now I want the name of the person who gave you those pictures. (*Young Steven shakes his head.*) Was it a man? (*He shakes his head again.*) A boy? (*He nods.*) Then that poor boy has to be helped, too. I must tell his parents, so they can help him in time, because if we don't, do you know what will happen to him? (*no response from Young Steven*) He'll get softening of the brain, and be put away in an insane asylum, just as you might, if I didn't stop this. Do you know what it's like in an asylum? Think of your friend, his mind gone, a gibbering idiot, not able to even dress himself, or go to the bathroom, filthy, alone, looked at with contempt by everyone, a despicable, lost, lonely creature, barely able to eat — like a pig — mumbling meaningless sounds, forgotten, lost? (*Young Steven buries his head in his hands. Mrs. Otis goes to him, takes his face, and forces him to look up.*) Look at me. I shall have to whip you until you tell me. Go get the whip. (*With leaden limbs Young Steven rises, stumbles into the shadows down right. Mrs. Otis follows him, and a moment later we see her hand swinging an imaginary whip, lashing at Young Steven's legs, each lash punctuated by a stifled sob from Young Steven, though we do not see him.*)

STEVEN

(*enters from up right*) Nancy'll be down in a minute. (*Mrs. Otis continues the lashing movement, still lost in her memory, then turns, dazed to Steven.*)

MRS. OTIS

Where's your father?

STEVEN

Mother!

MRS. OTIS

(*painfully walking into the room*) No, he's not here. He's — dead. I got lost thinking. Time gets confused, some days. Straighten your tie.

STEVEN

(*laughing, touching his tie*) You never change. (*Mrs. Otis walks to the sofa and sits.*) Are you all right?

MRS. OTIS

(*nods*) I don't exactly get livelier as I get older. Come and sit here. (*She indicates the hassock.*)

STEVEN

The hell seat? That's how I used to think of it. If you don't mind I'll stretch my legs. (*He walks to the French door, left, opens it.*) We could do with some air. The house has a stuffy smell. (*Mrs. Otis is watching him, absorbing him.*) Ever notice that old houses have their own particular smell? I wonder why. Damp in the cellar? What's been cooked over the years? Strange how much feeling you get out of a smell. Like grass. You just had the lawn cut, didn't you?

MRS. OTIS

Yes.

STEVEN

You should have waited for me. How I used to hate mowing the lawn.

MRS. OTIS

It was hard to make you. It took all week to drive you to it. By the time you finished, the first part was tall again. I was so ashamed. It would have looked better if I'd pastured a cow.

STEVEN

(*abruptly, still looking out*) Why didn't you ever let me have a dog?

MRS. OTIS

Because I knew I'd end up taking care of it. (*a moment's pause, then*) Do you like your work?

STEVEN

(*turning sharply from the door, suspicious*) Why?

MRS. OTIS

Is that such a strange question?

STEVEN

Does anybody like their work?

MRS. OTIS

I'd have liked anything better than keeping house.

STEVEN

Modern woman.

MRS. OTIS

Please sit down. (*She taps the hassock again. Steven grins, shrugs, and crosses to the hassock, sits.*) Tell me about your job.

STEVEN

You see magazines — newspapers — TV. You see ads. Ever wonder how they get there?

MRS. OTIS

They're mostly so irritating.

277

STEVEN

(*with quickened interest*) Well, good for you. Anyhow, I help to put them there.

MRS. OTIS

You write them?

STEVEN

No. I'm the catalyst, the conduit, the shining ribbon of road over which speeds the impulses of the man who has things to sell and the money to pay for ads. I am not the creator, I am the — ah — marriage broker.

MRS. OTIS

(*She doesn't understand this, so changes direction.*) What is your day like in the office? Do you have a secretary?

STEVEN

She can't spell.

MRS. OTIS

How does she dress? (*Steven shrugs.*) Is she a blonde or a brunette?

STEVEN

(*warily*) Blonde.

MRS. OTIS

Blue eyes? Brown?

STEVEN

I never noticed. One blue, one brown.

MRS. OTIS

Do you talk to her?

STEVEN

When you're with a person eight hours a day — !

MRS. OTIS

More hours than you spend with Nancy.

STEVEN

Not really. Nancy has insomnia and likes me to share it.

MRS. OTIS

Do you have twin beds?

STEVEN

(*rising, strolling right*) I think I'd better take the fifth.

MRS. OTIS

Now where are you going?

STEVEN

My legs got cramped sitting in the plane.

MRS. OTIS

We can't talk when you roam about and I want to *talk*. I get to see you precious little enough and I mean to *enjoy* it. I don't care how cramped your legs, you can suffer a little and sit by me. (*Nancy enters from up right with a lighted cigarette.*) Oh, fiddlesticks.

STEVEN

(*to Nancy*) That was fast.

NANCY

(*smiles vaguely at Steven, crosses, smiles at Mrs. Otis and goes to the French door*) My bad habit. I know you don't like it, Mother Otis. I'll stand here so the smoke will go out. (*Steven watches her, waiting. Mrs. Otis looks from Steven to Nancy.*) What a lovely day.

STEVEN

(*a stilted voice*) Yeah — I hope it's as good tomorrow.

NANCY

For the Centennial?

STEVEN

Yeah.

NANCY

(*equally stilted*) Oh, I hope so.

MRS. OTIS

What's going on between you?

STEVEN

Nothing.

NANCY

(*a purposeful hint in her voice*) Steven —

STEVEN

It's up to you.

NANCY

Well, I'm going on to California and Steven's going back to New York.

MRS. OTIS

Business?

STEVEN

Pleasure.

MRS. OTIS

What pleasure?

STEVEN

(*after a pause*) We're taking separate vacations.

NANCY

Steven!

STEVEN

Well, aren't we?

279

MRS. OTIS

Why? (*silence*) Is one of you interested in someone else?

STEVEN

Nancy likes California — I hate it.

MRS. OTIS

You didn't answer me.

NANCY

(*to Steven*) Coward! (*to Mrs. Otis*) We've decided to live separately.

MRS. OTIS

(*to Steven*) Your secretary.

STEVEN

It is not! Nancy's fed up with me, that's all.

NANCY

At least be honest! I offered to stay together. You wouldn't meet my terms!

STEVEN

(*outraged*) Generous-hearted girl! I sure wouldn't and I won't!

NANCY

All I asked was that he put himself under psychiatric care.

STEVEN

She likes steak well done, I like it rare. I like sports cars, she likes Cadillacs — so I have to go to a psychiatrist! (*to Nancy*) You never yielded on one facet of your preferences, of your stiff little middle-class rigidities. I don't like one damn thing you believe in!

NANCY

Go on, tell your mother more. Reveal yourself. Then let her be the judge.

STEVEN

She's not my judge, anymore! You and I have grown apart, that's all, so let's stop the shouting and — and —

MRS. OTIS

Of course you've grown apart. Marriage is a growing apart. It would be intolerable to continue the suffocating closeness of first love.

STEVEN

You and dad were apart — but were you ever close?

MRS. OTIS

Do you think you invented passion? Do you think I was always old? Or that you won't be like I am? Of course you grow up bursting with a hundred desires as untamed as wild horses. Well, growing up is penning them in, breaking them to harness. I thought by now you'd be controlled by your common sense!

STEVEN

Do you want me to go to a psychiatrist?

MRS. OTIS

Don't put it on me! I don't know the facts!

STEVEN

Why, you don't even trust doctors!

MRS. OTIS

(*abruptly*) What about the children? Do they know?

NANCY

No.

STEVEN

I told Jimbo.

NANCY

Cheating again!

STEVEN

I didn't intend to. The day I spent with him working on the boat — it just came out. It seemed right to tell him.

NANCY

Your story. With all your hatred.

STEVEN

No. And don't make a big thing of it.

NANCY

How did you explain it?

STEVEN

As I said now — we'd grown apart. You know, you bug him. You'd better lay off him. I tried to explain it was your nature to be bossy —

NANCY

I shall write him my side! And I think I shall write Pat!

STEVEN

Don't you dare! I'll wring your neck if you try that! Spoiling her summer! What I'll do is fly over there and see her!

NANCY

You haven't got the money! (*Steven is silent—he hasn't.*) He's been fired from his job!

MRS. OTIS

Oh, Steven!

STEVEN

I quit. (*Steven crosses to the French door, stares out.*)

NANCY

In the most obnoxious way!

MRS. OTIS

You've got another job in sight?

NANCY

No, he hasn't!

MRS. OTIS

I asked Steven!

STEVEN

Not exactly. Doesn't worry me. I won't starve.

NANCY

Tell your mother the way you quit! (*Steven gloomily shrugs.*) Mr. Foresman called him in to ask Steven to take a slight reduction because they'd lost an account, and I know he did it nicely, because we've had Mr. Foresman to dinner several times, and he's a delightful, witty —

STEVEN

Prick!

NANCY

Steven bellowed! Banged the desk — they had to call three executives to drag him out! And I know, because Mr. Foresman told me!

STEVEN

Ahha! Something going there between you and T. F.?

NANCY

You would think that! You can't get your mind off sex!

STEVEN

Perhaps you're not really so remote and mannered and formal and self-conscious and cool? But T. F.'s not the man to rape your virginal psyche.

MRS. OTIS

Steven Otis! I've never heard such language — not even from your grand-father.

NANCY

Now you're getting *facts*, Mother Otis.

STEVEN

Been undercutting me?

NANCY

The truth!

STEVEN

Want me to give her an earful about you?

NANCY

Fantasies out of a drunken haze?

STEVEN

Come off it! Gin is mother's milk to you.

NANCY

Never drunk! Never!

STEVEN

Not human enough.

NANCY

Not animal!

STEVEN

Vegetable! A cold fig-leaf, covering up every naked impulse that has life in it!

MRS. OTIS

(*rising, her voice strong and hoarse*) No! I don't have to endure this! You two noisy children, I'd like to knock your heads together! To do this to me, at this time! Oh, if I could play God I would put you in a trouble so real and simple and physical that stark fear would sweep away everything. Put you in a blizzard on the empty prairie!

STEVEN

(*alarmed*) Mother!

MRS. OTIS

(*seizes Steven's arm, shakes at him*) You sit down! There will be five minutes of calm! And I don't want to hear a word from either of you! (*She pushes Steven down on the hassock. Crossing toward the French door, she recites in a strong voice.*)

"Whet the bright steel
Sons of the white dragon!"

(*Nancy and Steven look at Mrs. Otis, startled. She is looking off left.*)

BENJAMIN

(*from offstage up left*)

"Daughter of Hengist!
The steel glimmers not for the carving of the banquet."

MRS. OTIS

(*walking toward them*)

"It is hard, broad, and sharply pointed;
Whet the steel, the raven croaks!"

BENJAMIN

"Light the torch, Zernback is yelling!

(*Benjamin swings about, Bet in his arms, puts her down, standing on the bench. Bet cries out in excitement.*)

Whet the steel, sons of the Dragon!"

MRS. OTIS

"Whet the steel, sons of the Dragon!"

283

BENJAMIN

"Kindle the torch, daughter of Hengist!"

(*Benjamin catches Bet up into his arms, kissing her on the neck; Bet squeals with delight as he carries her off down left. A moment later Benjamin returns.*)

STEVEN

Mother. Are you all right?

MRS. OTIS

(*turning back to Steven*) Steven — I want you to bring that coat over here. I want you to try it on. (*She points to the chair, left, where the frock coat is draped. Steven looks helplessly at Nancy, who shrugs and then nods. Steven goes slowly over to the chair, looks back at his mother, slowly takes off his coat, and puts on the frock coat.*) Stand straight. You look so silly in a bow tie. I never could stand one on Mr. Truman, either. Walk about. Over here. (*Steven hesitates, takes the top hat and puts it on jauntily, walks past Nancy, who is watching with amusement, to the French door and turns to his mother, his back to the door. Benjamin crosses to Steven and stands with his back to Steven's back, on the other side of the French door.*) You're about the same height. He was broader.

NANCY

Who?

MRS. OTIS

My father — Steven's grandfather.

STEVEN

(*crossing right, back to the library table*) A wild old sinner. I remember him with egg on his vest, food caught in his beard — (*Benjamin goes off up left.*)

MRS. OTIS

He was a strong and brilliant man! He established the first public library in the county.

STEVEN

I never heard anybody curse like he could. Never repeated himself.

MRS. OTIS

(*to Nancy*) He had a feeling for poetry! He knew whole poems by heart . . How many men today know poems by heart?

NANCY

Very few. Though I don't see what that has to do with anything.

MRS. OTIS

Nothing! And perhaps a good deal. Never mind. We are not going to have

284

another word about you two and your childish "separation." Whoever thinks that children are a comfort! I'll tell you what they are — children are a mortal illness! (*Steven starts to take the coat off, but stops as Mrs. Otis goes on.*) You know you're going to wear that for your part in the pageant. You're in the prologue.

STEVEN

(*amazed*) Are you joking?

MRS. OTIS

Didn't I write you?

STEVEN

About the pageant, yes — but —

MRS. OTIS

I promised you'd be in it.

STEVEN

You can't promise for me!

MRS. OTIS

I did! To honor me they're bringing the parade past this house. Odd — I can't quite get used to it — this family to be regarded as eminently respectable — but I mean to enjoy it for one happy day and you are not going to spoil it for me! The Mayor and the Lieutenant Governor will be right on our front porch. And Steven. You're in the pageant, as I promised.

STEVEN

But I don't know the part! (*The front doorbell rings. Nancy looks right, then at Mrs. Otis.*)

MRS. OTIS

Nancy, as for you and Steven — you'll be over this spat in a few days so I'm dismissing it from my mind before I get a headache. (*Nancy and Steven look at each other in a mutual feeling of helplessness and indecision. The bell is rung again.*)

NANCY

Someone's at the door.

MRS. OTIS

(*to Nancy*) Ask them in.

NANCY

(*crossing down right toward the door*) Please come in.

HOLLAWAY

(*entering*) You're Mrs. Steven Otis! Hello!

NANCY

(*uncertainly*) Hello.

285

MRS. OTIS

Now, Mr. Hollaway, I've no time for you. My son and his wife are here and I treasure every moment —

HOLLAWAY

I knew they were. The paper checks the airport for arrivals! (*crossing to Steven, who once more is starting to take off the coat and has one arm partly out*) No, no, put that back on! (*He helps the unwilling Steven back into the sleeve he has taken off.*) That's great on you! Too bad you haven't a beard but we'll fix that up.

STEVEN

You haven't.

HOLLAWAY

Oh, I'm an Indian. Look, I want an interview and a rehearsal. But the rehearsal first. Oh, it's a break you came early. Let's go through it once, right now! (*Hollaway takes two scripts from his inner pocket, sorts them over, hands one to Steven.*)

STEVEN

(*harshly*) What's this all about?

HOLLAWAY

(*pacing about with excited restlessness*) I'll give you a quick fill-in. First let me tell you about the parade. We're bringing it right past your front porch. You and your wife and your mother will review it from there — with the Mayor and the Lieutenant Governor, beauty contest winners and movie stars! After the united twenty Northern Iowa high school bands reach the front porch, they will enfilade — if that's what I mean — and the united high school choruses will fill in behind them. The three drum majorettes will put on an act, followed by dead silence. Then bands, choruses, led by the three drum majorettes will sing — it's dedicated to your mother. Like this — (*sings*)

> "Lizbeth Otis — from Iowa!
> We salute thee with this band,
> Because you tamed the land.
> You came to Iowa — Iowa!
> That's why the tall corn grows!"

(*He throws his hand high on the last line, pauses breathless for the reaction. His small audience is stunned.*)

MRS. OTIS

Did you write that?

HOLLAWAY

I guess I did. Not the music, of course.

I, ELIZABETH OTIS, BEING OF SOUND MIND

MRS. OTIS

Thank you.

HOLLAWAY

So — you see. Now on to the pageant. (*hands part to Steven*) Ready, Mr. Otis? (*Steven shrugs in resignation.*) Just read it. I'll do the stage directions. (*Hollaway looks about, decides on the top of the steps up right, crosses there, and continues.*) "Darkness. Then gradually a spotlight comes up on the figure of an Indian in warpaint holding a tomahawk and wearing the ceremonial bonnet." That's me. I speak first. (*with a slow guttural*) "Who is this white man that comes into our hunting grounds?" Then another light will come up on your tanned — I hope you'll agree to a false beard — tanned face, a strong face, like your father's, Mrs. Otis. Well — it's your face, Mr. Otis. You are in this frock coat and you have an axe over your left shoulder and a rifle under your arm. Now you speak. Up here with me.

STEVEN

(*Helplessly snared, Steven steps to the upper level. He reads, flatly.*) "I am English, Scotch, Dutch, German, Irish, Scandinavian. I am the bursting forth of the strength of Europe. I am the son of the Vikings and the Vandals. I bring progress."

HOLLAWAY

Of course you'll get more feeling in it when you're familiar with it. (*reverts to his Indian guttural*) "You are my enemy, for I believe in the changeless life. I am the hunter! The free man for whose pleasure and need this land of Iowa was created by the Great Spirit!" Now try to dominate me.

STEVEN

(*a bit stronger than before*) "The prairies shall be put to plough and this wave of the turning furrow shall be a wave that sweeps on across the plains and the corn shall grow and no longer the buffalo shall roam these empty wastes . . (*Mrs. Otis is bored. Her eyes are closing. We hear a fiddle playing the opening phrases of the "Arkansas Traveler" over and over in distorted variations as Frank, playing the fiddle, Bet, Benjamin, and Mary dance on from up left, in a square-dance pattern. Mrs. Otis rises and crosses to them, dancing around them. Meanwhile Steven continues, his voice fainter.*) From the rising to the setting sun the glory of a new civilization under God shall grow, and the waves of our great democracy shall wash the shores of the world."

HOLLAWAY

"I bow to the great white father as my friend and protector and we shall —"

(*Nancy has crossed to the chair where Mrs. Otis was sitting, still pin-pointed with a spot.*)

NANCY

Steven. She's asleep! (*Hollaway breaks off. He and Steven look and the lights dim rapidly out, the music fading a moment after. Darkness.*)

END OF ACT ONE

ACT TWO

The time is the afternoon of the same day. The place is the same as Act One, but the gingham dresses, frock coat, and top hat are gone. At rise, Mrs. Otis is lying on the sofa, her eyes closed. Steven enters, carrying his suitcase. He stops center. A light comes up on him. The effect is hazy.

STEVEN

I'm going back to New York.

MRS. OTIS

(*not opening her eyes*) Steven! You can't. Please, son, please, don't go.

STEVEN

(*in an even voice*) I'm sick of you. You're old and silly and I waste my time out here.

MRS. OTIS

I love you, son — doesn't that count?

STEVEN

Who cares? I've got so many interesting things to do back East.

MRS. OTIS

Wait over one day — please, son! You owe me that.

STEVEN

I didn't *ask* to be born.

MRS. OTIS

I nursed you.

STEVEN

Don't be disgusting. (*Steven leaves up left. The light that was on him goes out.*)

MRS. OTIS

(*her eyes still closed*) Steven, please come back. Steven! (*She starts to cry, softly mumbling over and over, "Steven, Steven." Shadows go across the room, then George enters from up right. He is younger than in Act*

288

I, ELIZABETH OTIS, BEING OF SOUND MIND

One, has a Grover Cleveland mustache, and is wearing a nightshirt. He is carrying a kerosene lamp. George speaks as he crosses.)

GEORGE

(in a loud, angry voice) I can't be away for two days but you make a mess! I told you the catch on that cellar window was loose and you was to check on it! You never did, did you? Blew open and the pipes froze. I been three hours trying to thaw 'em out! What were you doing? Playing the piano? Too scared of mice to go down cellar? Or just sitting thinking about yourself? You're so doggoned busy with yourself you don't care what trouble you make for me. You don't care for anybody but yourself — well I don't care about you! *(He turns and strides angrily off down left into the shadows. Steven enters up left, coatless and tieless, his sleeves rolled up and his hair disheveled. He is waving a black-snake whip. Mrs. Otis moans, her eyes still closed.)*

STEVEN

I finished mowing your old lawn, and look at what I found in the grass! Remember how you tried to make me cry? Now I've got the upper hand. I don't think I'll ever write to you again, and then you'll be all alone. Alone, alone, alone! *(He laughs, harshly, turns and exits, up right. The lights waver, flicker, turn to a greenish hue. Mrs. Cooms, in the dress of Act One, apron and all, hurries on from up right. She crosses left.)*

MRS. OTIS

Where are you going?

MRS. COOMS

Where do you think I'm going? Same place you're supposed to be at.

MRS. OTIS

I don't know! Please tell me!

MRS. COOMS

(pausing a moment) Your own mother, you old fool!

MRS. OTIS

Mother?

MRS. COOMS

She's laid out in her coffin waiting for you. Can't bury her, she says, till you come. It's nothing to me. *I* say, nail up the coffin. *I'm* not waiting. *(Mrs. Cooms exits, down right into the shadows. The stage darkens, then lightens, the dimming and lighting in the rhythm of a pulse — one pulse down, one beat up, back and forth, darkening a little more each time.)*

MRS. OTIS

(murmuring in her sleep) Mother. Mother. *(The lights go back to normal,*

as Steven, his tie on, his coat on, tiptoes in from up right. He goes to the basket. Mrs. Otis opens her eyes. Happy.) Oh, you came back!

STEVEN

(*puzzled, matter of fact, his voice gentle*) Back from where?

MRS. OTIS

(*raising up*) You didn't go, then?

STEVEN

(*laughing*) I just got here this morning.

MRS. OTIS

(*asking forgiveness*) I didn't want you to mow the lawn!

STEVEN

(*comforting*) Well, I didn't. You had it mowed. Remember?

MRS. OTIS

(*petulant*) Then why did you say you mowed it?

STEVEN

Mother, go back to sleep. I just want the keys to the Packard. I'm going to do the errands now.

MRS. OTIS

(*bewildered*) Oh. (*Steven pokes about in her basket. She raises herself further up — she is wide awake now.*) Take the car to go six blocks?

STEVEN

I like it. It's a wonderful old car.

MRS. OTIS

(*grasping her basket, moving it out of Steven's reach, clutching it to her*) Nonsense. The walk will do you good. You've messed up my things!

STEVEN

(*resigned*) Okay. Sorry I woke you.

MRS. OTIS

I wasn't asleep. I don't think so. (*Steven turns back toward the door right.*) You've got your list? You understand everything you're to do? (*Steven stops, turns back and nods.*) Read it over to me so I can explain anything you don't understand. (*Nancy enters from up right, pauses just inside the door. She is carrying an armful of file folders. Steven takes a paper out of his pocket, glances at it, then reads without expression, in the voice of a small boy made to recite a boring lesson.*)

STEVEN

"Look at the hall and the stairs of the apartment building —"

MRS. OTIS

(*interrupting*) Do you want something, Nancy?

290

I, ELIZABETH OTIS, BEING OF SOUND MIND

NANCY
I'll wait.

MRS. OTIS
Go on, Steven.

STEVEN
". . to see if they need varnishing."

MRS. OTIS
See if they're clean, too. I don't think much of our janitor. Put your handkerchief over your finger and poke in the corners.

STEVEN
(*nods and goes on reading*) "Find out if Mrs. Strunk in 2F is taking roomers."

MRS. OTIS
I heard she had two schoolteachers.

STEVEN
Will she tell me?

MRS. OTIS
Of course not. Look in the closets. The beds will probably be made up as couches but they'll have to keep their clothes somewhere. I won't have roomers kept. It runs down the building.

STEVEN
(*nods, resignedly, and reads on*) "In the business building, check Dr. Sommer's waiting room ceiling for water stains."

MRS. OTIS
He claims the roof leaks.

STEVEN
"If I see leak stains go up on the roof —"

MRS. OTIS
There's an iron ladder and a skylight at the end of the hall. Go up on the roof anyhow.

STEVEN
". . up on the roof and look at the general conditions particularly over the Doctor's waiting room."

MRS. OTIS
(*with animated interest*) That roof has been on for twenty-seven years — it was only guaranteed for twenty-five and the roofer I sent to look says it needs redoing — but he *would* say so. If a little tar here and there would make it last another year — we're that much ahead.

STEVEN
I don't see how I can do this last one.

MRS. OTIS

The down spout of the bank next door?

STEVEN

Just because they redid their roof and put in a new down spout last fall doesn't prove that the water in our cellar this spring —

MRS. OTIS

Can they prove it didn't cause it? Now be sure you see the president of the bank, Mr. Dunning. An underling would argue, but Mr. Dunning is young and puts on airs — he went to Harvard and he'll agree if you make it strong enough. (*Steven looks distressed.*) You don't have to be apologetic, either. I keep my checking account there.

NANCY

Mother Otis, why must Steven do such petty things?

MRS. OTIS

You never owned property or you wouldn't ask that! Profit comes from attention to details.

STEVEN

Goodbye. (*He starts out, down right; speaks to Nancy.*) Let mother finish her nap.

NANCY

I'll just be a minute. (*Steven exits. Nancy waits till he is gone, then speaks.*) Mother Otis, I'm beginning to feel you don't like me.

MRS. OTIS

I *always* admired you. I always wished I could be a businesswoman.

NANCY

Then sell the buildings! Buy stocks! As a businesswoman I advise it.

MRS. OTIS

Stocks are paper. Property is *real* — that's why they say *real* estate. Why do you care, anyhow?

NANCY

I don't intend to have the children's inheritance thrown away by Steven.

MRS. OTIS

Don't start that again! You two fight, if you must, but I won't be part of it.

NANCY

All right. But I warn you — I shall take him into court and prove he's incompetent.

MRS. OTIS

After I'm dead?

NANCY

Yes!

I, ELIZABETH OTIS, BEING OF SOUND MIND

MRS. OTIS

Do what you want, then! Tear each other apart — deal in scandal and hatred. I won't know.

NANCY

But you know *now*. I won't let you escape. You'll have that to worry over every day.

MRS. OTIS

And night! I sleep so little. You're cruel.

NANCY

So is a surgeon.

MRS. OTIS

What do you want of me?

NANCY

Sell the buildings. I'll stay over and talk to a real estate agent, if you like. Then set up a trust for the children — I can be one trustee and you can pick some levelheaded lawyer or banker for the other. Let Steven have an annuity.

MRS. OTIS

Why do you have to plague me?

NANCY

You've only a little time left to suffer. The children have their whole lives! I'm first of all a *mother*!

MRS. OTIS

What *are* you? All the dreams and hopes Mother and I had — women's suffrage, job equality for women, the things we longed for and worked for — and it comes down to a strange, brittle, nervous creature tormenting me in my own house! Please go out! Steven's been in here three times, and then Mrs. Cooms — and now you. If I don't rest today, tomorrow will be beyond me!

NANCY

I'm sorry. I really came in to ask where I could work — spread out these papers.

MRS. OTIS

Anywhere! — the dining room table.

NANCY

(*turns to go, then back to Mrs. Otis*) What did you mean — Steven came in before?

MRS. OTIS

Complaining about mowing the lawn! He didn't have to mow it. Now, did he?

293

NANCY

The lawn? (*She is startled and confused.*) I'll go, but let me help you get comfortable. (*She goes to Mrs. Otis, takes her basket, and puts it on the table. Mrs. Otis lies back with a sigh. Nancy takes the spread from the foot of the sofa and puts it across Mrs. Otis' feet.*)

MRS. OTIS

(*testily*) I'm fine.

NANCY

(*with a warm smile*) Have a good nap. (*She crosses up right.*)

MRS. OTIS

We used to do Gilbert and Sullivan.

NANCY

(*stops a moment*) That must have been nice. (*She exits up right. We hear the tinkling of a piano playing "Poor Wandering One" from* The Pirates of Penzance *and then a voice in the distance singing.*)

VOICE

> "Poor Wandering ones!
> Though ye have surely strayed.
> Take heart of grace,
> Your steps retrace,
> Poor wandering ones!"

(*The voice stops and the piano continues, fading into the distance as Frank enters from down left. He is wearing city clothes, now, but they are sloppy, careless. His hair is cut, his mustache shorter. He seems fifteen years older than in Act One. He carries his violin.*)

MRS. OTIS

(*laughing*) Come to play me a Sunday afternoon concert? I'd like that.

FRANK

Hello, Posie. Seen Mother?

MRS. OTIS

Not since after dinner when we did the dishes. How's Mamie?

FRANK

Always nagging! If I didn't have this fiddle to drown her out she'd have me looney by now. Don't ever dare leave it home or she'd bust it. Jaw, Jaw! I wish she'd let me stay on the farm. I ain't made for a banker, and Father jabbers at me every minute I'm with him, claims I'm too soft with folks. Well, I don't like bearing down on them poor people that come to get loans. And now there's trouble.

MRS. OTIS

What kind of trouble? What have you done?

FRANK

Not me. Father's been tomcatting again.

MRS. OTIS

I don't believe it.

FRANK

He was always fooling around with the hired girls. (*He laughs harshly.*) You musta known that.

MRS. OTIS

No. (*She rises and crosses to him, smells his breath.*) You've been drinking again.

FRANK

(*retreats*) Just a swallow or two. I was feeling dizzy. I think I got heart trouble, or consumption, maybe.

MRS. OTIS

What are you getting at? Do I have to shake you to get it out of you?

FRANK

(*lowering his voice*) This afternoon Mother caught him — britches down — in the woods, 'long side the River Road.

MRS. OTIS

I don't believe it. What would Mother be doing there on a Sunday afternoon? And we've no hired girl now, anyhow.

FRANK

Father and I foreclosed a chattel mortgage on a German couple down the River Road — the Blums. Took their milk cows, three pigs, and two horses because they didn't pay up. August Blum swore he'd get back at Father. He knowed Father was taking Mrs. Clapp down there Sunday afternoons whilst Lennie Clapp was on duty at the railroad station. Blum and his wife come and told Mother about two hours ago. She hitched up Old Red and drove down to see. She found them.

MRS. OTIS

Where's Mother?

FRANK

Gone to talk it over with the minister.

BENJAMIN

(*Enters down right. He wears the top hat and frock coat of the earlier scene, but his frock coat is open and streaked with dirt, his ruffled shirt is soiled, and his tie is loose. He is still a swaggering pioneer.*) Where's your mother?

FRANK

I don't know.

BENJAMIN

Posie? (*Mrs. Otis shakes her head.*) What in hell you doing here, Frank?

FRANK

Talking to Elizabeth.

BENJAMIN

How long have you been here?

FRANK

I was sleeping on the sofa, just woke up.

BENJAMIN

(*to Mrs. Otis*) That so?

MRS. OTIS

Father — I — Father! I didn't see Mother.

BENJAMIN

But you know? Frank told you?

FRANK

Not me.

BENJAMIN

(*stares at Mrs. Otis' guilty face, then at Frank*) You're a goddamned liar, Frank. I got a mind to kick your britches.

FRANK

(*frightened of his father*) Before God — I swear it!

MRS. OTIS

Frank!

BENJAMIN

(*grasping Frank by the arm, shaking him*) What did your mother say to you?

FRANK

You let me go! (*His father shakes him again.*)

BENJAMIN

She's been here, because Old Red is onhitched. (*He lifts Frank's arm and sniffs at his hand.*) You onhitched Old Red and wiped him down for her. What did your mother tell you? (*He twists Frank's arm so Frank goes down on his knees.*) I'm going to have it out of you! You sniveling, puling drunk. Don't think I can't smell your breath, either.

MRS. OTIS

Let him alone! (*Frank and Benjamin stand motionless. Mrs. Otis comes forward between them, speaks to Benjamin.*) You tormented Frank all his life! Made him weak too with your strength! Why were you so fierce with the ones you were supposed to love? (*She turns away. Benjamin starts to pace up and down, rolling his head slightly. Frank steals off down*

left. Mrs. Otis steps away from Benjamin, then turns to look at him again.)
What sort of a cancer was in you? Did you want pity? Sympathy? For
what? Did you ever try to tell me and I not listen? Now, perhaps we could
talk. Even your awful tomcatting seems less important. Like a drug you
took, to still the pain inside you. Was it? Why didn't you tell me about
yourself? I was gentle, wasn't I? I was ready to love you, Father, even
when you hurt Mother, I could have gone on loving you. I think I could.
I wanted to. Oh pace about! Pace! Walk — mutter — toss your head like a
wild animal! *(Mary Campbell enters from down right, stops at the top of
the steps. Benjamin turns to face her. They remain so, boring into each
other's faces, withstanding each other.)*

MARY

I've been to talk to the minister.

BENJAMIN

Then goddamn you and him! What right do you claim, damnit to hell —
you carnsarned —

MARY

(nodding) Having a tantrum like a child. Bullying Frank.

BENJAMIN

Unwifely creature! What in hell were you doing at the minister's?

MARY

Consulting him.

BENJAMIN

With the love that's been between us — the almighty great love — you
couldn't give me the chance to explain? No, you couldn't wait to damn
me. All right woman — I'm in hell. Are you happy to know I'm burning?

MARY

Are you trying to say that you repent?

BENJAMIN

Goddamn it, yes!

MARY

Then why can't you say what you mean in a simple way?

BENJAMIN

Simple! What is there that's simple? My God, do you think I'd be in this
trouble if *anything* was simple? Damn it, the trouble is you don't have the
least idea of how to be a woman! Damn it, a woman is soft and tender, to
console and comfort when a man aches from the struggle with this unholy
world! Where is your comfort? When last did you soothe my brow with
your white hand? When draw my aching head to your soft bosom that I

might weep out my anguish and sorrow and repentance that eats me? Are you made of granite?

MARY

I wish I were. (*rubs her forehead briefly*) Just tell me if you are repentant. Yes or no.

BENJAMIN

Yes. Heavenly days, yes, yes, yes.

MARY

Then you can be forgiven.

BENJAMIN

Well, praise God.

MARY

I'll tell the minister.

BENJAMIN

Him? How so, *him*?

MARY

According to church law you must come before the congregation to tell of your repentance and ask God's forgiveness.

BENJAMIN

Have you lost your mind? I will not, if I fry in hell forever. What kind of a mealy-mouthed, spineless fool do you take me for?

MRS. OTIS

Mother!

MARY

Stay out of this, Elizabeth.

MRS. OTIS

No — I won't! I won't have a church trial! I won't let you do it! I don't care what Father's done, I have my rights! I've put up with this house that you're too careless to make lovely or even decent, this great house that you keep like a barn! With your common, country ways coming between me and respectable people — just the same, Andrew Blythe wants to marry me! I'm almost sure!

BENJAMIN

I'll be damned.

MRS. OTIS

(*proudly*) Andrew Blythe!

BENJAMIN

He's got the mazoola and the high and mighty airs to go with it. I can't kick about him.

MRS. OTIS

So there can't be a church trial!

MARY

There has to be.

MRS. OTIS

Why — people would point at me, on the street. I won't dare stir from the house! I'd die of shame!

MARY

If he's got real feelings for you, it won't make any difference. You'll just have to make the best of things and wait and see.

MRS. OTIS

I will not! I'll break off with him. Do you think I'd lie awake night after night wondering how he's going to take it? Looking for signs he's changed? Wondering if he's pitying me? It'll be a clean wound, at least. Not dying by inches!

BENJAMIN

Posie, my heart aches for you. If your mother wasn't so cruel and hard —

MARY

I venture if he's anything of a man he won't let you go.

MRS. OTIS

All right — I'll give him a reason! That I'm marrying someone else!

MARY

Who?

MRS. OTIS

I've got others on the string — George Otis would marry me!

BENJAMIN

I'd see you dead first! Damn it, you know as well as everyone else in this town that his father run off with the town whore!

MRS. OTIS

Yes! And now I've something in common with him!

BENJAMIN

(wincing) Posie! Good God! Why — why he works in the Jew store! He boards with 'em!

MARY

Perhaps he likes them. I heard they set a good table. But I don't want you to marry him, Elizabeth. He's too good a boy to be grabbed up like a stray dog and tied to your fancy buggy, Miss Stuck-up!

MRS. OTIS

(cries out) Mother! (Mary and Benjamin are motionless.) Why were you so rough with me? "Strike glass against glass to loosen a bottle stop-

299

per," you said. But your glass was so much harder than mine! There's so much more pain in words than in a whipping! If only you'd been gentler — (*motioning Mary and Benjamin off*) Go away, both of you. (*They exit on opposite sides of the stage. The lights dim down, except on Mrs. Otis and on the couch. From up left George enters, coatless, stiff collar undone, tie undone, handkerchief tucked in around collar.*)

GEORGE

Well, I got the Paris green sprayed onto the cucumbers. I'm tired. Had a hard day. (*Mrs. Otis turns to look at him. He goes to the sofa, sits, takes off his coat, drops his suspenders over his shoulders, loosens his tie and his stiff collar.*) I can't wait to get to bed. (*He leans down to untie his high-laced shoes.*) I got word today from Illinois.

MRS. OTIS

I was not faithful to you, George. Did you ever suspect?

GEORGE

My father died. Funeral's tomorrow.

MRS. OTIS

All of your life you believed I drew back from you because of your father and the shame he put on you. Your goodness made up for him ten times over.

GEORGE

I sent fifty dollars. I said I didn't want any stone. It should be an unmarked grave.

MRS. OTIS

Is the adultery of the mind ever punished? I flinched from you, because you were not Andrew Blythe. It hurt something in me when you touched me. Handsome, gay, kind — but you didn't have a chance, George. Not after I decided you were going to marry me, and you did; and in my heart I hoped you wouldn't.

GEORGE

(*looking directly at her*) Point is, I mention the money because I was saving it to buy something nice for our anniversary. I apologize for using it to bury him, but it seemed I had to. I thought, I pretend to be a Christian, I got to forgive him — but then I saw I didn't have any feeling about him anymore, at all. It was like he'd died years ago. Funny what goes on in your mind. (*There is a pause as George regards his shoes. He rises, crosses to the French door, looks out. The lights fade to silvery moonlight. Mrs. Otis crosses to sit on the sofa. From a house next door we hear a piano playing "By the Light of the Silvery Moon."*) Oh dear, it's hot tonight. Mind if I put out the light and open the windows? Undress in the dark.

I, ELIZABETH OTIS, BEING OF SOUND MIND

These darn mosquitoes squeeze right through the screens. I should of kept up my piano playing. Don't know why I quit. I used to enjoy it, specially when you sang for me.

MRS. OTIS

Not for you.

GEORGE

(*turning back, sits on sofa, next to Mrs. Otis*) 'Lizbeth. You know what? It'd be easier on me if maybe we could get twin beds.

MRS. OTIS

Why, George?

GEORGE

It's hard not to come near you.

MRS. OTIS

Don't be silly! At our age?

GEORGE

Guess there's something wrong with me. Guess I'm — I'm over — over — you know. I'm sorry. Never mind. Night, 'Lizbeth. A good-night kiss?

MRS. OTIS

(*Turns her cheek to George who makes the gestures of kissing her, but his lips do not touch her. She rises and walks forward and the light follows her. In the darkness George makes his exit, left. Mrs. Otis touches her cheek. The music stops.*) Kisses never given — but well remembered. (*She touches her face, brow, and throat.*) So many years I waited, but not for you, warm in here, yet with a lonely chill. Unsure. Waiting for someone to force their way in and free me. (*Her hands go to her breasts.*) How grotesque that there's still roundness, and hope. All the years under these poor, sad breasts my faithful heart — with silly, unflagging devotion, like a dog no matter how abused, that goes on thumping its tail. (*Now her hands move slowly over her body. She crosses, passes through French door to yard.*) Can anything pluck at my nerves? Make me feel again? Only pain, now. My veins can throb but there'll never be anything to make me cry out in hope or joy. Well, my mind can dance, indeed it can — make up gardens and light them with a sliver of moon, and send me searching for fragrance in old memories so I can hide my face in them, tear out their petals — love me — love me not — while I dream — and dream — of daisies in the sunlight. Mother? Where are you? I want to come into the warm house! O-o-h! (*with this cry turns back into the living room*) I do believe I am getting senile.

(*Mrs. Otis crosses behind the sofa and picks up a white throw, which she puts over her shoulders. Organ music sounds and a woman enters from the left, followed by a couple. They, and all the congregation, are dressed in 1890 costumes. Two other women follow, then a man. The first woman sits in a chair by the library table, the couple sit on the sofa, one woman turns the coffee table to face the hall right and sits. The other woman sits on the hassock. George, now a young man of twenty-one, enters and sits on the coffee table. Still another woman enters and sits on one of the library chairs. At this point Mary Campbell enters, goes to the first chair by the table — this is evidently her accustomed seat. The woman obligingly moves to another chair near the table, and Mary sits. Now Benjamin Campbell, more resplendently dressed than we have seen him, enters. He stands, looking over the congregation, clears his throat to let people know he is there, and sits in the side chair down left. Almost at the same moment, the Reverend Zediah Jordan enters from down right and goes to the upstage edge of the hall platform, a Bible in his hand. Another woman hurries in from the left and sits on the sofa. The organ has continued softly in the background. Now a slight woman, Henrietta Clapp, wearing a heavy veil, enters from the left. She clings to the arm of her husband, Leonard Clapp. He is a slight, nondescript man in ill-fitting clothes. They stand, fearful, at the rear of the congregation.*)

JORDAN

Henrietta Clapp, Leonard Clapp, come forward. There's room at the front. (*Henrietta and Leonard Clapp come down the aisle. Leonard moves the bench up right to face Jordan and they sit, Henrietta on the down stage end.*) According to the laws of this congregation, which are in conformity with those of other congregations, we are met here after services to hear the confession and the plea for forgiveness of one repentant church member, guilty and admitting to a grave sin. It is with the deepest regret that I must announce that we are also gathered here to vote upon the excommunication of another member of this church, who has refused to repent, being a partner in the aforesaid act, and therefore must be tried before this congregation. Let me say that I have struggled long and earnestly with this unrepentant sinner and have prayed for him many hours, that his heart might be softened and his pride humbled before his Lord and Saviour Jesus Christ. Now at this last moment I again call upon Brother Campbell to arise and confess his guilt and offer his repentance. Benjamin Campbell — arise.

BENJAMIN

I'm sitting, and I see no reason to do otherwise.

MRS. OTIS

Stubborn, stubborn man!

I, ELIZABETH OTIS, BEING OF SOUND MIND

JORDAN

Very well. We shall proceed with Sister Clapp. Arise, Sister Clapp. (*Henrietta Clapp tremulously rises.*) I must ask you to remove that covering from your face.

HENRIETTA

Please!

JORDAN

There is no hiding from the face of the Lord. If you repent truly, you must open yourself to this congregation, for nothing of evil can be hid. (*Henrietta makes futile pawing gestures at her veil. Jordan steps forward and gently removes the veil, tossing it over her head. We see a pretty-featured woman, whose face now is swollen from weeping. Jordan steps back and speaks.*) And they brought before Him a woman who had been taken in adultery, and seeking to trap Him said, What shall we do with this woman? And He said, Let him who is without sin cast the first stone. (*He stretches out his hands, closes his eyes and raises his face. The congregation bows — all but Benjamin who sits up straighter, his head more erect.*)

MRS. OTIS

Bow your head, Father! But you never bowed your head, did you?

JORDAN

Our Father who art not only in heaven, but who walks among us, forgive the hurts that we do to Thee — through the hurts we do to each other. For each of us was made in Thy likeness and we are Thy children. We are today come to hear one of us, dear Sister Clapp, confess her sinning with Benjamin Campbell. Grant us the wisdom to know that her confession is a confession for every one of us! (*His voice thunders.*) May none let their pride set them above her! (*Now his voice turns gentle.*) Comfort this miserable woman, whose frailty we must expose. Grant us humbleness and give us the grace of mercy. Amen. (*Jordan opens his eyes and lowers his head to look at the congregation, who raise their heads. After a moment of silence he continues.*) Sister Mary Campbell, what did you see the Sunday afternoon of August twentieth in the willow grove on the River Road above Jason's Mill?

MARY

I was told by a German farmer and his wife that I would find my husband and Henrietta Clapp, our choir leader, there.

BENJAMIN

(*half-rising*) They owed me on a note.

MRS. OTIS

(*restlessly moving through the congregation as she speaks*) "One red jer-

303

sey pig and two black pigs, being all the pigs we now own, and one large roan cow dehorned. She is about seven years old. She is all the cow we now own and our horse Dan, a white gelding, eight years old weighing fourteen hundred pounds, and our dark gray gelding, Prince, thirteen hundred pounds being the only horses we own. Whereas the mortgagor is indebted to Benjamin Campbell in the sum of forty-two dollars and fifty cents, the above is hereby sold and transferred to aforesaid Benjamin Campbell."

BENJAMIN

It was their damned spite! 'Cause I took what they owed me.

MARY

Spite, maybe. But it was the truth.

JORDAN

Your turn to speak will come, Brother Campbell.

BENJAMIN

(*mutters*) Don't brother me!

JORDAN

Silence! (*controlling himself*) Continue, Sister Mary Campbell.

MARY

He had the team. I hitched up Old Red and drove down the River Road to the mill pasture, let down the bars, and drove over to the grove. I saw the team hitched to a bough. I walked into the grove and I found them there on the riverbank.

JORDAN

Who did you find?

HENRIETTA

Him — and me!

JORDAN

What were they doing? (*But even Mary can't go on.*) Were they in sin? (*She nods.*) That's all, Sister Mary Campbell, and may the Lord comfort you. (*She turns back to her chair, her head high. The heads of the congregation turn to follow her, then swing back to Jordan.*)

JORDAN

Sister Clapp, step forward and face the congregation. (*She haltingly does so, her eyes fixed above the congregation, and roaming restlessly.*) Is this the truth?

HENRIETTA

(*a small thin voice, practically inaudible*) Yes.

JORDAN

You've got to speak loud enough for the Lord to hear.

HENRIETTA

Yes! (*She starts to sniffle and cry, alternately, struggling against it.*)

JORDAN

No, no. We must wait until you're through with those tears. For your tears are for yourself — not for your sin. (*He waits while she controls herself.*) Was this the only time you have sinned?

HENRIETTA

Yes.

JORDAN

The truth to the Lord! You sinned with Benjamin Campbell before? (*She nods her head.*) Many times? (*She looks helplessly at Benjamin who stares up at the ceiling.*) Many times? (*She starts to cry again.*) Do you repent? (*She turns to Jordan and nods.*) To the congregation. (*She turns toward them but looks everywhere but at them and nods her head.*) Say after me: I sinned against the laws of God —

HENRIETTA

I sinned against the laws of God —

JORDAN

And against the laws of man —

HENRIETTA

The laws of man —

JORDAN

And against my husband.

HENRIETTA

And against — oh, Lennie! (*And now she breaks into unrestrained sobbing. Most of the women in the congregation start to cry now, too. Jordan steps down, extends his hand to Leonard Clapp, who rises.*)

JORDAN

Do you, Leonard Clapp, forgive this poor sinner in Christ? Will you take her back to your heart to forgive and to cherish? (*Leonard Clapp, wiping his eyes with a blue bandanna, bobs his head, yes. Jordan leads him by the hand to Henrietta; crying they fall into each other's arms.*) And do you the congregation forgive, and accept Sister Clapp back into the arms of the church?

CONGREGATION

Yes — yes.

JORDAN

(*starting to sing, inviting the congregation to join him*)
> "Shall we gather at the river,
>   Where bright angel feet have trod"

(*Jordan steps down from the podium, singing, the congregation joining in. Jordan goes to Henrietta and Leonard Clapp and embraces them.*)

JORDAN AND CONGREGATION

(*singing*)

> "With its crystal tide forever,
> Flowing by the throne of God?

(*Weeping women from the congregation move forward to embrace the couple — one man to shake Leonard's hand. Jordan brings Mary to Henrietta but Mary does not embrace her — she shakes her hand vigorously and turns away. The organ stops but the singing goes on throughout the next scene.*)

> Yes, we'll gather at the river,
> The beautiful, the beautiful river — "

(*The lights dim on the congregation. Mrs. Otis crosses out through the French door, left, her step and manner becoming younger. George follows her. The congregation goes on singing in a low voice, as dimly heard as they are seen. Mrs. Otis pauses, glances back at George who hurries to her.*)

GEORGE

You look so white! You're faint.

MRS. OTIS

(*taking his arm*) Help me! I need air. Let's walk. (*They stroll down left.*)

GEORGE

(*after a pause*) I'd cut off my right arm to help you! (*Mrs. Otis stops and looks at him.*)

MRS. OTIS

You say that! After this no one will care what happens to me. I'll go away somewhere and teach school and be an old maid.

GEORGE

(*horrified*) Oh, no!

MRS. OTIS

You don't care. (*takes her arm from George's, moves a few steps away, coquettishly*)

GEORGE

(*strangled*) I — I do! (*He steps toward Mrs. Otis.*)

MRS. OTIS

Really?

GEORGE

(*taking another step, now facing her*) Miss Elizabeth!

MRS. OTIS

Do you? (*He is speechless; she kisses him.*)

GEORGE

Oh! (*He kisses her passionately, his arms around her. Her arms are about him — but with the palms raised as though pushing away what is to come.*) Will you marry me?

MRS. OTIS

(*breaking from him, retreating*) No, no!

GEORGE

'Lizbeth!

MRS. OTIS

(*turning back to George, after a despairing look toward the congregation*) Yes.

GEORGE

(*crossing to her, waving his arms*) Oh, thank you! Thank you! (*He can't stand still — almost prances.*)

MRS. OTIS

(*alarmed*) What's the matter?

GEORGE

(*his voice strong*) I'm so happy! This is just like dying and going to heaven!

MRS. OTIS

SSSH!

GEORGE

(*putting his arm about her, walking with her*) Now I'll do everything! Oh, I've got it in me! Watch my speed now! I'll own a store. I'll set this town on fire! I've got it in me! All I needed was this!

MRS. OTIS

(*moving from his arm, facing him*) Oh, that's good. But we've got to go back. They'll notice. Come on. (*George tries to kiss her again, but she evades it and goes through the French door, looking back, with a fleeting smile. Now she reverts to old age.*)

GEORGE

(*following her*) I — I love you! (*George takes his seat, looking at her. The lights go up on the congregation, the singing is louder. They are seated, now. Mrs. Otis crosses toward Benjamin.*)

MRS. OTIS

(*over song*) Hallowed be Thy name, Father — who surely are not in heaven, nor is there a heaven (*crosses toward Jordan upstage, to left center*)

307

though I am sure of hell as a living truth. But afterward? Oh God — open the doors of silence, let the peace of nothingness receive us!

CONGREGATION

"Gather with the saints at the river
That flows by the throne of God."

(*Jordan steps back on the podium.*)

JORDAN

(*Leonard Clapp is drying his wife's eyes with his bandanna.*) I say unto thee — heaven rejoices over one stray lamb returned to the flock! But there is another lamb that has strayed.

BENJAMIN

You mean ram, don't you? (*Many of the congregation turn to look at Benjamin.*)

JORDAN

Benjamin Campbell, before this congregation, *again* I ask you, as I have many times before — I *beg* you — admit your sin!

BENJAMIN

I deny your right to interfere between me and my relationship to the everlasting, unknowable Power above that is my Creator.

JORDAN

I do not seek to interfere.

BENJAMIN

Then leave this matter to Him and me.

JORDAN

The stiff-necked cannot know God.

BENJAMIN

(*leaping to his feet*) I call on Him above to choose between you and me if you ain't a dang sight more stiff-necked trying to put your will onto me. It's *your* will trying to come between me and my God! What's your right?

JORDAN

As the chosen minister of this church —

BENJAMIN

(*moving toward Jordan*) You're no more than a man — unless you be taken by some papist ideas that you're a special fellow sitting in God's lap!

JORDAN

I am the minister —

BENJAMIN

You're a man!

JORDAN

A man of God!

BENJAMIN

(*turning to the congregation*) Listen to him boast. Well, who ain't a man of God — if as you said, we was all made in the shape of God? That God is in all of us? Why are you so special?

JORDAN

I am a humble servant of the will of God —

BENJAMIN

(*turns, steps toward Jordan*) God's let on to you that this is his will?

JORDAN

I won't argue with you.

BENJAMIN

Then be quiet and let me speak! (*He steps up on the platform, beside Jordan.*)

JORDAN

(*doggedly*) Do you deny the charges against you?

BENJAMIN

(*roaring*) I deny your right to stand in judgment — I deny your right to judge any creature of the Almighty — not even a fly!

JORDAN

(*intimidated*) This church has given me a responsibility —

BENJAMIN

All right. But don't go mixing church and God. (*He steps down, moves among the congregation.*) They're two different things. You folks are this church — you and me, because I'm a member until I choose to get out. (*turns to Jordan*) You are nothing more than another man that is our preacher — as long as we choose to keep you in the job. But you got no authority, or are you setting yourself up for a Protestant Pope?

JORDAN

The complaint against you was not my doing.

BENJAMIN

(*points to Mary*) You set my wife on to it.

MARY

(*standing, angrily*) He did not! When have I ever needed anybody to make up my mind?

BENJAMIN

You did it for spite, as I have testified!

MARY

For decency and honesty!

BENJAMIN

I ask all of you men — where would you be if your wife was to go to the preacher with every last suspicion and spite? I'll agree to a sin. I'll confess a sin! I never been able to make that woman cherish me and serve me as a true wife. She set herself above me! Where is your obedience — you false wife. (*Mary sits.*) The duty of a wife is to obey — and I warn every last man sitting here, and it's a pitiful small number there is, look out! If women are to be let judge their lawful husbands then you're in for trouble and the whole world turned upside down! Oh, wife of my youth — how could you do this to me? I don't say that I'm perfect — but ain't it the place of woman to comfort? To cherish? Look at us poor, damned men — having to struggle in the harsh, terrible, wild country. I been out in the Dakotas for weeks on end — sleeping on the ground, going without any food but hardtack, and having to eat prairie dogs to keep body and soul together — and why was I there? Taking the risk of death itself, of wolves in the night, of Injuns — I've been hunted by the Sioux! Woke from my bed on the frosty ground to find a rattlesnake bedded in the blankets. I been trapped in a prairie fire and I lived lonely — all to make money so my wife and children could have the good things of this life. For them. For my loving wife. Was she grateful that I made her life easy? That I risked my life and gave up my comfort? No, she ain't. She's as hard as flint. So in my dismay, in the sadness of my wounded heart I had a little innocent tenderness with a lovely-voiced, a golden-voiced, sweet-tempered young thing who was a true female and whose pity was so deep that she yearned over my lonely aching heart. She comforted with words — with mellow, beautiful words. That's my sin. I was lonely and I was comforted. Does Leonard Clapp say I sinned with his wife? (*He pauses, glaring at Leonard Clapp who huddles in his seat.*) No — for if he said it, he would be a damn liar and I would take such a slanderous statement out of his hide. In fact — why don't he say something in complaint? Leonard Clapp, dare you say that by word or thought or deed there was anything impure in my being with your wife? (*He pauses. Leonard Clapp is still more miserable, tries to make himself smaller.*)

MARY

(*rising*) I say it — for I saw it.

BENJAMIN

Then, and I am ashamed to say it, wife, you lie!

MARY

No man, woman, or child can say I ever lied in my life. (*to congregation*) Anyone can say it — speak up. There's those that don't like me because I spoke truth when you'd rather heard a lie — but not one can say I lied.

I, ELIZABETH OTIS, BEING OF SOUND MIND

BENJAMIN

I say it.

MARY

Elizabeth — I call on my daughter to testify. Elizabeth! (*George turns to Mrs. Otis.*)

BENJAMIN

Leave her out of this.

MARY

Elizabeth!

MRS. OTIS

Elizabeth isn't here any more, and whatever she said then — I shan't answer.

BENJAMIN

You heard what she said! (*Benjamin steps up on the platform beside Jordan.*)

MARY

Reverend Jordan, call this meeting to order and continue. I gave evidence. Mrs. Clapp has admitted it was the truth.

JORDAN

Henrietta Clapp — stand!

HENRIETTA

I — I can't. (*Jordan goes down to Henrietta, helps her up.*)

JORDAN

Don't be feared of this wild man. You are in the house of God. Did you sin carnally with Benjamin Campbell?

BENJAMIN

Don't let this preacher browbeat you!

JORDAN

Did you — I say before the Lord and Jesus Christ and in his name, I command you to say did you sin with Benjamin Campbell? (*Henrietta starts to cry.*) In the name of our Redeemer, speak up! Did you go with Benjamin Campbell to the grove by the river and did he then disrobe you in certain ways and places and did you there submit to him in an evil and adulterous way? Answer me, woman!!

HENRIETTA

(*screams*) Yes! (*And she sinks back on the bench, sobbing.*)

JORDAN

Members of this congregation —

BENJAMIN

I will be heard!

311

JORDAN

(*stepping up on the platform, to command the congregation*) All in favor of excommunicating Benjamin Campbell from this congregation — say aye!

CONGREGATION

(*Mostly women's voices, joined by Mary who is as straight as ever. George looks at Mrs. Otis, and is silent.*) Aye. Aye. Aye.

BENJAMIN

(*shouting, simultaneously*) I resign from this goddamned church!

JORDAN

Go!

BENJAMIN

I will!

JORDAN

Man of Satan!

BENJAMIN

(*to Jordan*) You mewling, lady-pleasing, spineless blabbermouth! Half-jelly, half-pap. (*Benjamin steps down toward the congregation.*) May God be pitied for what you say in his name! (*Benjamin strides left through the congregation.*) May God pity all men who bow down to women!

(*The lights go out as Benjamin exits through the French door. The organ thunders wildly. In the darkness the congregation exits. As soon as they are gone the lights come up on Jordan, on the platform, Mrs. Otis and George facing him, Mrs. Otis with the white throw from the couch over her head, like a mantle, Mary behind her. Benjamin is entering from the left. The music breaks off as the lights go up.*)

JORDAN

(*his Bible in his hands*) Dearly beloved —

BENJAMIN

Elizabeth! I got Judge Bigelow coming to marry you!

MARY

She wants a minister.

BENJAMIN

Not him! He makes me puke! I told you not to have him!

MRS. OTIS

(*to Benjamin*) Yes, I want Reverend Jordan. I will have him.

BENJAMIN

(*between Mrs. Otis and George*) Posie — I can't stay then. Don't you want your father at your wedding? With that stench in my nostrils I can't stay!

I, ELIZABETH OTIS, BEING OF SOUND MIND

MARY

Behave and stay. Or go. You're spoiling your daughter's wedding. (*Mrs. Otis signs to Jordan to begin.*)

JORDAN

Dearly beloved, we are gathered together —

BENJAMIN

(*crossing to Jordan*) Oh, God Almighty. (*He snatches the Bible from Jordan's hands.*) Daughter — I'll never forgive you this! (*Benjamin raises the Bible to throw at Jordan.*)

MRS. OTIS

And I'll never forgive you! Never! (*Benjamin's arm drops — he lets go of the Bible and it drops to the floor. He looks at Mrs. Otis and, sagging for the first time from his jaunty prideful bearing, he goes slowly off right as lights swirl again. Jordan is stooping to pick up the Bible when all goes dark. The front doorbell rings. In the darkness all exit, except Mrs. Otis who staggers to the armchair.*) Where's my pill? (*Mrs. Otis fumbles in her basket, finds a small bottle, takes out a pill, puts it under her tongue, and sinks back. The doorbell rings again. Nancy enters from up right, goes down right to the door, opens it, and Hollaway hurries in.*)

HOLLAWAY

Hello. (*He comes into the room. Nancy follows him in, catching at his sleeve.*)

NANCY

No, she's resting!

MRS. OTIS

I'm awake —

HOLLAWAY

(*to Mrs. Otis*) Sorry — but I've got a problem. I need an interview with your son.

NANCY

I'll give you the interview!

MRS. OTIS

What is it?

HOLLAWAY

My deadline — and I want a piece on your son. We've got a feature on you —

MRS. OTIS

He's downtown on business.

NANCY

(*to Hollaway*) I can give you the story on Steven.

MRS. OTIS

(*alarmed*) No, Nancy — please —

HOLLAWAY

I have to clear what I use with you.

MRS. OTIS

That's right. I'll talk to him, Nancy. (*But Nancy isn't leaving.*)

HOLLAWAY

Instead of an interview I suppose we can run a bio — with some general comments on his impressions of the city. (*He takes out folded paper and a pencil.*) He's in advertising?

MRS. OTIS

Yes.

HOLLAWAY

What company?

MRS. OTIS

(*rattled, uncertain*) Well — I've got it here in my basket. (*She turns to her basket.*)

NANCY

(*stepping forward*) I'm sorry — you can't give unauthorized publicity. They insist on every mention of the company being cleared in New York. Just say it's one of the top four.

HOLLAWAY

What account?

MRS. OTIS

Automobiles. He's always loved automobiles. Even my old Packard —

HOLLAWAY

What make?

NANCY

(*crisply*) Not authorized to reveal it. But top selling in its class.

HOLLAWAY

You sound like he worked for the CIA.

NANCY

I don't make policy for his company. Write them a letter.

MRS. OTIS

(*to Nancy*) Perhaps we shouldn't say anything about Steven's work. Not right now.

NANCY

(*gaily*) Why not? And I know Mr. Hollaway will want to know that Steven's been made a vice president.

314

MRS. OTIS

(*shocked*) Nancy!

NANCY

After all — if we don't name the company, who's going to make a fuss? Not Steven.

HOLLAWAY

That's good. I'll put that in the headline. Now — hobbies?

MRS. OTIS

He was president of the Hi-Y in high school.

NANCY

Racing sports cars.

HOLLAWAY

Hey, hey!

NANCY

He cracked up at Watkins Glen.

HOLLAWAY

That's color. Grandson of pioneer seeks new frontiers.

NANCY

And he bred Irish wolfhounds. Took a ribbon at the Westminster. That was when he had a dogfood account. But the wolfhound made a face at the dogfood on TV and that was the end of *that* account, and of his kennels.

HOLLAWAY

(*laughing*) Great story. But I think I'll skip it for this piece.

MRS. OTIS

He had a straight A average in high school. And went through the University of Chicago in three years. Then later he went to Harvard Business School.

HOLLAWAY

(*laughing*) That's good background — but I think we'll concentrate on now. What about children?

MRS. OTIS

I've two *wonderful* grandchildren.

NANCY

James Richard Otis, a senior next year at Harvard.

MRS. OTIS

On the Dean's list! That means —

NANCY

(*going on*) And Patricia Otis, sophomore at Wellesley. Patricia's on a bicycle tour of France this summer, and James is on a sailboat retracing the path of Columbus' first voyage in the Indies.

HOLLAWAY

Good! That descendant of pioneers angle again.

MRS. OTIS

Would you like a picture of Steven?

HOLLAWAY

Yes. I'll run it next to yours. (*Mrs. Otis fishes in her basket.*) Now if I could have a quote on his impressions of Boue City.

NANCY

A sparkling town — warm, progressive. It makes him happy to be here.

HOLLAWAY

Are you kidding? I live here. (*Mrs. Otis has found a picture of Steven which she holds out, but Hollaway doesn't notice.*) You've given me the cue, though. I know what they like to read. Corn is the basis of Iowa life. (*He sees the picture, crosses, and takes it, looks at it.*)

MRS. OTIS

Well, he *does* like it here. Now be careful of that picture. I want it back.

HOLLAWAY

Okay. Thanks, Mrs. Otis. Sorry I had to butt in. (*Hollaway moves toward the door down right, takes Nancy's hand, holds it a moment with evident pleasure.*) Goodbye, Mrs. Otis. Suppose I call you Nancy? I think of Mrs. Otis as a sort of title belonging to Steven's mother. You know, I'd like a story on you, when things calm down.

MRS. OTIS

She's a *very* important executive.

NANCY

Oh, Mother! Not really. Goodbye, Mr. Hollaway. I'll be seeing you, I hope.

HOLLAWAY

You can't avoid it. (*He exits down right.*)

MRS. OTIS

Nancy Otis! I don't understand you. So many lies! So kind to Steven.

NANCY

Why not? I'm fond of Steven. Separated, I can love the man. It's only his reality that's impossible. Anyhow, this may lift his ego, which is currently around his shoetops. (*Steven enters from down right, pulling an unwilling Hollaway after him by the arm.*)

HOLLAWAY

Now wait a minute!

STEVEN

(*who is hot, a little disheveled, and, as we begin to suspect, rather drunk*)
I want to know what's going on here.

NANCY

Steven! Let go of that poor man!

STEVEN

What tricks have you been up to?

HOLLAWAY

I met him on the porch — I told him you'd given me a story on him —

STEVEN

What a sweet darling. I bet that's a dilly of a story!

MRS. OTIS

Whatever is the matter with you, Steven? Let go of Mr. Hollaway.

STEVEN

(*letting go of Hollaway*) I've got a right to know. Nobody's printing anything about me without my okay. Now let's get that straight.

HOLLAWAY

(*angry*) Okay!

STEVEN

So what's your story?

HOLLAWAY

I don't know what's wrong with you — your wife bent over backwards.
She wouldn't even give me the name of the company where you work! Nor
the account you work on. All she said was they were among the biggest
and you were a vice president.

STEVEN

(*laughing too loudly, putting his arm about Nancy*) That's my girl. You're
a sweetheart. Isn't she a sweetheart?

HOLLAWAY

Yes.

STEVEN

(*giving Nancy a shake*) Now where's the trap?

NANCY

(*putting his arm away, stepping from Steven*) Calm down and be quiet.

STEVEN

What do you mean by that?

MRS. OTIS

Steven, you're all hot and excited.

NANCY

If that were all.

STEVEN

That's more normal, darling. A dig. Dig we must for the glory of a greater Nancy.

NANCY

Oh, quit it. Why don't you go, Mr. Hollaway?

STEVEN

(*catching Hollaway's arm again*) He's not going anywhere. Until I get to the bottom of this. What story did she give you? All sweet and lovely? I'm a great guy? A world beater?

HOLLAWAY

She certainly did.

STEVEN

But that's not true.

MRS. OTIS

Steven, I want you to stop right now. I want you to sit down and count to —

NANCY

About five hundred.

STEVEN

I don't think I choose to be a great man in Boue City.

HOLLAWAY

All right, all right.

STEVEN

They used to say — syphilis must be good — because the *Chicago Tribune* is against it.

MRS. OTIS

Steven! I will not have this!

NANCY

What a fool you are!

STEVEN

I'm always safe if I go against you, darling. Hollaway, let's have a little fun with the citizens of this lousy little town. Let's tell them the truth. Now write this. I've got no job. I'm unemployed. Fired. Given the heave-ho. Print that. Want the details?

MRS. OTIS

Mr. Hollaway. Please go! (*He would, but Steven has too firm a grip.*)

STEVEN

It's so damned hot in here. Now where was I? Lead for your story — "Boue City boy given the gate by top advertising firm." And I got a subhead too — "Mr. Otis confided in us that his second marriage" — got that? — "second marriage has also gone down the drain." (*Mrs. Otis struggles to her feet.*)

MRS. OTIS

Nancy! What's wrong with him?

NANCY

He's drunk!

STEVEN

Like hell! And it's not sunstroke, either. (*giving Hollaway a shake*) Now, fella, you got that straight? You want a story, you got one. A dilly, right? Now go and write it, old boy, old boy! (*gives him a shove*) That sun was hot, though. (*Hollaway runs off down right. Steven moves left, into the room. Mrs. Otis goes past him to the hall platform, right.*)

MRS. OTIS

Mr. Hollaway! (*But he is gone. Mrs. Otis stops with a gesture of futility. Nancy runs to her, steadies her.*)

NANCY

(*to Mrs. Otis*) Darling — oh, I'm so sorry! (*over her shoulder to Steven*) I could kill you! (*to Mrs. Otis*) Come, sit down, dear. (*But Mrs. Otis shakes her head, absently.*)

STEVEN

(*to Nancy*) What's that all about? "You could kill me."

MRS. OTIS

(*turning to look at Steven, speaking to Nancy*) Put coffee on and get a basin of cold water and a washrag. It always helped Frank.

STEVEN

Frank. Frank who? (*remembering*) Uncle Frank? Who drank himself to death at the age of eighty-five? Elixir of bourbon should do as much for me. (*Nancy exits up right, with a scornful look at Steven. Mrs. Otis is watching Steven, looking back through her memories of him, wrestling with the insoluble mystery of the male. Steven takes out his handkerchief to wipe his forehead, shakes it out and observes that it is soiled with smudges of dirt.*) Reminds me. Dirty hall. Get a new janitor. As to Mrs. Strunk and the rumor that she has a roomer. I believe she has, for the feminine apparel in one closet was lightly perfumed with lilac, whereas sniffs about the person of Mrs. Strunk revealed an effusion — effluvium — of carnation. Saw the president of the bank. Good fellow. Success, there. After the third martini he agreed to take down the drainpipe. Oh, oh! I wasn't to mention his private bar to you. Don't betray me. Don't move your account to another bank. Prohibition is over — even for bankers. (*Steven sways, takes a step to balance himself.*)

319

MRS. OTIS

(*harshly*) Sit down before you fall down!

STEVEN

(*backing to the sofa, sitting*) All right, but it's the heat, not the humility.

MRS. OTIS

(*walking toward him*) I am *ashamed*!

STEVEN

Yes? Well, I'm rather proud of myself. I lived in this town like a frightened shadow, as though God were a schoolteacher, and I'd be beaten with a rubber hose if I transgressed any one of His sour commandments.

MRS. OTIS

That's nonsense!

STEVEN

As though you were God, the schoolteacher. Let me tell you, God is masculine. That's why frustrated women worship at His knee, enjoying loving caresses in the privacy of their dreams. But today, like Saul on the road to Damascus, I had a revelation — a blinding light struck me as I passed the Golden Oak Pool Room. And I went in and I stood at the bar with farmers and carpenters and truck drivers and other lowly characters —

MRS. OTIS

You didn't!

STEVEN

(*paying no attention to her interruption*) There they stood, broad, tall, and unafraid — drinking beer. And I thought — this is Boue City. Not that other neat, middle-class, proper women's world I grew up in. And I said to God the bartender, give me a beer. And I saw that they looked at me, because today I am a man. (*He pauses, defiantly returning his mother's outraged glare.*) No use, Mother. Can't stare me down. I'm not afraid. Not again. Not ever.

MRS. OTIS

You wallow in words like a pig in mud. Lie down. Take off your shoes — do you want me to take them off?

STEVEN

I shan't do it, and I won't let you. Didn't you hear me? Can't you grasp it? I'm the master of me, you're not. (*Nancy enters right with a basin of water and a washrag.*) Nor my niggling, economy-souled wife. I'm in full command, here. (*Steven pats his chest.*)

MRS. OTIS

(*turning to Nancy*) Give it to me. (*She takes the basin and washrag and goes to the sofa.*)

STEVEN
(*shouting*) Don't touch me!

MRS. OTIS
The coolness will feel good.

NANCY
I put ice cubes in the water. (*Steven hesitates, takes the basin, puts it on the couch beside him, wipes his face with the washrag.*)

MRS. OTIS
Tomorrow you'll be yourself.

STEVEN
What a black curse! (*Mrs. Otis gives him a last, appraising look and turns toward the French door, left.*)

NANCY
Where are you going?

MRS. OTIS
(*controlled*) Out into the yard.

NANCY
(*to Steven*) Aren't you ashamed of yourself — to do this to her when she's so frail. To hurt her so! At least say you're sorry! Say it!

STEVEN
Oh, shut up . . I'm sorry, Mother. (*Mrs. Otis hesitates a bare moment and goes on toward the door. With the petulance of a boy he hurls the washrag after her, striking the floor behind her.*) I'm goddamned sorry! (*The lights go out.*)

END OF ACT TWO

ACT THREE

The next morning. The living room. There is a huge bouquet of red and white peonies on the table down right. At rise, Mary Campbell is sitting in Mrs. Otis' armchair, sewing on a quilt. She is much older, now, and wears glasses. Mrs. Otis is at the open door, down right, speaking to someone offstage, who has evidently just left. Mrs. Otis wears an elegant "walking gown" from the 1890's which she has resurrected from an attic trunk.

MRS. OTIS
Goodbye, Doctor McEwen . . No, I'm not upset . . I understand, but I won't promise . . Certainly. Now that you've warned me, no blame can attach to you . . Thank you. Remember me to your wife. (*Mrs. Otis*

321

takes a deep breath of the June morning, then speaks to herself.) What a lovely day. (*She turns back into the room, speaking to her mother.*) What would you say to me, now, if you were alive?

MARY

My yellow rose bush needs manure.

MRS. OTIS

(*laughs*) Yes. And I'd say to you, "There was a robin on the porch rail, cocking his head at the doctor," and you'd go on sewing and say —

MARY

Doctors are fools.

MRS. OTIS

(*touching the peonies on the round table*) How clearly I see everything, as it was when I was little — the prickly point of a blade of grass, a white cloud that looked like a fat man laughing. I used to think the sun was God's eye . . Am I afraid? . . I don't think so. George was. He clung to me like a frightened little boy, tears in his eyes. Father made such a fuss —he resented death. It seemed as though his temper was the last part of him to die.

MARY

When your father and I were first married, no two people were ever so much in love. (*grimly*) That changed.

MRS. OTIS

I know it wasn't just the trial . .

MARY

Being in love and falling out of love are things that happen to us, and we don't have much to say about it. When your father died I mostly was relieved.

MRS. OTIS

(*to herself*) Frank was glad to go. It was good you weren't alive to see it. Living in filth, half-blind.

MARY

Frank's the best boy. Your other brothers were wild.

MRS. OTIS

I don't remember.

MARY

Jason died at sea. Bruce was shot in Mexico. I never knew more than that about it. Somebody sent me his watch with a note that just said he'd been shot. Arthur, of course, died ordinary in Salt Lake City.

MRS. OTIS

I don't feel as though I were going away. It's more as though everyone else is leaving me. I'll be alone. (*Benjamin enters from up right. He is grizzled, almost white. He is wearing a food-splattered vest, black pantaloons, and a collarless, white shirt with a gold stud. A heavy gold chain hangs from vest pocket to vest pocket.*)

BENJAMIN

Hello, Posie.

MRS. OTIS

You've got food all over your vest again.

BENJAMIN

(*brushing futilely at his vest*) Just come in to talk a little.

MRS. OTIS

Why don't you find some of your old friends?

BENJAMIN

(*proudly*) Outlasted every one of 'em! (*wistfully*) I'd be glad of just one old fool. (*putting his hand to his belly and giving prolonged groans*) Posie — I got a pain, here.

MARY

(*brusquely*) Want a cup of tea?

BENJAMIN

(*forgetting his pain in his irritation*) Not from you!

MRS. OTIS

(*scolding, as though he were a small child*) It's because you won't put your teeth in when you eat, and gulp everything down. Why don't you go rest awhile?

BENJAMIN

I'll find something to do. (*turning away*) Read my Bible, maybe. (*turning back to Mrs. Otis, his voice alive*) Know what? Just you read Matthew, nineteenth chapter, twenty-eighth verse. I got proof there that even Judas was saved!

MRS. OTIS

That's good. You go along, now.

MARY

"The mouths of fools pour out foolishness."

BENJAMIN

(*his voice deeper and stronger*) "Of woman came the beginning of sin and through her we all die!"

MARY

(*dry and impersonal*) "The candle of the wicked shall be put out." 'Cause Judas was saved don't mean you will be.

323

BENJAMIN

(*roaring with his old vitality*) "The churning of milk bringeth forth butter and the wringing of the nose bringeth forth blood." (*He stamps off, up right.*) "So the forcing of wrath bringeth forth strife."

MARY

Poooh.

MRS. OTIS

(*with sudden compassion*) Father! (*But Benjamin leaves without responding. Nancy enters at the same moment, from down right. She is wearing a smart dress of the present day and is carrying an armful of peonies.*)

NANCY

(*with concern*) Oh, Mother Otis!

MRS. OTIS

(*turning to her*) That vase won't hold any more.

NANCY

I'll put them here. (*putting her peonies in the vase on the hall table*) You should be lying down.

MRS. OTIS

Not if I feel like standing up. Sometimes I eat in the kitchen standing up, off the top of the gas oven. It's a good height.

NANCY

(*soberly, crossing to Mrs. Otis*) I talked to the doctor.

MRS. OTIS

You weren't here!

NANCY

I saw him leaving and I followed him. I made him tell me. Mother Otis, I know.

MRS. OTIS

Know what? That I'm old and somewhat worn out?

NANCY

At least sit down, Mother. (*She takes Mrs. Otis' arm. Mrs. Otis resists.*) Please!

MRS. OTIS

(*unsuccessfully trying to free her arm*) Where's Steven? Does he know?

NANCY

Never mind Steven. He doesn't know. You sit down, dear. Please.

MRS. OTIS

I don't want him to know. (*She allows herself to be led to the sofa where she sits.*)

324

NANCY

Isn't that better? (*She sits on the hassock.*) And I want to talk to you. A good, last talk.

MRS. OTIS

Don't try to hustle me into my grave.

NANCY

(*quickly*) I mean before I have to go away.

MRS. OTIS

Talk. I've nothing to say. (*Mrs. Cooms has entered up right. She is wearing the gingham dress Hollaway brought in Act One, and she is carrying a large chocolate layer cake on a platter. As she comes up to the peonies she pauses for a sniff and makes a face.*)

MRS. COOMS

They stink, don't they? I'd never have peonies in my house. (*She comes downstage so Mrs. Otis can see the cake.*) The cake's iced. Where do you plan to serve? Out on the porch?

MRS. OTIS

The dining room will be best. Remember, we're having strawberries and cream, too. (*to Nancy*) Thick cream.

MRS. COOMS

I hulled 'em.

MRS. OTIS

Let me see the cake. (*Mrs. Cooms brings it to her. Mrs. Otis takes a smidgen of chocolate icing on her finger and licks it off.*) Oh, that's good. I could eat a piece right now.

MRS. COOMS

(*indignantly*) Before the company sees it? Not on your life! (*Grumbling to herself she hurries off up right with the cake.*)

MRS. OTIS

I'm hungry. Do you suppose she'd let me have a piece of that cold chicken from last night?

NANCY

(*as to a child*) Oh, not between meals. (*taking Mrs. Otis' hand*) I'd like to talk to you just as though I were your own daughter. With complete honesty.

MRS. OTIS

That means it's something unpleasant.

NANCY

What's going through your mind, now?

325

MRS. OTIS

That I don't like to have my hand held. (*She pulls her hand away.*)

NANCY

(*laughing placatingly*) You're a delight.

MRS. OTIS

Get to your point.

NANCY

I was thinking — I've made *my* will. I suppose you've made a will?

MRS. OTIS

What if I have?

NANCY

Perhaps you'd tell me —

MRS. OTIS

You don't give up. Oh, you might as well know. Everything goes to Steven. Or did. I've about changed my mind, however.

NANCY

You'll sell the property?

MRS. OTIS

No. But I'll set up a trust. Mind you, Steven is to have the income for his life.

NANCY

Not *all* of it! He'll waste it!

MRS. OTIS

Yes — all! When he's old he *shall* be independent! I've seen too many old people shunted off by selfish children, callously put away to die in some cramped, smelly "home." Steven *shall* be *independent*!

NANCY

Shall we call the lawyer now?

MRS. OTIS

Don't hurry me! In spite of the doctor I shan't go till I'm ready.

MARY

(*rising, taking her sewing, crosses toward right*) Elizabeth, I'm going up to rest. I've been meaning to tell you I want "Rock of Ages" sung at my funeral. (*pause, looking back at Mrs. Otis*) It's God the rock that gives us the grace of stubbornness, without which I don't see how anyone could last through a life. (*She exits up right. Mrs. Otis looks after her.*)

MRS. OTIS

(*to Nancy*) One afternoon Mother went upstairs to rest and never waked up. Her face was peaceful, more soft than I ever saw it. You see, she be-

326

lieved in heaven; if she had a warning she probably thought, "At last I'm going to be happy. God will take care of me now."

NANCY

(*nervously rising, moving away*) What a wonderful way to die!

MRS. OTIS

Believe in God, believe in heaven — that's all you have to do.

NANCY

But you can't?

MRS. OTIS

Can you?

NANCY

Perhaps — when the time comes.

MRS. OTIS

That'll be too late.

NANCY

You don't believe?

MRS. OTIS

I'm willing to go halfway. I can believe in God, but I don't care for him. (*Rising, she crosses to the armchair.*) "So God made man in his own image," it says. That's what shook me. He made a world of fools — in his own image! (*She smiles at Nancy, who is rather shocked. Mrs. Otis sits.*) Then there's heaven. Imagine sitting on the edge of a cloud singing the same songs forever. Unless it was Gilbert and Sullivan. (*She breaks off as Mrs. Cooms enters up right.*)

MRS. COOMS

Where's your son?

MRS. OTIS

(*turning to look at her*) Upstairs, asleep, I suppose.

MRS. COOMS

He is not. He came down before eight o'clock all got up in that fancy coat and top hat. I offered to make breakfast and he said he was going downtown first, be back soon. Well, where is he? I've kept breakfast waiting over two hours now and he can starve for all of me! Or I'll quit, if you like!

MRS. OTIS

Nancy, you didn't tell me.

MRS. COOMS

I'm not going to miss that parade for no man.

MRS. OTIS

Never mind. You're quite right. Just clean up. He can go hungry.

327

MRS. COOMS

Well. I can give him a little something. (*She marches off, exits up right. Mrs. Otis watches her, waits until she has gone.*)

MRS. OTIS

Why didn't you tell me he'd gone out?

NANCY

I couldn't bear to talk about him. I knew how he'd hurt you.

MRS. OTIS

Where do you suppose he is? (*Nancy indicates helplessness.*) What is there to do in town at eight o'clock? I should think he'd have slept — after yesterday.

NANCY

He was awake in the night. Writing something.

MRS. OTIS

With the light on?

NANCY

Of course. I took a sleeping pill and pulled the covers over my head.

MRS. OTIS

If I only had twin beds to give you. George wanted them. Oh dear! What do you think was on his mind?

NANCY

(*bitterly*) I never know what he's thinking.

MRS. OTIS

Nor did I, with George. You have to go on trying to be sensible and logical anyhow. When you married Steven I expect you loved him — but did you like him? What did you really think of him? Or did you think? (*Nancy shrugs helplessly.*) Was there another man before Steven?

NANCY

(*startled*) Do you mean was I — a virgin?

MRS. OTIS

That wasn't what I meant — but were you? Oh, well, you wouldn't tell me anyhow.

NANCY

If you're really interested —

MRS. OTIS

No. There's always some other man, in our memory. *He* never goes without shaving, never has dirty underwear, never is vulgar or silly in public. What comfort in this make-believe! This dream husband. With him we know how marriage could have been, the peace, the everlasting heaven of being understood — and understanding.

328

NANCY

How touching! But I understand Steven — all too well.

MRS. OTIS

Really? I don't. Yet he was the sweetest baby, and we were *so* close — up to the time he started to talk.

NANCY

What about the lawyer?

MRS. OTIS

I want to tell Steven first. Mother taught me if you're going to do something that will hurt someone — do it to their face. (*There is a* THUD *on the front porch, down right, the heavy special edition of the newspaper, thrown at the porch by a passing newsboy.*)

NANCY

(*startled*) What's that?

MRS. OTIS

Must be the paper. Better take it in. We might as well see what they made of it — though I've prepared myself. (*Nancy rises, goes out down right onto the porch, and in a moment comes back with the rolled, string-tied issue, the Centennial Edition. She brings it to Mrs. Otis, puts it in her lap.*) You open it. (*Nancy unties the string and the seven sections of the paper sprawl out, some falling on the floor.*) You look.

NANCY

(*looking at the first section*) Your picture's on the front page, with a whole story.

MRS. OTIS

Not Steven's picture?

NANCY

I don't see it.

MRS. OTIS

Look.

NANCY

(*scanning the pages rapidly*) Nothing yet. (*She continues looking.*)

MRS. OTIS

(*reaching out and snatching the paper from Nancy*) Don't, I'm a coward. I'd rather not know.

STEVEN

(*on the porch left, calling to someone in the street*) Thank you! It's been a real pleasure. I'll see you tomorrow if I don't catch up with you at the pageant. (*Nancy looks toward the door. A moment later Steven, in top hat, frock coat, frilled shirt, silk vest, and wide tie, enters.*)

329

MRS. OTIS

(*looking at him*) Father, what have you been up to? (*Steven stops short. Nancy, concerned, puts her hand on Mrs. Otis' arm.*)

NANCY

(*to Mrs. Otis, louder than usual*) It's Steven. He's dressed for the pageant.

MRS. OTIS

(*pulling her arm away*) I know! (*pleading to Steven*) Where have you been!

STEVEN

I went out. How do you like this outfit? (*He turns about, turns back, smiling at his mother.*)

NANCY

You don't have your beard.

STEVEN

(*taking in his mother*) You look more like Paris.

MRS. OTIS

Son — I was worried.

STEVEN

I'd made an appointment and it took longer than I expected. (*He is in high spirits.*) What a great day. Why aren't we all outdoors?

NANCY

Don't you have *any* guilt?

STEVEN

(*warily*) Why?

NANCY

After what you put your mother through yesterday?

MRS. OTIS

Never mind, Nancy.

STEVEN

Where did you get the dress?

MRS. OTIS

Out of the attic.

STEVEN

I surely do like it.

MRS. OTIS

(*pleased*) You do? I couldn't *stand* gingham.

STEVEN

This is much better. The Queen has to dress for the occasion. You look wonderful.

MRS. OTIS

Thank you! Steven — you haven't had breakfast. (*starting to rise*) I'll get you something.

NANCY

(*rising herself, motioning Mrs. Otis back into her chair with a significant nod toward Steven*) I'll get it.

STEVEN

(*to Nancy*) What a lovely memory this will be!

NANCY

Shut up and talk to your mother. (*She crosses to up right.*)

STEVEN

Just coffee — darling. (*Nancy exits.*)

MRS. OTIS

That's not a proper breakfast — especially after not having supper — (*Mrs. Otis sits on the sofa.*)

STEVEN

(*pacing about*) I'll live off my fat. Anyhow — I had breakfast at the Green Mill —

MRS. OTIS

I go out for Sunday dinner there, sometimes. Was it good?

STEVEN

All right.

MRS. OTIS

Then what did you do?

STEVEN

(*stopping, facing his mother from the right*) Mother. I'm going to stay here for a while.

MRS. OTIS

You're not joking?

STEVEN

I was born and brought up here — yet it's a new world to me! And not a bad world.

MRS. OTIS

(*anxiously*) You made this decision — in the cold light of morning?

STEVEN

Yes. In fact, I've a business venture going.

MRS. OTIS

(*pleased*) And live here with me? (*He nods.*) Steven, come here. Sit with me. (*Mrs. Otis pats the hassock, Steven hesitates, then crosses behind her*

331

and looks down at her. Mrs. Otis looks up at him.) You look so like your grandfather.

STEVEN

It's the coat and hat. (*He gently pets her shoulder. She takes his hand in her hand and presses it to her cheek, then starts and drops his hand. She speaks in a strong, deep voice.*)

MRS. OTIS

Steven Otis! You've been in the barn. You took Old Red out! (*then in a puzzled, worried voice*) But I don't have a horse! I *smell* a *horse* on you!

STEVEN

(*coming around down right of Mrs. Otis*) I want to talk to you about that.

MRS. OTIS

(*bewildered*) About a horse? I think I'm mixed up.

STEVEN

(*laughs, sits on the hassock*) No, you're not. I've bought a horse. (*Mrs. Otis stares unbelieving.*) Nothing immoral in that?

MRS. OTIS

You don't know anything about horses! I used to know horses. *Both* your grandfathers knew — (*She pauses.*) Not a *racehorse*?

STEVEN

(*nodding*) That's right.

MRS. OTIS

(*holding her hands to her head*) I must wake up. This is one of those dreams again. Like yesterday.

STEVEN

No dream. It's simple. I've bought a trotter.

MRS. OTIS

How much did you pay?

STEVEN

I signed a note.

MRS. OTIS

How much?

STEVEN

Five thousand dollars, but —

MRS. OTIS

You're out of your mind.

STEVEN

Now, wait. I went out to the fairgrounds this morning. I timed her.

MRS. OTIS

(*woodenly*) You timed her.

STEVEN

Two-nine!

MRS. OTIS

(*repeating*) Two-nine.

STEVEN

And that was after only two circuits — she was practically cold, I checked her records. It figures. Three years old, a rangy roan. A big filly, but dainty — clean, powerful action and real spirit. She's a sweetheart!

MRS. OTIS

Five thousand dollars. Who did you buy it from?

STEVEN

I mentioned, I think, that I dropped in at the Golden Oak yesterday. One of the men was a trainer — and we got talking racing. Mother — that's a world out of the past! I felt as though I'd been taken back sixty years — those people live with their horses, nothing else matters.

MRS. OTIS

Whose horse?

STEVEN

I met the owner this morning. A Mrs. Martin.

MRS. OTIS

Pretty, dark hair — with blue eyes?

STEVEN

I think so. At least her name was Mrs. Martin. She's a widow?

MRS. OTIS

Yes, she's a widow.

STEVEN

Amiable, witty woman.

MRS. OTIS

So, you bought the horse.

STEVEN

I'd have bought her if Mrs. Martin had been cross-eyed, dumpy, and stuttered.

MRS. OTIS

But you'd have paid less. Steven — what possessed you? Don't you have any common sense? You haven't any money — and you sign a note for five thousand dollars — no job —

STEVEN

Look, I went over the races — the fairs in Iowa and Minnesota and the purses. I'll pick up more than her cost in this one season — given any luck at all.

MRS. OTIS

What makes you think the owner of a racehorse ever had luck? (*Nancy enters from up right with a tray on which are two cups of black coffee. She takes one to Steven, goes to the table, sits, and sips the other.*)

STEVEN

Thanks. (*He sips it.*)

NANCY

(*to Mrs. Otis*) You told him?

STEVEN

What?

MRS. OTIS

No. Steven talked.

NANCY

About me?

MRS. OTIS

About a horse.

NANCY

A horse. (*She gives a little social laugh.*) Always something new.

MRS. OTIS

He's bought a racehorse.

NANCY

That certainly drives the nail in.

MRS. OTIS

Yes.

NANCY

You'd better tell him.

STEVEN

This is terrible coffee.

MRS. OTIS

Steven —

STEVEN

What?

MRS. OTIS

The doctor was here this morning.

STEVEN

(*concerned*) Why? Did you call him?

MRS. OTIS

I didn't feel well in the night.

STEVEN

What did he say? You look fine. How do you feel now?

I, ELIZABETH OTIS, BEING OF SOUND MIND

MRS. OTIS

(*with a slight smile*) Just the same as yesterday!

STEVEN

(*deceived*) Well, good! (*He sips coffee, frowns over the taste, then, looking at his mother, goes on.*) Don't think this racehorse is going to take up all my time. I'll be watching for other opportunities. I'd like to get this town by the tail and — (*He breaks off as Hollaway enters from the porch, down right. He wears a splendid Indian headdress and is wrapped in a Navaho blanket. He carries a newspaper, the Centennial Edition. He holds up one hand in an Indian salute.*)

HOLLAWAY

How! (*Steven turns. They all look at Hollaway in silent amusement.*)

STEVEN

Good Lord.

HOLLAWAY

You two look great. (*noticing the paper on the floor*) Oh, you saw the paper!

STEVEN

I forgot to look for my interview.

HOLLAWAY

It isn't there.

STEVEN

(*ironic*) Too late for the deadline?

HOLLAWAY

(*stiffly*) We didn't have the space.

STEVEN

Come off it.

HOLLAWAY

I didn't get it written in time.

NANCY

Thank you! Oh, thank you!

HOLLAWAY

This is *your* day, Mrs. Otis. I didn't want anything to take away from it.

STEVEN

The warm soul of the heartland.

MRS. OTIS

Thank you, Mr. Hollaway.

NANCY

It was so good of you to come, Mr. Hollaway. You probably have a hundred things to do. We won't keep you.

STEVEN

You don't have to rush him out. I've got something to take up with him. Cup of coffee, Hollaway?

HOLLAWAY

No thanks. But I've got something to take up too — a couple of things. First of all, I think we ought to go over your lines again.

STEVEN

What I had in mind. (*He takes some folds of paper from a pocket.*) I did a little rewriting of my speeches.

NANCY

Steven!

HOLLAWAY

Now look —

STEVEN

Yours wasn't bad, but I think I've given it a little more power.

HOLLAWAY

No, I'm afraid I can't allow that!

STEVEN

(*starting to put the paper back*) Okay. Get another pioneer. What was the other thing you had in mind?

HOLLAWAY

Well — suppose you read it.

STEVEN

(*blandly*) Sure. (*opens up his rewrite*) Spotlight on my strong, tanned face. (*He opens his frock coat, moves about as he reads.*)

STEVEN

"I am English, Scotch, Dutch, German, Irish, Scandinavian, Italian, Negro, Chinese, and Greek. I am the bursting forth of the hunger, the starvation of miserable men everywhere, driven to a wilderness by a last hope. I bring guns to kill, greed to harvest what I can wrest from the Indians or from my neighbor."

HOLLAWAY

That's a little strong.

STEVEN

Cue!

HOLLAWAY

"I believe in the changeless life — I am the hunter, the free man for whose pleasure and need this land of Iowa was created by the Great Spirit."

STEVEN

"The prairies shall be put to plough, your hunting grounds destroyed; for we shall inoculate you with our diseases and the turning furrow shall be a wave that buries you and your women and children. For we believe in the divine right of force. Our corn will grow, and yours wilt, and there will come a day when the buffalo, slaughtered for our gain, will disappear, and you shall starve by thousands; from rising sun to setting sun you shall know the misery of the weak, as our American Dream is built on your bones, for we shall triumph with ruthlessness; and the smugness of our comfort will be a curse that washes the world."

HOLLAWAY

Good Lord, that would stand them on their ears!

NANCY

It denigrates our history!

MRS. OTIS

Isn't it true?

NANCY

No, it isn't. It's one-sided. The Indians were savages.

MRS. OTIS

Steven, I like it. It's good to have a little truth in the midst of glorifying ourselves.

HOLLAWAY

You really think so, Mrs. Otis?

MRS. OTIS

Yes, I do.

HOLLAWAY

It's all right with me — but it sure brings me to my second point with a bang. I want to get a job in New York, and after they hear that I may have to. Mr. Otis, if you could give me ten minutes sometime, about the best way to get started in New York.

STEVEN

Fifteen minutes for that.

HOLLAWAY

Seriously — would you talk to me? I've read about you ad executives — you bounce around, and always end up in a better spot, because you know the answers.

STEVEN

I do? Okay, it's a date. I'll tell you what not to do.

HOLLAWAY

(laughing) See you then. (glances at his wristwatch) Oh, oh. Not long to parade time. I'd better round up the Mayor and get him here. Goodbye, everybody. (With a wave Hollaway exits left.)

337

NANCY

Mother Otis — do you want me to tell Steven?

MRS. OTIS

What? Oh — (*remembering*) No, no. I'll talk to him.

NANCY

You didn't. You didn't even tell him the truth about what the doctor said.

MRS. OTIS

"Doctors are fools." Mother said it, and they are.

NANCY

Steven. Your mother's life is hanging by a thread.

MRS. OTIS

Doctor McEwen never said *that*!

NANCY

He said we can't tell how long!

MRS. OTIS

But I'm not hanging by a *thread*. It's a strand of steel.

STEVEN

Suppose you take a walk, Nancy.

NANCY

But, I —

STEVEN

(*takes Nancy by the arm and leads her down right, toward the front door*)
Take a walk, darling. If you want to sit, that's all right. But get out, darling! (*Nancy exits. We hear organ music, played as a dirge, and from up
right four pallbearers enter, walking with measured step, two by two, as
though carrying a coffin. They advance into the room. Mrs. Otis rises and
walks toward them, between the first two. She turns and walks with them
as they move toward the French door.*)

MRS. OTIS

No! (*She stops, steps from them, downstage. The organ music ceases, but
the pallbearers walk on out the French door and exit up left.*) I didn't
have music at my wedding and I don't need it at my funeral!

STEVEN

(*coming from down right, amused, smiling at her*) You won't care, will
you?

MRS. OTIS

(*smiling back*) I suppose I won't. You know Nancy is terrified at the idea
of death?

STEVEN

(*gently, moving toward Mrs. Otis*) Between us — what did the doctor say?

338

MRS. OTIS

He said he couldn't guarantee how long I'd live. I asked him if he was giving guarantees to other people and how much they cost. He was annoyed.

STEVEN

(*laughs, then*) I'm glad I'm going to be here with you.

MRS. OTIS

It's true?

STEVEN

I told you I was.

MRS. OTIS

Thank you for not carrying on about what the doctor said.

STEVEN

(*sitting on the hassock*) I carry on about things that can be changed.

MRS. OTIS

I wonder if you'd feel that way if it were you.

STEVEN

Perhaps. I have an idea you don't want to live forever. I don't.

MRS. OTIS

That would be intolerable.

STEVEN

Know the difference between the pessimist and the optimist?

MRS. OTIS

(*sitting on the sofa, near Steven*) Tell me.

STEVEN

The optimist says, "This is the best of all possible worlds." And the pessimist says, "You're right." (*Mrs. Otis is amused, enjoys her laugh.*)

STEVEN

What did you want to say to me?

MRS. OTIS

(*troubled*) I'm worried about — how you'll take care of things. The property. Nancy thinks —

STEVEN

That it ought to be left so I can't touch it?

MRS. OTIS

Yes.

STEVEN

(*Head in his hands. There is a moment's silence. Steven looks up.*) All right. If you'll feel easier. I won't starve. I suppose you want to be sure the children will get it?

MRS. OTIS

Yes. And that it won't be wasted.

STEVEN

If that's going to make you more at peace — okay.

MRS. OTIS

(*rising, moves about*) I don't know what to do! I don't want you to be dependent on them in your old age!

STEVEN

(*laughs*) I'll never be that old. That's my trouble.

MRS. OTIS

You will though! Oh, Steven, then you'll need comfort and *money*!! If you don't have it, you'll be pushed around, humiliated. Why do you think I'm getting all this royal treatment? With the Mayor coming and perhaps the Lieutenant Governor? Do you think that if I were living in an old ladies' home they'd do this?

STEVEN

You're more cynical than I am.

MRS. OTIS

Perhaps I could make that banker you seemed to like a co-executor? Would that hurt your pride?

STEVEN

My pride has calluses.

MRS. OTIS

I wish I knew you better. I wish I knew the children. I could understand them, now. I'm even on the edge of understanding you. (*Mrs. Otis moves to Steven, puts her hand on his cheek.*)

STEVEN

(*passes his hand over his eyes, then excusing himself*) It's not that I'm sorry for you. I'm going to be sorry for myself.

MRS. OTIS

Why?

STEVEN

Miss you.

MRS. OTIS

You will?

STEVEN

Who'll I argue with in my mind — and hate? That's been a great comfort, you so firm and always there. I could blame so much on you.

MRS. OTIS

You didn't really hate me? (*Steven shrugs — smiles. Mrs. Otis crosses to*

340

the armchair and sits.) Because of the whippings. But I never punished you in anger!

STEVEN

(*rising*) No. Always cold and reasoning — like an enemy.

MRS. OTIS

I was trying to do what was best.

STEVEN

(*moving restlessly about*) And all the blessed feeling without thinking shut out of your face.

MRS. OTIS

I don't understand. All cruelty and evil come from acting on emotion.

STEVEN

No.

MRS. OTIS

War and plunder and killing —

STEVEN

No. In war you kill in cold blood. On orders. No hate there, just stupid cold reason. Business is the same — war with all the comforts, and token bloodshed. And cold — how cold!

MRS. OTIS

Businessmen are cold?

STEVEN

Of course not. The poor, half-frozen bastards are the friendliest men in the world. Starved for warmth.

MRS. OTIS

You never wrote me anything about the war, except unimportant humorous things.

STEVEN

(*sitting at the table*) What would have been the point?

MRS. OTIS

Your Uncle Bruce, whom you never knew, was in the Civil War.

STEVEN

Perhaps that was different.

MRS. OTIS

Mother said the only battle he was in, he fired his gun in the air so he wouldn't hit anyone.

STEVEN

Independent type.

MRS. OTIS

Then he felt a blow. He said to the man next to him, "Stop hitting me."

341

And the man said, "You're shot." There he was bleeding. Then he got mad and wanted to shoot somebody, but they took him back to the hospital and when he was well, his three-month enlistment had run out.

STEVEN

What an easy, personal world! His enlistment ran out.

MRS. OTIS

Later he was drafted, but Father paid for a substitute. Steven, you won't buy the horse?

STEVEN

I must, if we're going to be friends. You mustn't try to boss a friend.

MRS. OTIS

Aren't there any other dreams you have? I so wanted you to study law —

STEVEN

And be Governor and President? Not that one. I've had dreams —

MRS. OTIS

What?

STEVEN

Floating down the Mississippi, living on the country.

MRS. OTIS

That's a childish dream!

STEVEN

Yes, and now it's full of industry's crud — excuse me, Mother — industrial waste, and it's dangerous to eat the fish. Well, we'll see. Perhaps I'll find an answer in Boue City.

MRS. OTIS

(*who has been following her own thoughts*) Steven — I know Mrs. Martin. She is a *shallow* woman.

STEVEN

(*laughing*) It's her horse I want.

MRS. OTIS

You won't live a month without a woman to depend on — and quarrel with — and resent.

STEVEN

I've got you.

MRS. OTIS

I should be satisfied, if I have you, at last. Even if you resent me — as your father did. Steven, if I last till fall — could the children come out to see me?

STEVEN

Why not? If you wouldn't be annoyed by them. It's a very different world they live in — even different from mine.

I, ELIZABETH OTIS, BEING OF SOUND MIND

MRS. OTIS

(*rises, moves to Steven*) This moment I have the feeling I could reach across to them. Steven — I could know them better than you! Oh, everything is crowding in — I see so much! I suppose you think I'm senile. The truth is my mind was never so bright, so farseeing, so understanding! I see everything, just as it is, not confused by hope. And then it gets to be too much to stand, like looking at the Gorgon's face, and so I turn my mind off. That's what they call senility. Now I see you. (*She puts her hand out in a timid gesture, toward Steven, and he takes it in both of his.*)

STEVEN

(*after a moment*) I love you.

MRS. OTIS

I'm glad, even if it isn't true. I've waited a long time. Buy the horse, if that's what you want.

STEVEN

(*his arm about her*) I'll take you with me to see her race.

MRS. OTIS

Just for now, leave this horse out of it. Let's pretend we agree about everything, that you don't resent me, and that I know you'll do what's right.

STEVEN

(*takes her hands*) That's a good dream.

MRS. OTIS

When I was growing up I thought being married might be like this.

STEVEN

I know.

MRS. OTIS

(*exhilarated by her thoughts, moves away from Steven*) The strangest thing! I feel quite young. All of a sudden I'm one of them, on their side. I hate the old, too. The old are always wrong, aren't they? It's only the dreams of the young that last forever. (*We hear a band faintly playing a march. Mrs. Otis holds up one hand for silence.*) Listen! (*Steven obediently listens.*) I think I hear the band. The parade must have started.

STEVEN

I don't hear it.

MRS. OTIS

(*crosses to Steven, takes his hand*) Oh, you do too. I wish Mother could be here for it.

NANCY

(*Entering from the porch, down right. Steven and Mrs. Otis break their clasp, like young lovers surprised.*) The Mayor's here!

MRS. OTIS

(*patting her hair*) Well, ask him in!

NANCY

(*looking searchingly from Mrs. Otis to Steven*) You talked — you settled things?

MRS. OTIS

(*gaily*) Yes, we did. (*Steven grins at her.*)

NANCY

(*puzzled*) I don't understand —

MRS. OTIS

Well, we do. Now where's that Mayor of yours?

NANCY

(*turns back toward the porch, calls*) Won't you come in for a minute, Mr. Jordan? (*The Mayor, Mr. Jordan, enters. He too has a frock coat. He is silver-haired, pleasant. As he enters little Bet enters slowly from down left and goes to Mrs. Otis. The Mayor has crossed to Mrs. Otis, puts out his hand. She takes it.*)

MRS. OTIS

I once knew a Mr. Jordan, a fine man. (*Benjamin, as we first saw him in Act One, enters from down left and stands in the shadows.*)

MAYOR

Perhaps my grandfather? It's an honor to be here, Mrs. Otis. We've a number of distinguished people out on the porch whom I want to present to you. (*Mamie and Frank, as they were at their wedding, enter up left and stand, watching.*)

MRS. OTIS

He was a minister and I think I was in love with him when I was a little girl. (*She absently pats Bet's hair.*) When I was grown up, he married us.

MAYOR

I think that must have been my great-uncle.

MRS. OTIS

Where's Mother? (*She looks back at the figures of the past.*) I don't want her to miss this.

STEVEN

Would you like to go out now?

MRS. OTIS

(*to the figures of the past*) I know that this parade and this pageant aren't going to be like it really was. We can't imagine that today.

MAYOR

We've tried.

MRS. OTIS

Let me lean on you, Steven. Sometimes talking so much makes me dizzy. (*Steven supports her. Mrs. Otis still fondles Bet's hair.*)

MRS. OTIS

I had such long red hair. I hated it. They called me Carrot-top. (*The band is louder.*) Where's Mother?

MAYOR

I think I hear the band.

MRS. OTIS

I've heard it for some time. (*But she doesn't move, though everyone is anxious to be on the porch.*) Father used to tell about the Sabona massacre. I think you ought to put this in the pageant. (*She turns to the figures of the past, walks toward them.*) The Indians killed everyone, but they saved the finest, strongest man till the last. They cut open his stomach and fastened one end of his intestines to the pump, and forced him to walk around it. Walk he did, but laughing and jeering at the Indians every step until he fell down dead. (*looking at Benjamin*) Father used to say, "*That was a man!*" Whenever I complained about something, like having to go out and gather eggs after dark, or bring the cows in, he'd say, "All right, Bet, walk around the pump, but be sure you laugh while you do it!"

MAYOR

That's a great story. Shall we go out now? (*Mrs. Otis steps forward, one hand on Steven's arm, the other on the Mayor's. Bet follows close behind. The figures out of the past move toward the right, the door. Mrs. Cooms comes from the kitchen and briskly heads for the door. Mary comes from the shadows at the left and stands, watching. Mrs. Otis looks back and sees her. Her face lights up.*)

MRS. OTIS

(*relieved*) Oh, Mother — I was waiting for you! (*She turns to the door with Steven and the Mayor, goes firmly out, head high, a bright smile on her face. George and Young Steven, as we saw them in Act One, enter from up left and follow the other ghosts of the past, George's arm about Young Steven. The band swells louder, playing "The Iowa Corn Song." As Mrs. Otis steps through the doorway, the lights dim swiftly out.*)

THE END

I, Elizabeth Otis, Being of Sound Mind by Philip Barber was presented on December 1–3, 9–11, 1966, at the Theatre in the Round, Minneapolis. It was directed by Mac Harris.

Cast of Characters

MRS. COOMS	Mickie Dickerson
ELIZABETH OTIS	Virginia Harris
MARY CAMPBELL	Nancy Grill
BENJAMIN CAMPBELL	Charles Russell
HOLLAWAY	Gregory Filas
BET CAMPBELL	Phyllis Kramer
FRANK CAMPBELL	Don Laube
MAMIE	Sandra Bucholtz
STEVEN OTIS	John Regan
NANCY OTIS	Tamera Andersen
YOUNG STEVEN	David Morrison
GEORGE OTIS	William Zenker
REVEREND AND MAYOR JORDAN	Leo Miller
HENRIETTA CLAPP	Margaret Kramer
LEONARD CLAPP	Norman Rudd

CONGREGATION: Barbara Morison, Gene Miller, James Hickey, Marge Rudd, Catherine Hickey, Jo Hicks, Dwight Hicks.

PALLBEARERS: Dwight Hicks, James Hickey, Gordon Mac-Nabb, Norman Rudd.